Charles Clement Post

Ten Years a Cowboy

Charles Clement Post

Ten Years a Cowboy

ISBN/EAN: 9783743324718

Manufactured in Europe, USA, Canada, Australia, Japa

Cover: Foto ©ninafisch / pixelio.de

Manufactured and distributed by brebook publishing software (www.brebook.com)

Charles Clement Post

Ten Years a Cowboy

TEN YEARS
A COWBOY.

BY C. C. POST.

ADDENDA
BY
TEX BENDER, THE COWBOY FIDDLER

CHICAGO:
RHODES & McCLURE PUBLISHING COMPANY,

Entered according to act of Congress, in the year 1898 by the
RHODES & McCLURE PUBLISHING COMPANY,
in the Office of the Librarian of Congress, Washington, D. C.

All Rights Reserved.

PLYMOUTH
PRINTING & BINDING CO.
CHICAGO.

Brown on Guard

CONTENTS.

THE STORY, ROMANCE AND ADVENTURES OF A LIFE ON THE PLAINS WITH THE VARIED EXPERIENCES AS COW-BOY, STOCK-OWNER, RANCHER, &c. &c. PAGES..17 to 358

	PAGE
THE PLAINS.	359
From the Missouri River to the Rocky Mountains	363
The Trees	365
The Herbage	367
The Buffalo	369
The Indian Warrior and his Pony	371
The Insects	374
The Mirage	375
Water	377
The Wichita Mountains	378
The Indian	380
CATTLE.	385
The Gains in Cattle Ranching	386
How to start in the Cattle Business	387
The Stock Country	389
The Cattle Ranches	389
Settlers' Rights	390
The Dashing Cow-Boy	391
Cattle on the Ranges	392
Cattle in Winter	393
Advantages of Cattle over Horse Raising	394
The Round-Up	395
Movricks	395
Cutting-Out	396
The Cow-Ponies	397
Branding Calves	399
Branding Cattle	403
On the Trail	406

CONTENTS.

Night Watching..408
Shipping by Rail......................................410
The Journey to Chicago................................412
Queens of the Ranch...................................415
California as a Cattle Raising State..................417
California Laws.......................................419
Water Rights..420
Profits on Cattle-Raising in Texas, as the Business was
   formerly Conducted................................422
Profits on Cattle Raising as at present Conducted.....424
Advice to the Cowboys.................................427

SHEEP. 429

Sheep Driving...429
Spanish Merinos.......................................430
Certificate for Taxes.................................431
The Outfit..431
Taking Horses through the Mountains...................433
Hiring Drivers..434
Sheep Shearing..437
On the Road...437
Scab..439
Dipping...439
Sheep Driving from California to Sonora...............443
Tolls...446
Crossing the Sierras..................................448
The Bedding Ground....................................450
The San Antonio.......................................451
Driving Sheep in Nevada...............................453
Food in Camp..453
The Cook's Duties.....................................454
Clothing..455
Bathing...457
Beds..458
Temperature...459
Sleeping in Camp......................................460
Shepherd Dogs...462
Prairie Dogs..465
Driving Sheep in Idaho................................466
The Laramie Plains....................................467
Near Salt Lake..468
How to make money in Utah.............................469

TEN YEARS A COW BOY.

CHAPTER I.

A LITTLE OLD TOWN ON THE WABASH.

A few years ago when even in the middle Western States land was to be had for the taking, a bit of a town pre-empted a site on the banks of the Wabash river, in the State of Indiana, and proceeded to establish itself and settle down to business, squatter fashion.

I say squatter fashion because it took on the air of not being very certain of its claim to permanent ownership, and so not eager to make improvements beyond such as were necessary to its immediate wants.

This feeling about permanency of title may have been owing to the fact that the Wabash was a river of unsteady habits, and liable to get on a rampage at periods more or less frequent and unexpected, depending somewhat upon the state of the weather and other causes. This, you understand, was before the government had established a bureau at the national capital with orders to regulate the weather, and so render such conduct on the part of the Wabash and other streams of similar habits entirely without excuse.

But, whatever the reason may have been, the town always had the appearance of having no permanency of title to the site it had fixed upon. The streets—if you choose to call them streets—were wide enough, and they would have been beautiful plots of green if it had not been that they were white instead, white with mayweed, except where the hogs rooted holes in the earth for purposes of their own; for the town did not keep its hogs shut up. So great was the people's sense of personal liberty in this village of wide spaces, that there were none among the inhabitants who had ever suggested an abridgment to the unlimited freedom of the hogs. On the contrary, they were permitted to wander about at their own sweet will, and they put in their time about equally in hunting for such food as was to be found in the river bottom, and in maintaining their rights as free and independent citizens, by rooting up the streets, and such apologies for gardens as the people felt incumbent on themselves to attempt making, for the town was not more thorough in its manner of fencing in its gardens and yards than in anything else. A fence of "palins," thin strips of timber split from some straight grained ash or oak tree, and pointed at the end, was occasionally erected about a bit of ground, being nailed on perpendicularly, pointed end upward, and an attempt at the cultivation of what was called a "truck patch" made. But as nails were scarce and high, and the town did not know exactly how long it was going to stay there, these palings were seldom securely fastened, and appeared as if put there for the purpose of affording the hogs amusement for their leisure hours in rooting them off, more than for any real protection to the vegetables planted within the inclosures.

There were several dogs, also, and children, connected with the town. I do not think I ever quite understood what the town considered to be the rights or duties of the children, or whether they were supposed to have any, but those of the dogs were plainly to be perceived by any one at all observant of such things. Their duties were to assist the hogs out of the truck patch whenever they wandered in and were unable, in the excitement of the moment, to find their own way out at the hole by which they entered; this, and to stand in front of the houses and welcome any chance stranger who sought an interview with the town for any purposes. I think they also assisted at the obsequies of such game as the inhabitants secured from time to time from out the surrounding woods or adjoining prairie. And as for their rights, why they were the same as those of the other citizens, which appeared to consist principally in sitting around discussing the probability of another rise in the Wabash, and occasionally going out to a cornfield on the outskirts and spending a half day or so in cutting down weeds and chasing squirrel and chipmunk depredators on the aforesaid cereal.

There was one other difference between the apparent duties of the men and the dogs which I ought to mention; the dogs did not fish and the men did. The men appeared to think it a duty to fish, and would frequently sit a half day at a time upon a log in the sun, holding a pole with a line attached when it was too hot to hoe corn or weed the truck patch; something the dogs never did. On such occasions the dogs usually lay in the shade and caught fleas, which was perhaps their fair share of the labor. I think neither could boast greatly over the other of the success attending their efforts; the men and boys certainly caught a great many fish, but then the dogs also secured a great many fleas.

I never knew for certain why the town remained

there. May be, after all, it had a clear title to the site on which it stood. It was not a very big town ; a dozen or score of houses, most of them of logs, some of rough boards, some a mixture of the two, one part being of logs, with a crazy little lean-to of boards at the back, some whitewashed, but more with the color which nature and the elements had given them.

Looking back at it now I more than half believe that what made the town stay there was the ferry.

This might seem to have furnished good reason why it should *not* stay there, since it could evidently have gotten away by means of the ferry if it wanted to. But I do not think it wanted to.

May be it would have done so if it had thought of it, but if so it was evident that the thought had never come to it; the town was not greatly given to thinking, but I do not really believe the reason for its staying was that it never occurred to it that it could go by way of the ferry if it wanted to. Possibly it expected the Wabash to rise high enough some time to take it away and so save it the trouble of going; I can not say positively as to that. I am inclined to think it stayed because it liked to stay.

And why not ?

In the first place, it was a good location for such a town.

There was the river with plenty of fish to be had for

the taking; the woods upon its banks abounded with game, and was also a capital range for hogs. In the prairie, a bit back from the river, the prairie chickens raised their young and waxed fat. There were sand banks for the children to play upon; there was the periodical rise in the river, not to speak of passing flat-boats and an occasional steamer to furnish topics for discussion. And then there was the ferry—the ferry, which gave the dignity and importance to the town and a reputation throughout the country for miles on both sides of the river. Yes, I think it was the ferry which kept the town contented and happy and prevented any disposition on its part to wander away.

The ferry boat was not unlike other ferries—the boat part of it, I mean. It consisted of what was known in those days as a "flatboat;" a low, flat boat constructed of strong timbers heavily planked over, and slightly turned up at either end, like the front end of the implement known among farmers as a stoneboat, and used by them to draw stone off their fields. It swung from shore to shore by the force of the current. There was a line of canoes, perhaps a dozen in number, the one farthest away only being fastened to a stake driven securely into the earth at the bottom of the river, midway between banks and some twenty rods above the ferry. To this canoe was attached, by means of long ropes and at equal distances from each

THE FERRY.

other, other canoes, the last of which was in turn attached by a rope to the ferry or flatboat, which in size was perhaps ten or fifteen feet wide by twenty long. Now when the ferry boat was pushed out from either bank, the force of the current would tend to carry it down stream in a straight line, but being held from above by the long line of canoes and their attachments, it could only swing in a circle. The water, pressing both against the side of the larger boat and of the canoes attached to it, propelled it to the middle of the stream with considerable velocity, sufficient, when the water was high, to compel it to make the other quarter of the circle and bring up at a point on the other shore exactly opposite from where it started, when it would be made secure by a chain thrown over a strong post set in the ground. Then a plank would be pushed out, upon which passengers and teams could walk dry shod to the land.

If the river was low, and the current failed to bring the boat quite to shore, as it sometimes did fail of doing, the person in charge was ready, standing in the stern of the boat, to push it ashore with a long pole.

Now this ferry belonged to a person by the name of McKinley. *Mister* McKinley he was called; and he was the only citizen of the town who was ever honored by having this prefix attached to his name;

which fact argues that Mr. McKinley was a man of importance and influence in the community, as indeed he was.

For, was he not the owner of the ferry from which the town received its dignity, and upon which it depended for its fame? Had he not held communication with the dignitaries of the State itself and been granted authority—*legal* authority—to run the ferry, as aforesaid? And did he not have proof of the fact in the shape of a paper, printed in three or four sizes of type, signed by the secretary of State, tied with a red ribbon and sealed with the great seals of the States both of Illinois and of Indiana, declaring that "having confidence in the patriotism and integrity of Mr. William H. H. McKinley, he is hereby granted authority, etc., to run a ferry across the Wabash river, etc., etc.; the same being a river navigable by boats, etc., etc., and also constituting the boundary line between the two States, as aforesaid?"

This charter Mr. McKinley had had framed and hung up in the rough porch in front of the log cabin in which he lived with his family of six, not counting the dogs, which would have raised it to a round dozen at least.

This cabin of McKinley's stood near the banks of the river, on the Indiana side; the banks on this side being several feet higher than on the other side.

The house was only a few rods from the ferry landing, and any one entering the cabin could hardly fail to observe the charter where it hung in its frame by the door.

The children used, when it was first hung there, to come about the porch and gaze up at it in open-mouthed wonder and silent awe, and go away with minds full of imaginings of the many great things Mr. McKinley must have done to cause the authorities of two States to certify to their confidence in and admiration of him, to be to the trouble, too, of having it printed in big letters and little ones, and putting the great seals of the States upon it, so that no one might so much as dare to doubt that its possessor was indeed a great man, having the confidence of all of the great men of the country—one to whom it was proper and right should be given exclusive authority to run a ferry boat and charge people for riding on it.

Of course such a man must never be addressed too familiarly, hence the children always, and the men generally, addressed him as *Mister* McKinley.

Occasionally, some man in whose cranial development there was a hollow where his bump of reverence should have been, would speak to him as "McKinley," simply, or even as "Mack," but he seldom appeared to hear when thus spoken to, and children hearing him thus addressed would drop whatever employment they were engaged in and look and listen, and seem to wonder whether Mister McKinley would feel sufficiently offended to ask the authorities to mete out proper punishment to the man who thus failed to render the respect due to him in whom the State reposed such unbounded confidence and desired to see honored.

Children are quick to catch the spirit of the teachings of their elders, and in proportion as their imaginations are more active and their knowledge of the world more limited than those of older persons, so are they more intensely affected by the things which they see and hear. To the children of this little town upon the banks of the Wabash the State represented all earthly authority and power and dignity; and knowing nothing of its duties or limitations, and nothing of legal forms or customs, they regarded any one who had held communication with it, or been given any commission under it, as partaking in a very great degree of the grandeur which in their minds attached to it, and they looked upon such a one as entitled to demand about what he chose from other people, in the way of homage at least.

If any shall say that reverence for their fellow-men or being greater or more worthy of honor than themselves, is not a feeling natural in man, or that by nature every man is inclined to regard himself as possessing equal rights with every other man, I answer, that possibly it may be as you say some time—when generations have come and gone in which, from the cradle to the grave, men shall have been taught by society, both by precept and practice, that all are at birth equal before the law—but at present the belief of past generations in the divine right of some to better birth than others shows itself in our children, and causes them not only to yield to oppression too easily, but to regard with awe and reverence any who put forth a claim to superiority of birth, or to having been given authority by those entitled to exercise it.

And so these barefooted, straw-hatted (when they had any hats at all), and linsey-clad children acknowledged the claim to honor and dignity put forward by the man to whom the State had granted a commission to charge for ferrying people across the Wabash, as being natural and proper. They may, and, I think, did assist in increasing the estimate which Mr. McKinley at first felt disposed to put upon the honor done him, by the readiness with which they acknowledged his claim to be valid and proper.

Be this as it may, Mr. McKinley enjoyed the dignity of his position and the honor accredited him of being the only man in the community with a prefix to his name, and being contented with the honor he left the work of running the ferry to any other member of the family who chose to attend to it.

At first most frequently it was his wife who shouldered this duty in addition to the care of her household. Then the oldest of the children began to perform this service, and finally and by degrees the sole charge of the business was given over to her, or rather appeared to settle about and devolve upon her naturally; probably from the fact that no matter what the weather, or the state of the water in the river, she was always ready to answer the call of any one who desired to be set across, and equally skillful and courageous in the management of the boat.

I say "she," for the boatman of the ferry was a girl.

At the time of my introducing her to the reader she was nearly thirteen years old, tall, slim, graceful in her motions as one of the willows which leans over the river and dips its twigs in the clear water just below the landing there, and equally as unconscious of the fact.

See her now as, standing upon the stern of the

ferry, she exerts her strength to push it well up to the landing with the flatboat pole. Her feet are bare, and feet and ankles are tanned as brown as that dead leaf floating with the current there. Her sun bonnet has been thrown aside; her arms are bare and brown half way to the shoulder, and a mass of soft brown hair that would curl beautifully, if only it had proper attention, hangs about her neck and shoulders. See now, as she bends her supple body to the work of forcing the boat ashore, how like to the willow she is. Yes, that is she. That is Nettie McKinley, or "Net," as she is familiarly called, for the reverence which attaches to her father as being commissioned by two States to run a ferry boat does not descend to her who runs it. Familiarity, you know, is the road by which dignity vacates the premises. If Mr. McKinley was to run the ferry and speak cheerfully and laugh and chat with everybody who crossed with him as his daughter does—great man though he is—he would prove the truth of my saying and cease to be addressed with more respect than that bestowed upon his fellow villagers, and the evidence of his being a great man, and wise withal, lies in the fact that he does not run the ferry, and does not permit people to address him too familiarly.

And now let me introduce another friend of mine; one whom you must know if you are to go with me to the end of this story, from the Wabash to the Rio Grande, and maybe back again. Dear reader, I present to you the three P's, Phineas Philip Philander Johnson, eldest born of Mathilda S. and Abraham T. Johnson, aged fourteen.

I say eldest born, but there is some question about that, as also whether he is most Phineas or Philander or Philip.

It all comes about in this way:

He was one of triplets born to the Johnsons two years after the town was located and the same spring that the ferry was established. When it became "norrated 'round," to use an expression common to the residents along the Wabash and in some other localities as well; when it became "norrated 'round" that Mrs. Johnson had three babies, all born on the same day and all boys, every married woman within ten miles of the ferry struck straight out for the Johnsons' the moment they heard of it; and every one of them when they saw the new arrivals declared that they "looked as near alike as three peas in a pod;" and old man Johnson, who had a touch of the humorous in his composition, finally declared that that was what they should be, and straghtway named them Philip, Phineas and Philander, but when some one asked him which was Philip and which the others, he replied that "he had not decided yet, and it didn't make no difference no way, since nobody could tell tother from which, but as soon as they got growed up a bit he 'lowed to separate 'em out and mark 'em, and have the mark recorded same's they do calves and pigs."

But alas and alack! two of the innocents crossed over to the land of eternal sunshine before a short month had gone by; and as no one knew which of the P's it was that passed over and which remained, and as people said that anyway the one that stayed was properly the heir of those who went, it was finally decided that this one should have all the names—hence Philip Phineas Philander Johnson, or more commonly Phil, or the three P's.

Now if any of my readers are inclined to metaphysics and the study of the occult, I suggest to them that here is a field for thought.

What, probably or possibly, is the effect upon the two P's who passed over before being distinguished in the minds of their parents from the one who remained, and what will be the effect upon him of thus receiving the appellation by which his brothers are entitled to be known? Will the confusion of things and names and persons here affect the *karma*—I believe that the term—which our young friend to whom I have just introduced you will be able or compelled to create for himself? And will the *aura* of those who passed over be in any way affected by the acts of him who remains, and who not only bears the names to which they are entitled, but is indistinguishably and permanently mixed up with them in the minds of the parents and the community in which the latter is still living?

You will note that Phil is not greatly different from other boys of his age and surroundings. I may as well tell you here, so that you may not suffer any disappointment later on, that now that he is a man he is not greatly different from other men. This is just a plain narrative of the lives of plain everyday people possessed of plain everday virtues and weaknesses; and that there has been anything worth recording in their lives is due rather to the circumstances by which at times they have been surrounded than to any extraordinarily heroic qualities possessed by them. There are thousands equally heroic by nature of whom the world never heard, for the reason that heroism is so common a virtue among the people.

That which is not of the common only is made matter of history.

The everyday life of the common people of this and most other countries is filled with acts of heroism;

heroic forbearance under multiplied wrongs; heroic self-denial, growing out of love for country and family and friends. I do not write this narrative because there was or is anything worthy of chronicling in the people of whom I write, but rather because of the events by which they were surrounded and in which they played their part by reason of being there.

Phil Johnson, now, is, as you see, a common enough looking boy, in blue jean overalls and hickory shirt. His straw hat has lost half its brim, but so have the hats of half the boys of his age throughout the town, and the other half will be gone in another week. What would you expect of hats that serve the purpose of footballs nearly as much as of head gear among a crowd of growing young savages, such as most boys are?

If you do not believe Phil is growing, look at his pants—half-way up to his knees, now, exposing the calf of a well-turned leg, and preparing to show still more of it before the first frost.

Yes, his face is freckled and tanned with the sun, and his hair has been given a lick and a promise to-day—probably for several days; possibly the promise without the lick; but if the lick, then it was given with a coarse comb that was lacking half its teeth, and the promise was of a more thorough combing some other time, and will probably be kept next Sunday, when his mother compels him to put on a clean shirt and overalls and slick himself up generally, preparatory to going to "meetin';" for I would not have you think the town wholly without gospel privileges. On the contrary, services are held with considerable regularity every third Sunday—in the open air if the weather permits, and if not, in the house—the only one, by the way, builded wholly of boards of which the town can boast—in which, during the winter months, the district school is kept.

One thing I wish to remind my reader of, lest he or she may have forgotten.

We forget so many things as we get along up in years.

I would not be a bit surprised, now, if you, dear reader, would deny that you were ever in love with a freckled, sun-browned girl with bare feet and a calico frock, but everybody knows you have been.

Why, I'll wager a box of the best Havanas that I can go with you back to the old neighborhood where you were raised and get proof enough to convict you in a justice's court of having been in love with a dozen such in your boyhood days.

And you, dear madame, to my positive knowledge you were in love a half dozen times at least, or thought you were, before you got out of short dresses.

Some of your sweethearts were fair skinned, tow-headed little men in nankeen waists that buttoned onto their pants, and some of them wore roundabouts and some wore coats and tucked their pants into their boot legs so as to show their red tops; lords and knights, worthy to rank with the greatest and noblest of earth. Oh, you can not deceive me. I have the wisdom which comes of years and experience, and I know all about it.

Now, if you want to recall old memories and see yourself as you were before the cares and burdens of life existed for you, just you watch what's left of the P's for a little while.

There, didn't I tell you?

He has left the crowd of youngsters with whom he was playing and is off in the direction of the ferry.

He has heard a halloo which he knows comes from some one on the other side of the river wanting to be ferried across, and is off like a shot to help Nettie with the boat. No, no, don't stop him. Let him go; there is nothing in nature more innocent than the loves of children, of boys for girls and girls for boys. For pity's sake do not do anything to make them ashamed of their love. A knowledge of what sin is and its possibilities comes soon enough; let them be innocent while they may.

"WHERE IS YOUR BROTHER."

CHAPTER II.

STARTING OUT TO MAKE A MILLION.

As Phil came over the bank Nettie was just in the act of pushing the boat off shore, having already loosened the chain with which it was fastened, and thrown it upon the boat. She had purposely delayed a little in doing this, making pretenses that the chain would not unfasten, but the moment she heard the sound of running feet on the bank above, the difficulty vanished and she began to push off.

Phil gave a shove at the prow and sprang on board, going at once to the tiller for the purpose of so turning the rude craft as to get the best use of the current in forcing it across. Evidently he was well acquainted with the handling of it. The truth is, he seldom spent much time any where else than on or about the ferry unless on compulsion from his parents. Ever since Nettie began to manage the boat Phil had been her assistant as often as he could escape from the tasks assigned him at home.

"'Spect he's down to the ferry," was always the reply of any member of the Johnson family when any other member inquired where Phil was.

As for the children of his own age belonging to other families, they never inquired of his own people of his whereabouts; if he was not in sight on the premises, neither cutting wood in front of the door, weeding the truck patch or picking up chips, they knew at once that he had been sent off on an errand, in which case it was no use to ask for him, or he was at the ferry; and it was there that they went to make their inquiries.

"Phil's got to chop wood this afternoon;" "Phil's got to hoe the onions;" "Phil's father made him go hunt the hogs down in the bottom; they're goin' to get 'em home and finish fattin' 'em." All these among other reasons Nettie herself had been heard to give in answer to questions as to where Phil was; which simply goes to show the existence of a pretty good understanding between them, and that Phil was in the habit of reporting to her any pressing engagements made for him by his parents in advance of his meeting them.

In fact the intimacy between Phil and Nettie had been of so long standing that no one had observed its beginning, or appeared to notice its existence any more than if they had been brother and sister. To the children themselves it appeared—as it certainly was—the most natural thing in the world. Nettie's first memory of the ferry, which was her first memory of anything, was of playing with other children about it, and Phil's memory went no further back.

When Nettie first began to manage the ferry boat Phil was by to encourage her in her ambition, and when the boat made its first trip with her in charge Phil went along to assist.

That was years ago now, and Phil had always been her chief assistant since. Not that he was the only one she had, for every child in the village was more or less at the ferry, and not one of them had reached the mature age of twelve years without having, one time or another, stood at the tiller and tried to guide the boat. But none of them seemed so greatly to enjoy the fun or labor—which ever you desire to consider it, or to so persistently hang around the boat as Phil. And so it was that gradually he came to be looked upon as in some way one of the managers of the ferry, having rights if not duties there.

All this, I say, had seemed natural enough to everybody, and to none more so than to Phil and Nettie.

That there could be any reason why they should blush to acknowledge the intimacy which existed between them had never occurred to either, or at least not until a few days previous to the time of which I write, nor did either understand why it was so now.

Only recently a strange feeling had sprung up in their hearts; one which made them shy of each other in the presence of older persons. Just why it was so, neither could well have told; and indeed they would probably have denied its existence. It began when a short time before a couple of gentlemen, one of whom lived in a railroad town ten miles away, but who occasionally had business which required him to travel the road to the ferry and so was known to Nettie by sight, and another, a young man she had never seen, had crossed together.

Phil was away at the time, and having as it chanced always seen them together when he had crossed heretofore, the gentleman noticed his absence and inquired of the girl if her brother was sick that she was tending the ferry alone.

"Who, Phil?" she asked in reply; adding: "He ain't my brother. He's Mr. Johnson's boy, and he couldn't help run the boat to-day 'cause he has to hoe in the truck patch."

"But isn't he hired to help you tend the ferry?" asked the gentleman. "I supposed you were both Mr. McKinley's children."

"Oh, no," answered Nettie, "Phil isn't hired; he

just helps me because he likes to run the boat, and because—because—"

She blushed and stopped. She was going to say "because we like each other," but something, perhaps it was the amused smile playing around the mouth of her questioner, caused an embarrassed feeling before unknown to her.

The gentleman finished the sentence for her by adding:

"Because he is your sweetheart, eh!" And for the first time in her life she blushed. Just why she blushed she could not have told. Indeed, I suppose she did not know she was blushing, but she knew that her face felt suddenly uncomfortably warm, and she turned away and pretended to be busy with the tiller, and never once again looked at either gentleman, neither replied to their smilingly pronounced "good byes" as they left the boat. And when, after completing his stint for the afternoon, Phil joined her at the ferry as usual, she greeted him less boisterously than was her custom, and when any one was by appeared shy of him, and as if she wished to avoid being seen sitting or standing by his side. Phil felt this shyness rather than saw it with his natural eyes, and instinctively tried to keep closer to her than ever, which only seemed to make her the more anxious to keep away from him. When he went home and to bed that night he had for the first time in his life a feeling that there was something wrong with the universe some way, as if the world was out of kelter and needed fixing, though just how or why he could not say.

But the next day when he went again to the ferry the feeling had all passed away and the world had resumed its natural brightness. Nettie, too, appeared to have forgotten, if she had ever had anything to remember, for she hailed him with accustomed familiarity, and they spent a pleasant half day together, though once or twice when grown people were around there was something about Nettie quite indefinable to Phil, yet which caused a slight return of the feeling of the night before.

But the feeling, whatever it was, passed in a moment. When he went to his dinner and his afternoon stint of weeding in the truck patch he was light hearted as a boy could be and did an unusually good job of weeding; and the next day when he had chopped and split enough wood for his mother to bake with and was again at liberty, and hearing the halloo of some one wanting to cross the river, he darted away as we have seen, with heart as light as his heels.

As we have seen, too, Nettie was waiting and hoping for his coming; even pretending to those who wished to be brought across that she was having trouble in unfastening the boat, in order to give Phil time to get there before she cast off.

Had she been straining her eyes in an effort to recognize the parties waiting to come over as intently as she was straining her ears to catch the sound of Phil's approaching steps, she would have seen that the travelers were the same gentlemen who had crossed over two days before, to one of whom she owed the knowledge of her ability to blush; in which case she would probably have hurried to push off before Phil's arrival, instead of making an excuse to await his coming.

When Phil had taken the tiller after jumping aboard, Nettie went and stood by him, and, all unconscious of the strangers watching them, laughed and chatted merrily, their eyes meanwhile observing the motion of the boat, and Phil moving the tiller this way and that almost mechanically, as long practice in a thing enables any one to do.

As they neared the opposite shore Nettie picked up the chain, and the moment the boat touched sprang ashore, ready to throw it over the post placed there for that purpose, when, glancing up, she recognized the travelers, and was instantly covered with confusion. All the old feeling of embarrassment came back to her, and she stood for a brief space of time with her hands extended as if in the act of letting the ring drop over the stake, but forgetting to let go of it, while the blood suffused her face and neck.

"So the captain's mate has returned, has he?" interrogated the elder gentleman, glancing from Nettie to Phil and back again; and then added, laughingly, "The brave knight performs the service required of him by the powers which be, and instantly flies to the presence of his sweetheart;" at which his companion laughed also.

Neither Phil nor Nettie knew just what he meant by his remark, but they did know that in some mild way they were being made sport of for being so much together, and instantly they became silent. Only once during the few moments they were swinging back to their starting point did either speak, and then Phil asked some simple question in a low tone, which Nettie answered in a still lower one, and without looking at him; and when the gentlemen had left the boat and ridden up the bank and out of sight, she also went up the bank and into her father's cabin, and did not return for more than an hour, and not until Phil had gone home.

The next morning, when Mr. Johnson, standing at the foot of the ladder which led up into the loft of his story-and-a-half log cabin, and looking up at the open landing above his head, called first, "Phil," and then

"Oh, Phil," two or three times, and getting no answer had climbed to his sleeping place with the intention of waking him by some more vigorous measures, he found the loft empty. Phil was not there.

"Blamed if the youngster ain't up and out a'ready," he said aloud, as he descended to the lower floor again; "wonder what's on hand to make him turn out without being called?"

"Phil's up a'ready," he said to the boy's mother, as he passed from the log part into the frame kitchen in which she was preparing breakfast. "Where d'ye s'pose he is; ain't gone down to the ferry before breakfast, I reckon?"

Whether Mrs. Johnson felt a sudden premonition of evil, or whether she thought her husband had been mistaken in supposing that Phil had arisen, I can not tell, but she laid down the knife with which she was turning her corn cakes and went into the other room and up the ladder, as her husband had done. She was gone some minutes, and returned with a scared look upon her face. She held in her hand a piece of paper, evidently the blank leaf torn from some school book, on which was scrawled in a big hand:

"Tell Nettie I've gone away; when I've made a million of dollars I'll cum back and marry her.'

"Phil."

Two weeks later, a letter addressed in the same

schoolboy hand arrived, and was given to Mrs. Johnson. It ran as follows :

"DEAR MOTHER:

I'm going to go to Kansas to herd cattle for a man. We are goin' through with teams. When I get a good farm and lots of cattle of my own I'll come back after you all.

Your affectionate son,

PHIL.

Post skrip. Tell Nettie."

IN FRONT OF THE STAMPEDE.

CHAPTER III.

IN FRONT OF THE STAMPEDE—RIDING THE TRAIL.

Ride! ride like the devil; ride for your life, man! Stick spur in your pony's flank, and press hard and press long; lean low over your saddle bow—speak quick, sharp words of encouragement and command to your beast, and ride for your life! for behind you, like the waves of a mad sea, are ten thousand frightened steers, and you are scarce the length of your horse ahead of them! If your pony stumble—if in the darkness of night made black by overhanging clouds his foot shall strike a prairie dog hole, or if he fail to clear at a bound the ruins of some deserted corral, the location of which neither horse nor rider knows anything of—if anything happen by which his speed is checked but for one short moment—the hoofs that are thundering at your heels shall tramp every semblance of humanity out of your body before you can utter a prayer or curse!

It was in the spring of 188– that Maxwell's big herd

started up the trail from the Rio Grande country on their long journey through Texas and the Indian Territory to Kansas. For months the Maxwells, aided by their men, had been rounding up and branding and preparing for the trip, and finally all was ready, and the herd was started North. Herds starting from as low down as Laredo, or anywhere in Southern Texas, must start early in the season, as it is an all summer drive if cattle are to be brought through in good condition.

Maxwell had in this drive a good round five thousand longhorns, or Texas steers, mostly three-year-olds. The plan was to take them North by easy stages to well up in the Indian Territory, winter there, and push them into market as early as they could be got into fit condition.

The outfit consisted of ten men, besides a cook.

Each of the ten men was supplied with several Spanish ponies for riding; for on such drives frequent changes of horses are absolutely necessary. The cook was furnished with a pair of stout mules, a wagon for "chuck" or provisions, consisting principally of beans and black coffee, though a steer is always killed when needed on such expeditions, particularly when passing through strips of country where there are cattle at range.

Cattle men, as a rule—to which there are exceptions —much prefer having men in their employ, when they want fresh meat, kill a steer or heifer bearing some brand other than their own, and applaud it as a good joke—a sort of sharp trick. Human nature is not much different on the plains than elsewhere; neither are cattle men or cowboys worse than others; but those who engage in the business as employers or employed do so either from a desire to acquire wealth rapidly or a love of freedom from the restraints of law, and it is natural among such that a disregard for legal rights, even a pleasure in disregarding them, should manifest itself; but let the sympathies of this class be appealed to—let a companion, or even a stranger, be in need, and none so ready to extend a helping hand; and the most ready of all is often he who is most prompt on occasion to wrong another in the killing of a steer or branding a maverick.

The drive had been on the road but two or three days, and was hardly broken in—long-horned steers that have never been handled except as they were caught with a lasso, thrown to the ground and branded with a hot iron, never get very well broken in, even to driving in a bunch—when, just as night approached, a rain storm came up accompanied with wind, and at once the herd began to drift, that is, to work slowly ahead with the storm.

The only thing to do when a herd begins drifting, and especially if it be a large one, is for the herders to keep with it, riding in front and at the sides; keeping it from breaking up into bunches, and so becoming separated. Cattle do not travel very rapidly in such cases, but they keep moving steadily, with heads down, noses close to the ground, and any effort to stop them is likely to result in the thing most to be dreaded—a stampede, and a division of the drove into bunches, whereby it is likely to become mixed with other herds.

When the storm came up, the men, a few at a time, went back to the cook's wagon and secured such provender as they could for themselves, caught and mounted fresh ponies and resumed their places in the line which they had formed about the drifting herd, endeavoring by the singing of songs and by keeping even pace with the cattle as they drifted to keep them from becoming uneasy, and so hold them together.

And now, reader, if you have ever hankered after the free and easy life of a cowboy, this is a good time to think the matter over and arrive at a decision.

Fancy yourself one of Maxwell's hands on this drive and the night in question. You have been in the saddle all day and have changed horses twice; the night is black, but you have been out on dark nights, and on rainy nights and on horseback before. Very well. Now recall, if you can, the darkest night in which you were ever out. Imagine the rain falling steadily and every now and then rustled and rattled about by a gust of

ALONE IN THE DARKNESS. 51

wind, yourself **astride of** a Spanish pony, who would feel insulted if he thought you considered him thoroughly **broke, even to the saddle, and** by **you.** We are on a **prairie** miles, **yes hundreds of** miles, **in** extent over **which neither of us has ever** ridden, **and we are two** of but a handful **of men in charge of** some thousands of half wild steers **drifting** with the storm.

We separate here; **you turn your** pony's head with the storm and ride slowly **in** advance of the drifting herd. I continue on **out** of your sight and hearing, **and** then do as you **have done,** turn my pony's head with the wind, and drift.

You are alone **now; you see** nothing, unless perchance a flash of lightning discloses for an instant a sea **of** horns, **of** long slim horns above **a** mass of black moving beasts liable at any moment to become frantic with fear and rush at you and over you, trampling you down and mangling you beyond possibility of recognition.

Hour **after** hour the storm beats down and the cattle drift. **You** were soaked through and through hours ago. For hours you have **not so** much as seen the pony's head upon which you ride; you do not know which way or where you are going, or how going, only that you are drifting with **the** storm and the herd. You hear the tramp of feet, **the rattle** of horns knocking against each other, **and** occasionally the voice of another herder singing, or **rather** yelling, for the double purpose of keeping the steers as quiet as may be and of letting his companions know about where he is.

You attempt to lift up an answering voice, but the wind comes with a gust, snatches your sombrero from your head and whirls it away in the darkness. If there was only the least bit of light it would look like a great dusky bat sailing through the air, but it is too dark to see anything; and besides, the same gust of wind that robbed you of your sombrero drove the words you were trying to speak back into your mouth and down your throat, choking you and forcing you to turn aside your head to catch breath again as you ride to-night with Maxwell's drive of Texas steers.

And just as you turn your head, and before you can catch your breath, the steers stampede. Your hat carried by the wind and skimming over their backs has done it. You feel the first mighty impulse, the first frightened thrill of that compacted mass; the ground trembles, and for an instant, with the wind in your throat, you are confused and imagine yourself in a storm at sea. Only the agility of your pony saves you from instant death, for you are in the lead and the herd that is coming down upon you is as blind with fear as are you with the darkness.

Only ten minutes since the stampede began and it seems an hour; you are a mile, miles from where you started and still alive but not out of danger. A Texas steer is almost as fleet of foot and long of wind as a cow pony, and you had but a few yards the start, having kept close up to them that your presence might quiet them. You are gaining on them, however, and they may slacken their pace any moment now.

But no, they have taken fresh fright and are rushing on faster than ever. And—what's that? **Great** God! they are closing in on the sides. In the darkness the edges of the drive have moved faster than the center and you are flanked upon both sides, and in their fright now they are closing in instead of scattering.

Something touches your stirrup as you ride; you feel the presence of something beside you, keeping even pace with you; you think it a steer and that the herd has quite closed in on you; but no, it is another rider and another pony. In the race we who separated in front of the drive hours ago are driven together by the pressure of the herd upon our right and our left. We are still behind the leaders upon both flanks. We do not see this, we feel that it is so; there is something in the air, in the trembling of the ground, in the efforts of the animals we ride to put forth increased speed that tells it to us.

But how dark it is. We lean forward upon our saddle bows; we strain our eyes; we drive our rowels afresh into the flanks of our steeds, we fly through the darkness.

There comes a flash of lightning, not vivid, but enough to show us the ground in front and the herd closing in upon us. There is but a little space on either side not filled by the black mass of moving bodies and horns.

The light has vanished now and we can feel the darkness around and about us; and now we feel the touch of warm bodies against our legs; the herd has closed in upon us; we are a part of the mass of surging brutes, surrounded, doomed.

Only for an instant. Another flash of lightning and an opening appears; we lack but a length of being in the lead, our ponies see it, understand it, put forth new strength and clear the press. We are saved. No, one falls, his pony's foot caught in a prairie dog hole, and the mass surges over him. To-morrow search will be made and a mass of blood and mangled flesh will be found and given such burial as is possible, but for that he who rides has no time to think. He is out of the mass and again in the lead and a good ten miles from the point where the stampede began, and the surging mass of bodies and horns behind is beginning to recover from its fright, to check its speed. He is saved.

But how do you like to ride the drive? Has the wild free life of the cowboy the same charm for you it had before you rode this night with Maxwell's herd?

When the morning came after the stampede and the ride from which one never returned, the drive was found to have been kept well together, considering the distance and the character of the night. It had divided into two parts, but luckily both had taken the same general direction and had come to a halt when the storm ceased near daybreak, not more than two or three miles apart, so that the difficulty of gathering them together was not great. But it was noon before all the herders had opportunity to get anything to eat or to change their tired ponies for fresh ones.

Among the last to show up at camp was one of the men who was in front of the drive when the stampede began. What remained of the other had been buried two hours before and a rude mark placed over the hastily dug grave.

"That was a close call you had last night, Phil,' remarked one of the men. "I thought you and Bob had both gone on the long drive. I knew you and he were in front, and was afraid the brutes had pushed ahead at the sides so as to flank you. I was half way back on the side to which the wind was blowing and could hear you while you couldn't hear me, but I kept calling to the boys in front of me to keep singing or calling so we could each know where we all were and keep the steers as much together as possible. When the cattle started I thought of you and Bob, for I wasn't in any special danger myself, not more than common at such times; and when that flash of lightning came I saw you both, just for a second; must have been on a bit of a rise just then, so I could see the whole mass of brutes and you and Bob bein' closed in on, but only a few lengths behind the foremost of the drive. I hoped then you'd both come through, but I reckon Bob's pony must have stumbled. Well, everybody's got to ride that trail sometime, but I'd rather die some other way than be trampled to death by a lot of longhorn steers."

"I, too," returned the other. "I don't believe I'm a coward, but there are things about this business that are a little bit too rocky for comfort. I've more than half a mind to say that this will be my last drive. Soon's we round up in Kansas guess I'll settle up with the company and take what's coming to me and start in for myself somewhere."

"Goin' back to the States?"

"No; at least not yet. I must make a stake first; a little one, anyway. I was only a boy when I left home—ran away, you know—and I promised not to go back until I was worth a million. Then I dropped down a peg or two, and fixed the line at a big ranch and lots of cattle; and I must at least have a little ranch and a few cattle, or I'd be ashamed to show myself in the old neighborhood."

"Well, you came mighty nigh being saved that trouble. I calculate you were only one jump ahead of death last night, and not much time to spare to make it in. But what's the use of whinin'? Better eat our chuck while we can get it." And the two turned to the lay-out provided by the cook, and proceeded to satisfy their appetites.

And this is Phil Johnson, the man who so narrowly escaped death last night, and is now sitting on a bit of limestone rock, drinking black coffee from a tin cup and eating grub from a chuck wagon; the boy you used to know when he lived in that little town on the Wabash, and 'tended ferry with Nettie McKinley when not engaged in weeding the truck patch, bringing in wood for his mother, or hunting hogs or cattle in the river bottoms. He has not got the million dollars yet, you see, not even the ranch and big lot of cattle, but he has been to Kansas, as he said in his letter to his mother that he was going to do, and from Kansas has drifted to the Lone Star State, where we now find him drifting back again, a rider for Maxwell, one of the largest cattle men of the West.

Yes, he has grown. He is a man now. Let me see— it was five, six, eight years ago that he ran away from home because his little sweetheart left him one day without saying good-bye, and hid away in her father's cabin. How time flies. Eight and fourteen—that makes twenty-two. Phil is a year past his majority now, and Nettie herself is past twenty.

The accidental reference of Phil's companion to the States called up memories which haunted Phil all that day and the next and the next. He could not forget the old home; oh no, he had never forgotten it, nor the ferry, nor Nettie; neither his purpose of going back some day and surprising them all by the amount of wealth he would display; but the desire to return had never been so strong upon him as now.

Perhaps it was because of his narrow escape from death in the stampede, though, as for that, he had been near death often before in those eight years.

Ever since he left home—or, at least, ever since arriving in Kansas with the emigrant he fell in with a few days after leaving—he had lived upon the frontier; most of the time as a herder of cattle. Twice he had formed one of a little company that had followed a party of cattle thieves across the Rio Grande into old Mexico, and retaken the stolen beeves after a smart skirmish, in which men had bitten the dust upon both sides; and once, when with a herd in New Mexico, he had had a brush with the Comanches, and came near getting his scalp lifted. And all this time he had kept in mind his promise of some time going back to the old neighborhood and Nettie.

He had not, however, made much headway toward the million or even the ranch and cattle. He had lived in the main the life of other cowboys, which means getting anywhere from fifteen to fifty dollars a month and spending it whenever opportunity offers. What could one expect of such a boy and such companions?

Yet Phil had not been drunken or wild, as many are; he had simply spent freely when he had anything to spend and a chance to spend it. Nothing is so hard to resist as the temptation to spend when among those who are in the habit of spending freely; and nowhere in the world, or among any class of men, is one more meanly thought of for niggardliness than among cowboys.

Phil's outfit was always of the best. His saddle cost fifty dollars. His spurs were of silver; his pistols finely mounted; his blankets were made in old Mexico, and were thick and heavy and fine, and he dressed in the best of cowboy style. He generally owned a pony or two besides, but ponies are cheap—from fifteen to fifty dollars—a month's wages. And this was the extent of Phil's savings to date; this the start he had made upon his million.

But now, as he rode day after day, or stood his

lonely guard at night, his thoughts turned more seriously to the past and also to the future. For the first time he realized fully that the years were passing, and that if ever he was to make good in any considerable degree his boyish boast of securing a competence and returning to the village of his birth, it was time he set about it. He had not really intended for earnest what he had said to his companion the morning after the stampede about this drive with Maxwell being his last. That was said without consideration, or at least without any very great consideration, but it proved in the end to be a prophecy. The more he thought of the words he had spoken, the more he determined to make them good, and he resolved to leave his employer the moment he could do so with a few hundred dollars ahead, and to begin in earnest the work of making a home for himself and—and, yes, Nettie ; that is, if she had not forgotten him—if she had not married some one else.

He wondered if she had forgotten, if she had married. Sometimes he fancied she had and tried to picture her living in the little old town on the banks of the Wabash as the wife of one of his former playmates. At first this idea rather amused him ; he had been gone long enough and had seen enough of the world to have a realizing sense of what a quiet, out of the way place it was. Not even a flatboat floating down with the current any more, to break the monotony of life in the little town. True, there had not been many such when he was a boy, but he could remember a few; could even remember seeing an occasional little steam vessel working its way to the small city forty miles up the stream. But all that was over now; no steamers, no flatboats even; the railroads had caused all that to cease being profitable, and at the same time by building up larger towns at short distances away, had left this little town without a thing to furnish excitement or even to stimulate conversation. Thinking of it he could not help wondering if the inhabitants were still talking of the last flatboat which floated down the river four years before he left and got snagged and sunk a half mile below the ferry.

Ah, yes, the ferry. He had gone with Nettie and a lot of other children to see the boat where she lay. Joe Bronson was among them he remembered. He wondered if Joe lived there still, and if he hadn't been making up to Nettie during these years of his own absence.

Then he began to be jealous of his probable rival. The thought which had but a moment ago provoked but a mild species of curiosity, a wanting to know, had, now, that it took different shape and a personality, excited an uneasy feeling which reminded him of the time he noticed Nettie's shyness, and he felt half tempted to quit the drive at once and break for home then and there. But he remembered his boast of coming back rich and he felt ashamed to return empty handed. Then came thoughts of his mother and all her kindness and self sacrifice. He remembered how she had worked and economized in order that the family might be kept together and comfortable. He did not realize it at the time, but he understood it all now, and he compared her labors with his own and her spending with his, since he started out for himself, and he felt ashamed and humiliated. Hard as he saw his own life as a cowboy to have been, he felt that her life had been incomparably harder; for it was a life of ceaseless toil, of duties never ended and without a thing to break the monotony from year end to year end.

"No wonder the folks used to talk of that flatboat getting snagged four years after it occurred," he muttered. "Why, hang it all, that's the only thing that ever did occur so far as I can remember; there wasn't anything else they *could* talk about."

"And how mother used to scrimp and save every penny and go without things herself for us children;" so his mind ran on. "I believe the twenty-five cent pieces we used to get to spend at Christmas and the fourth of July cost her more self-denial than it would me to have sent home a thousand dollars."

"And father, too, he must be getting old now; how jolly he used to be with us youngsters. Think of his naming us triplets Philip, Philander and Phineas. He must have thought it a huge joke, and so it was. Wonder now what became of the other two—the two that died? Reckon they ain't cowboys? Reckon they wouldn't have run away as I did just as I was getting big enough to pay for my keep, and never let 'em know where they were all this time? Hang me if I ain't a worse brute than one of them longhorn steers."

You see he was getting tender hearted if not sentimental, thinking of the past and all it had been and might have been.

Such thoughts come to us all at times, I think; thoughts of the goodness and sweetness of our mothers —of the sacrifices which they have made for us—of their love for us and sorrow endured because of us; and it is well that such thoughts do come. They seem to break up the crust of selfishness which forms about one's heart in contact with the world, and make room for kindly feelings toward all mankind.

The result of Phil's thoughts was to change to a fixed purpose the impulse which came to him that morning to save his earnings, and as soon as he could, with credit to himself, return to his old home and do what was possible to compensate his parents for his long absence. And he clenched his good resolution on the spot by sending from the first town he reached a long letter to his father, telling them of his wandering, of his present whereabouts and firm purpose to begin "laying up a stake," and ended by sending with it every dollar of money he had at the time.

MR. BROWN, OF NEW YORK.

CHAPTER IV.

IN WHICH MR. BROWN, OF NEW YORK, IS INTRODUCED TO THE WILD WEST. AFTERWARD HE BUYS SOME STEERS.

The long, warm months of summer passed slowly away, with the herd moving steadily nothward, and September saw them still on the road. But early in October the drive reached the vicinity of Caldwell, Kansas, and were bedded for the last time by the men who had brought them through from the Rio Grande, for here they were taken in hand by partners of Maxwell, who shipped them East by rail.

Phil had expected a letter from home to reach him here, but none awaited him. He had settled with his employer, receiving his season's pay in a lump, having religiously refrained from drawing any on the long drive; being determined to have at least a nest egg with which to start out on his own hook when the drive should end.

He drew wages for seven months, amounting to over three hundred dollars, more money than he had ever possessed at any one time, and had he received a letter from home, as he fondly expected, I am not sure he would not have weakened in his purpose of not going home until he had made his fortune. Even as it was he felt strangely inclined to go. Then his pride arose, and he began to feel himself deeply wronged.

They had forgotten him, he said, or had never forgiven him for running away.

As if a mother could ever forget her child.

He had not said anything in his letter about Nettie.

At first he had thought he would, then concluded not to, thinking his mother would probably mention her in the letter she would write to him, and so he would learn whether she was married or not, without having asked. Not getting any letter discouraged him, and after giving up the idea of going home he felt tempted to go on a lark, and blow in every dollar of his earnings, and return to his old life again. But better thoughts intervened, and, after lying around for a few days, he entered into partnership with a "tenderfoot," as a man unacquainted with frontier life is called.

This stranger, whose name was Samuel Brown, put in four thousand dollars against Phil's outfit, valued at three hundred, and his ready cash, three hundred more, each to receive equally of all profit; Phil's superior knowledge and experience being considered an equivalent to Mr. Brown's extra quantity of capital.

Thus elevated to the character of a capitalist, Phil's ambition took a fresh lease of life, and his self respect went up several degrees; nothing now could have tempted him to blow his money in at a gambling hell.

Brown, his partner, although an Eastern man, and unacquainted with the business, was evidently a man of pluck and endurance.

He had been bred in the city, but having a natural love for a life of freedom, and hearing of the fortunes being made in the cattle business, had turned his little capital into money and gone West for the purpose of investing it. Happening to meet Phil he took a fancy to him; and learning from the Maxwells that he was trusty and experienced, struck up a partnership with him, and, ten days after arriving in Caldwell, Phil and Brown started back along the trail the former had just passed over, on their way to buy a drove of cattle for themselves.

Nothing of special interest occurred on their way down; that is, nothing of interest to the reader. Everything was interesting to Phil's partner, Mr. Brown.

from the start. Even the pony he purchased to carry him on the trip proved a subject of absorbing interest for a time.

The pony also appeared deeply interested in Mr. Brown.

Evidently he recognized him as a "tenderfoot" at sight, and the moment Mr. Brown swung himself into the saddle the pony proceeded to introduce him to the ways of the country which he was invading.

First he reached around and took Mr. Brown by the leg, as if feeling for his muscle, in an endeavor to ascertain the probabilities of his being able to walk to Texas in case a necessity for doing so should arise.

Apparently satisfied on this point, and being invited by Mr. Brown to proceed, he proceeded; that is, he proceeded to place all four of his feet close together, put his nose with his feet, and jump into the air.

Brown went up with him but forgot to come down when he did. Instead of coming down with the pony he kept on going up, and when he did come down he landed on his head—not the pony's head, but his own.

He lay doubled up in a heap for a second or two, and then got upon his feet and put out his hand and spread his fingers wide apart and beat the air faintly, as if feeling around for something, he did not seem to know just what. Then he came to, and straightened himself up and looked at the pony with blood in his eye; there was blood on his nose also, but that is not worth mentioning. Then the pony turned his head to one side and looked at him, brought his feet back to their first position and shook himself as if he had said: "Well, my young tenderfoot, what do you think of the Wild West by this time?"

Then Brown made for him, and got him by the bridle, and crowded him up against the corral, and spoke to him in language which encouraged a bystander to remark that "Brown would make a success as a cowboy yet."

Then Brown argued with the pony some more, and finally succeeded, with the help of two other men, in getting mounted again; upon which the pony proceeded as before to bring his feet together under the center of his body, put his nose to the ground and spring about eight feet into the air.

This time Brown was expecting something of the kind and was prepared for it. He rose with the pony and also came down with him, doing both in good style; but as the pony struck the ground stiff-legged and as this was what Mr. Brown was not expecting, he immediately rose again, and when he came down this time it was on the ground on the spot where the pony had stood a second before. Recognizing the fact that Mr. Brown had gone up into the air again, and his experience with tenderfeet not enabling him to determine whether or not he intended coming down, and, if so, whether he had any particular spot selected on which to alight, he considerately moved forward a few yards and went to nibbling grass until wanted.

Again Brown arose from the ground and made for the pony, but so far from being able to mount him was he that Phil had first to catch him with his lasso, after which, with some help, Brown again climbed on, "prepared to stay with him," he said; but the pony, who had done nothing for a month, evidently felt that simply pitching Brown off was not sufficient exercise, and so instead of bucking he started off at a run, whereat Brown straightened up in the saddle and having the bridle to hold on to succeeded in keeping his seat. Phil followed after at the same rattling pace and the two passed out of the town in what Brown felt to be pretty good style. In fact I think he considered this part of the performance quite creditable, as that night, sitting about their first camp, he remarked to Phil that he wished he could have had taken a photograph of themselves as they came out of town, to send back to his folks.

This, however, did not prevent a feeling of un-

THE PRICE OF YEARLING STEERS. 71

certainty regarding his ability to stay with the pony in case he began bucking again, and when they saddled up the next morning, Phil, observing with what suspicion Brown eyed the pony, and knowing from experience just how lame and sore his partner must be with this first day's riding, had compassion on him and offered to exchange mounts until his pony was thoroughly broke in, a proposition which Brown acceded to with some apparent reluctance but much inward satisfaction.

In time Brown became a fearless and fairly good rider; but I doubt if the remembrance of his introduction to the ways of the "Wild West," or at least that portion of it represented by bucking ponies, affords him any especial pleasure even yet.

Arriving in Texas the two men bought four hundred head of yearling steers, paying eight dollars apiece for them, and proposed to push out into New Mexico, where Phil felt certain of being able to find a range suitable to their wants.

They accordingly bought a wagon for the transportation of provisions, ammunition, and the few tools they should need to build a permanent camp with. They bought a pair of mules and harness, and hired a cheap hand to act as cook and to drive the team on the journey. They also bought a number of ponies, about half of them being three-year-old mares, so that they might be making a start toward raising their own cow ponies while their herd of steers was growing.

Of course they had to go well armed.

While there is really far less lawlessness and disregard for human life among the cattle men and cowboys along our frontiers than the blood and thunder stories told of them would lead people to suppose, there are yet a sufficient number of reckless characters among them to make it wise to go armed.

There are two ways of avoiding the probabilities of war; the first one is for no one to carry any of the weapons of war; the other is for everybody to carry them. The former is undoubtedly the best way provided all agree to it, but as everybody can not be induced to do so, a proper regard for one's own interest in life and long-horned steers and Spanish ponies is best exhibited in the purchase and wearing of a brace of revolvers, to which—if two or three are intending to strike off by themselves with a small herd—it is well to add a good repeating rifle.

I have noticed that the Indians especially have a profound respect for a repeating rifle. Such as do not understand its workings regard it as a device of the Evil Spirit to assist in driving the red man from his native plains, while such as do understand it have a realizing sense of the danger involved in stealing cattle or ponies from those in possession of so formidable a weapon.

Having completed the purchase of their herd and laid in a good supply of provisions, the two men set out for their destination, which point was, however, a little indefinite, even in Phil's mind.

He felt confident that he should find plenty of feed on the route he had marked out for them to take, and therefore was not uneasy about the matter, as they could move leisurely and settle down whenever a good bit of unoccupied range with plenty of water presented itself; and for this purpose they had reserved a few hundred dollars to be used, if need be, in buying out some one who had enough of this kind of life and was anxious to go back to civilization.

Accordingly they struck across country until they reached the Pecos river, which stream they followed up for a time and finally crossed, in order to secure the better pasturage skirting the foothills of the Guadaloupe range of mountains, thus avoiding the staked plains with their scarcity of water—for which they are only too well known, as many a hapless ranger and cattle man can testify—crossed the Big Bonita river, and finally pitched camp on a little stream which enters the Pecos river fifty or seventy-five miles above the Bonita, and not far from opposite old Fort Stanton, which is on the other side of the Guadaloupe range.

They were more fortunate in this than they had hoped, as they found the range unoccupied and unappropriated, and they at once took steps to enter it, at the government price of a dollar and a quarter an acre. That is, they entered three hundred and twenty acres lying along the head waters of the creek, thus securing control of the water privilege, which meant virtual control of the whole range adjoining for as many miles as would suffice to pasture what cattle could be watered at the stream.

True, this is hardly what the spirit of our institutions is supposed to intend or sustain, but such is the letter of the law, and such its application throughout the West generally. Nor is this all, nor the worst of it; in many places the continued sole occupancy of great tracts by large cattle owners and syndicates of owners has led them to presume to a permanent and absolute ownership of the whole tract, and in many cases they have erected barbed wire fences hundreds of miles in length, inclosing hundreds of thousands—even millions of acres, and are prepared to defend their claims in the courts. That they should deem it possible to do so successfully will doubtless appear ridiculous to the reader until he stops to consider the fact that the control of so much land and of the capital necessary to stock it, thereby making it profitable to inclose it, is quite

PREPARING TO BECOME CATTLE KINGS.

sufficient to make and unmake courts in most countries, and may well prove to be so here.

This was something, however, upon which neither Phil Johnson nor Sam Brown felt compelled, or even greatly inclined, to moralize.

They had come for the purpose of finding a range for their steers, and they sought for and secured it in accordance with the letter of the law and the custom of the country. They intended laying the foundation of a business that should grow into something big by and by. They meant to herd their yearlings here two years and then put them on the market, and use the proceeds of the sale to buy another and larger lot, and so continue until they had a big herd and could afford to hire men to care for them, while they took things easy "*a la* cattle king."

This was the expression Brown used one night as they sat chatting about the camp fire, while the steers lay quietly resting in front of them.

Phil did not understand exactly what "*a la* cattle king" meant, but he was too sharp to "give himself away"—in the current slang of the time—and quietly listened for some other expression which should throw light on it.

Having fixed on a location for their permanent camp, the next thing to do was to erect a log house, which was no very difficult job, as scattering timber lined the creek bank.

A rough stockade, sufficient to hold the steers at night and thus save the trouble and exposure of night watching, was a work of more difficulty, but was finally accomplished—being built partly of timber and partly of rock gathered along the creek bank, and where the underlying ledge cropped out upon little ridges here and there over the prairie.

And then the "pards" settled down to what they were inclined to regard as solid comfort.

As there were no other herds, or at least no large ones, very near them, they had little fear of the cattle getting mixed up with others and so taken off their own range; and with a stockade to which they could be driven at night, whenever it appeared desirable, the labor of herding them was very little and left plenty of time for hunting.

They therefore discharged the hand who had acted as cook and teamster, turned the mules out to graze with the ponies and did the cooking by turns between them.

Their principal fear now was of Indians.

The chief range of the Apaches was to the south and on the other side of the mountains; but they were known to be in the habit of making excursions far north of the spot where Phil and Brown had located, and the sight of a bunch of young cattle is a temptation not always, if ever, resisted, provided the danger of appropriating them is not too great.

However, the partners decided not to let this fact worry them or cause them to enjoy in any less degree the situation, which to Phil, after his years of harder services, seemed to be an exceedingly soft thing; while Brown, for the very opposite reason, he having no previous experience, was charmed with the variety of his surroundings and the freedom of the life he was leading.

Deer and antelope abounded; herds of buffalo were by no means unfrequent, and jack rabbits were everywhere, so that there was lack neither of sport nor of meat in variety for the daily fare; and with the addition of corn meal, with which to make bread, coffee and bacon for a change and seasoning, the partners lived like kings and enjoyed life to the utmost.

Among other incidents of their daily life was one in which Sam again figured, in connection with that bucking pony.

Riding slowly along near the quietly feeding herd one fine morning, a mule-eared rabbit suddenly sprung up from behind a sage bush almost at the pony's feet, and started off with that peculiar lope for which he is noted, when Sam took it into his head to have a little sport racing him; accordingly he gave the pony a dig with his spurs and away they went. The race had continued for a mile or so when the rabbit darted behind, or rather into, a clump of sage brush growing on the edge of a bit of a ravine which headed but a few yards or rods away, but which at the place where the sage brush grew was possibly six feet across and three or four feet deep, the water having washed out the earth from what was evidently a seam in the limestone rock, leaving nearly perpendicular and very solid walls.

Now, Sam had never chanced to cross the ravine at this particular spot, or if he had done so he had forgotten the locality, and when the rabbit darted into the clump of sage brush and squatted, Sam thought him still making time on the other side and so came ahead full tilt; but just as he reached the bushes where the rabbit sat, and was expecting his pony to clear them at a bound the pony concluded that there was no use of his going any further until the rabbit started on again, and stopped; but his rider, who was standing up in his stirrups endeavoring to get sight of the game, continued going right along and landed on his stomach on the other side of the ravine. Now, the rabbit, which had squatted in the brush, decided to start on again just at this time also. Possibly it was a glimpse of Sam as he came sailing over that induced him to start just as he did. Be that as it may, he did start and just in time to land upon the opposite side at exactly the same instant that Sam landed, but unfortunately for the rabbit, as fortunately for Sam, the rabbit was under, and while serving to break the other's fall had the life crushed out of him by the performance. It is probably the only instance of a man being thrown from a bucking pony upon the game he was chasing, and the result of the accident helped Sam to forgive the source of it.

CHAPTER V.

A COTILLION AT THE CAMP, DURING WHICH THE MUSIC
SUDDENLY CHANGES.

What with the care of their herd, the pleasures of the chase and an occasional visit to or from the owners of other herds, the time passed swiftly enough, and the yearlings which they had bought in Texas at eight dollars a head were become two-year-olds, and having had good range and good water were worth nearly twice what they cost, and the partners were beginning to count the months before they should commence their long drive to some point East where they could sell to advantage or ship to Chicago by rail.

They could sell their cattle on the spot—that they knew very well—and quite probably, too, for as good a figure as they could get in Kansas or Chicago, making allowance for cost and possible or probable loss on the drive, for two or three thousand head

DEFENDING THE RANCH.

can be driven a long distance almost as cheaply as four hundred where pasturage costs nothing; and there were plenty of buyers for a fine bunch, such as they had. It would be difficult indeed for a man with a likely bunch of steers to get into so remote and inaccessible a nook of country that no one wishing to buy them should find him out, and these friends of ours had not sought to do such a thing as that.

There were other ranches within distances easily covered by a pony in the space of a few hours, in either of three directions, and all these, of course, knew of the Brown-Johnson ranch and of their likely bunch of cattle, so that if it had been understood that they wanted to sell either cattle or ranch, they would easily have found a buyer.

But the partners had about decided not only to drive but to ship their cattle. Brown especially urged this every time they talked together on the subject. He wanted to make the trip East and see the folks once more, he said; then he would come back and they would start in afresh, and stay two more years without going out, by which time they would be pretty well fixed.

Phil did not know which he wanted to do; of course he was anxious to sell to advantage, and at times he felt favorably inclined to his partner's proposition to take the cattle clear through themselves, when the time came. These were the times when the desire to know what had become of the old place and Nettie were strongest with him. At such moments he felt that he must go back to the litte old town on the Wabash, and see for himself what was the cause of his getting no answer to his letters—I say letters, for he had written a second letter home soon after locating their ranch, and had ridden forty miles to mail it.

In it he had expressed his regrets for the manner of his leaving, and still deeper regrets for having remained so long silent after leaving, and had asked, humbly enough, that he be made acquainted with the condition of things in the family and the neighborhood, making special mention of Nettie. But, though he had twice ridden the same road which he took to mail his letter, and had twice sent by others, he received no reply nor in any way obtained the slightest information from home. Hence his changeful feeling about a trip which would bring him so near the old familiar spot that no possible reason could exist for his not visiting it.

At times, as I have said, he determined to go; at other times he was equally decided in his feelings that he had nothing to go for, inasmuch as his family and friends ignored his effort to establish communication with them, and appeared willing to forget that he had an existence.

Before any necessity for a final settlement of his mind on this point arose, it was settled for him in a way he had not taken into his calculations.

He was alone with the herd one day, Brown having ridden over to one of the neighboring camps to borrow some coffee, of which they had run short, and everything being quiet and the steers feeding in a bunch, he concluded to gallop back to the cabin, about three miles away, and get himself some dinner.

His doing so quite probably saved his life. He had gone only about a half mile, when glancing back over his shoulder, he discovered the whole herd flying in wild confusion across the range in the direction of the mountains, followed and urged on by about fifty Apache Indians mounted on ponies. They were on one of their periodical raids, and the Brown-Johnson ranch being among those nearest to the mountains, where alone they could expect to escape the pursuit that was sure to follow, had been selected by them as one to be stampeded.

Fortunately, or unfortunately, as the case may be, they had struck the ranch on the day when Phil was alone in charge of the herd, and, keeping on the opposite side of a ridge of some prominence, had approached within a short distance of the cattle unseen, and were about in the act of making a dash over the ridge and upon the herd and Phil, when he suddenly took it into his head to ride back to camp for his dinner. Had he remained it is not at all impossible that a bullet would have found its way to his heart before he could have sheltered himself behind anything or gotten out of range of their rifles. As it was, his first impulse was to turn back and give battle single handed to the whole pack of them, but in this he was given no option, for, even as he hesitated whether to follow his inclination and sell his life, if need be, as dearly as possible, or obey the dictates of his judgment and endeavor to escape and notify the neighboring ranchers, a dozen or more of the Indians turned their ponies' heads and made a dash straight for him.

Phil knew well enough it would not do to permit himself to be surrounded there on the open prairie, for while with his long-reaching Winchester he could keep a large number at bay when approaching him in front, yet, if he became surrounded they would crawl upon him from all sides, concealed by bunches of high grass and sage brush that were scattered about, and before he knew of their exact location some of them would get in their work, and his days of cow punching would be over.

Besides this, his experience told him that if he expected to get back more than a scattering steer or two of the cattle they were stampeding, the thing to do was to raise a crowd from the neighboring camps and make pursuit as quickly as possible. Accordingly he turned his pony about, and putting spurs to his flank dashed away at the top of his speed, still in the direction of his camp, beyond which, at a distance of fifteen miles, lay the camp nearest his own.

But before he had covered half the distance between himself and his cabin, it became evident that the race was to be a close one. The Indians were well mounted, and, encouraged by the knowledge that their intended victim could not turn in his saddle and fire at them with any great precision of aim, came riding down upon him whooping and yelling like so many fiends let loose from pandemonium.

They were within long rifle shot when the race began, owing to Phil's momentary indecision, and if they were to gain on him, even by so much as a few rods, he stood a chance of being hit by the volley which he knew would be fired the moment they believed the chance of killing him worth the trying it. Things began to look serious; it was bad enough to lose the steers—it would be worse to lose his scalp. He glanced back over his shoulder. They were gaining on him, sure as fate. Three or four of their best mounted had perceptibly lessened the distance between him and them already, and the camp was yet a long mile away. Once there he could make a stand and hold them at bay—he did not doubt that; one good man behind entrenchments and with a Winchester rifle and plenty of ammunition, could hold twice that number of Indians at bay for almost any length of time—but could he reach there?

He struck with his spurs anew and mercilessly; he raked his pony's sides with the cruel steel, but the poor brute was already putting forth his best efforts, and could add nothing to his speed.

Again Phil turned his head and glanced back, and as he did so he heard the sharp crack of a rifle, and a bullet whizzed past him. They were already within range and a half mile still lay between him and the cabin; a half mile, and a dozen savages raining bullets about himself and pony; for now that the ball was opened every one of them appeared anxious to furnish music for the cotillion, and all began firing.

But none of the bullets touched either the rider or his pony, and now that the reds had emptied their rifles Phil felt that his chances had improved greatly.

What he had feared was that they would reserve their fire until they were so close that he would have short time to take shelter, even if he reached the cabin or the stockade; but now, unless they could reload, he knew they would slacken their pace the moment it became evident that he was going to reach shelter ahead of them, and thus seek to avoid a return shot at too close quarters.

"Just let me reach shelter and I'll furnish some of the music for this fandango myself," muttered Phil as the bullets whistled past his ears. "You devils have had your time and played your tune—next comes my time to play, and if I don't make some of you dance the dance of death I'm mightily mistaken!"

But Phil was wrong in his calculation when he thought the savages had emptied their weapons in that one discharge. Several of them were possessed of repeating rifles equal to that which Phil himself carried— rifles captured in a raid they had made some months previous on the settlers upon the other side of the mountains—and the first volley was followed by another and another and another, until bullets appeared as thick about him and his pony as bees about a hive at swarming time; and just as he neared the cabin and began to congratulate himself upon his escape, there came a stinging sensation in his side, and at the same time he felt his pony sinking to the ground beneath him. In an instant he had withdrawn his feet from the stirrups and sprung from the saddle.

He feared that he would fall to the ground when he lit—feared that he had been seriously wounded, but instead he found himself firm on his legs, and his legs making double quick time for the shanty now only a few yards away.

The savages greeted the fall of the pony with renewed yells and came straight on, firing again, but ineffectually, and were within pistol range of the cabin around the corner of which Phil was darting, when "crack," "crack," rang out the report of two rifles within, and two of the Indians, throwing up their arms wildly, fell.

"Crack," "crack," "crack," "crack," came the shots from the cabin in swift succession, and "crack," "crack," went Phil's Winchester from the corner, and two more reds swayed back and forth and then fell forward, as their ponies swerved sharply to the right or left in the wake of their companions, whose riders were now urging them to as great speed in their efforts to get away from the cabin as a moment before they had urged them toward it.

"Told you the music was going to change," yelled Phil as he lowered his Winchester, after seeing that the last of the Indians was out of range. "This is a quickstep of another kind, you see; sorry you can't stop and enjoy it."

"Are you hurt, Phil?"

"Where are you hurt, Phil?" came in the same breath and from two different voices, and the next instant Sam Brown and a man by the name of Peters, a cowboy from the ranch which Brown had started to ride over to in the morning, rushed out of the cabin and up to him.

"I reckon I ain't seriously scalded yet," answered Phil, "but I'm mightily obliged to you fellows for being here just at this time; I only wish you had come a little earlier. I doubt if them devils of Apaches would have raided us if there had been three instead of one. But I'll not complain, though I think I've got a scratch that will help me to remember this little scrimmage. Here, boys, you've done me one good turn, now do me another; help me to ascertain the extent of the damage done by that Apache's bullet."

On examination the wound proved to be no more than a scratch, and of no serious consequence. The ball had been fired from a line a few feet to the right of directly behind him and had passed under his arm as he leaned forward in his saddle and cut a furrow half its own thickness and three inches long, in the flesh over his heart, and then buried itself in the neck of his pony, who nevertheless recovered from the wound given him and is still in service, or at least fit for it.

As soon as the extent of Phil's hurt had been ascertained, a hasty consultation was held and a course of action decided on.

First a cautious examination into the condition of the fallen savages was made, and three of them found to be dead enough. The fourth was severely wounded but not dead, neither likely to die immediately; hence came the question of how to dispose of him, and as neither of the men could get his own consent to dispatch him, it was decided to carry him to the cabin, bind up his wounds the best that could be done under the circumstances, place food and water where he could reach it and leave him to take his chances and live or die as the fates should determine, while an effort was being made to retake the stampeded steers.

As the three men stood over the wounded Indian discussing place for his disposal he watched them with immovable features and without uttering so much as a groan. They thought him too badly wounded to be capable of any effort, either offensive or defensive; and he evidently thought them discussing the manner in which they would put an end to him. Either that, or his hatred of them was superior to his fear of death, for as they stooped to pick him up he suddenly made a vicious lunge at one of them with his knife. His arm was weak, however, and the knife was knocked from his hand by Peters without any one being injured, and without so much as a word of comment he was carried —though I fear not too gently—into the cabin and laid on one of the bunks. He was shot through the body just above the hips, and his chances did not appear worth any great amount of money for live stock, so the men decided; but such as they were he was to be permitted to keep them all. A bandage was therefore put about his body over the wound, and food placed within reach, as also all the vessels in the house which would hold water, so that the savage might not only have drink but to dampen the cloths over his wounds, and then the three men mounted their ponies and rode away; Phil on the animal which had brought Peters to the ranch, Brown riding his own pony, the two striking out on the trail of the stampeded herd, while Peters took Phil's wounded pony and made back as rapidly as possible under the circumstances to his own camp, where he could get a fresh mount and from where messengers would be sent in hot haste to all the surrounding camps, putting them on their guard and raising a crowd from among them to follow on and aid, if possible, in re-taking the stolen cattle, and in punishing the thieves.

Once, when relating to a number of gentlemen the incident of the wounded savage, one of the number expressed to the writer his surprise at the feelings of common humanity displayed by Brown and Peters and Johnson in the matter. I wish, therefore, to say here, that while on general principles a cowboy hates an Indian, and accepts, and may often be heard repeating, the old saw—

"Live Indian bad Indian,
Dead Indian good Indian,"

it does not follow therefore, that the cowboy is a brute devoid of all feelings of pity or humanity, or that he takes pleasure in or can even be induced by anger or by the blood and thunder stories of writers who have never been within a thousand miles of danger from a redskin, to do so contemptible or cowardly a thing as in cold blood to kill a wounded enemy, even though he be an Apache Indian and engaged in stampeding stock. There may be some such men in the regular army. I have heard it so said; I do not know if it is true or not, but there are none such among the cowboys of Texas and the Territories, at least I hope not and I believe not.

The regular army and the army of cowboys are differently made up. Men may enter the former who are too lazy or too cowardly to earn a living at any other calling, and once in they have to stay; but

A GOOD INDIAN. 93

cowards and lazy people never engage in the business of punching steers on the great plains, or if by chance such a one starts in, it is safe to say he throws up the job within forty-eight hours. The man who sticks is neither lazy nor cowardly, and though the life they lead makes them coarse and sometimes, nay, generally, cruelly indifferent to the suffering of animals, they yet are not so hardened that any need express surprise at an act of common humanity done by them to a wounded savage.

Neither have I introduced this incident or this particular Apache to the readers of this narrative for the purpose of having a grateful Indian upon whom I may depend for help in getting my hero out of the hands of the tribe just as their braves hold a council and decide to burn him at the stake, after the fashion set by the blood and thunder novelists. I have no hero and no heroine; I do but tell of things that have been, and he who writes of incidents as they actually transpire and of men as they are has no need of such aids in the making of an interesting book; and I may as well state now as later, that when Phil and Sam returned to the cabin, after their absence in trailing the stampeded cattle, the wounded Indian was dead; upon the discovery of which fact they set fire to the cabin and cremated the body in the best style possible under the circumstances. Doing it, not because they had any prejudices against the ordinary method of burial, but because they preferred building a new cabin, when they should need it to the work of removing the remains of the dead savage.

"I'D BE CONTENTED TO LIE AMONG THE ROCKS A WHOLE WEEK SHOOTING, IF THE TARGETS WERE APACHES."

CHAPTER VI.

ESSFUL STRATAGEM—SAM TELLS HOW HE AND PETERS CHANCED TO BE AT THE SHANTY.

Phil and his partner galloped along on the trail of ampeded herd, keeping a sharp lookout, not only ndians but for any cattle that might have broken from their captors, they had little opportunity and uch disposition to talk. In such situations men little and talk less of the business immediately in and when there is no need of their talking of that talk not at all. When one knows that behind each or bush that he sees may lurk a foe in wait to put let through his heart, one uses his eyes rather than ongue.

am and Phil had no fear of an open attack or of an k by great numbers.

he main body of Indians were undoubtedly with stampeded herd, rushing them along toward the mountains, but they could well spare a few of their number to scout along in the rear and endeavor to check pursuit, or if the pursuers were too numerous for that, to notify their companions and enable them to take advantage of the knowledge in making their escape, and the possibility that at any moment they might be fired on from cover necessitated the utmost caution consistent with the making of reasonable progress.

They therefore rode in almost absolute silence; now, with eyes sweeping the prairie on every side for straggling steers; now, scanning closely every bush or stone or bunch of tall grass capable of giving ambush to a lurking foe.

Neither did they follow the trail too closely, but turned to the right or left around each little elevation behind which their enemies might be awaiting them, for, as Sam laconically expressed it, their cattle were not worth exchanging their scalps for, and if he could not have both he proposed to let them keep the steers while he kept his scalp; a sentiment not difficult to understand or appreciate.

They, however, saw no Indians and no straggling steers until the afternoon had worn well away, and they were entering the foot hills which led up to the mountains, when, coming up over a ridge, the first of a series of ridges or long, low hills, they saw, away in the distance, the herd of stolen cattle, followed and half surrounded by the Indians, who were urging them forward as rapidly as their now tired condition would permit.

And now the partners determined upon a bold move. They knew—or, at least, they thought they knew—that as the Indians approached the mountains they would split the herd into three or four branches, and, dividing their own forces, take different routes to their fastnesses, thus confusing their pursuers, or, at least, compelling them to divide their forces also, and so make almost certain their ability to escape with at least a portion of their plunder. Thus, if the pursuit grew hot on one trail, the savages could abandon that portion of the herd, and having divided the pursuing force, cross, by trails known to them, to some other point and join their companions, and either aid them in overpowering the party in pursuit of them, or hold it at bay while the others escaped with their portion of the drove.

Anticipating this attempt to split the herd, Sam and Phil resolved to make a bold dash at the right moment and endeavor to cut off a portion of the cattle, and so save it if possible.

To do this it was essential that they approach very near without being seen by the Indians, and be ready to take advantage of the opportune moment when the Indians would be most intently occupied, and in some confusion from their own efforts to divide the herd.

Accordingly they made a detour of several miles to

the right, following such a course as best served to conceal them from the Indians, and in the dusk of early evening came upon them from the side instead of in the rear, and just as, by riding in among the herd and shouting and yelling, the savages had succeeded in breaking it up in bunches and sent the steers flying in a dozen different directions. Fortune favored the partners still further, for the largest bunch—about one fourth of the herd—broke in their direction, followed by a half dozen of the savages only, the others being engaged in efforts to unite the smaller bunches and start them in the different directions they were desired to take.

Weapons in hand, the two men sat upon their ponies in the shadow of a bunch of chaparral, and watched the steers rush by; held their breath and let pass the unsuspecting savages; fingered the locks of their Winchesters, and waited until all were well over the ridge, and for the time out of sight of their companions, and then put spurs to their ponies and followed after.

If the Indians saw, they mistook them, in the gathering darkness, for members of their own band, and not until the sharp crack of rifles sounded the knell of two of their number did they realize that an attack upon them was being made; and then, not understanding the source of the attack, and not knowing how small was the attacking party, they fled precipitately and rejoined their now excited and demoralized companions, leaving

RECAPTURED STEERS. 99

Sam and Phil to push on after the flying cattle and gradually turn them in the direction of home, without so much as a return shot.

Until midnight the two men kept the now almost exhausted steers moving, and then allowed them to lie down and rest, while they kept watch.

Rifles in hand and holding the ponies by the bridles, they stood guard until the morning, but nothing of a suspicious character occurred.

When daylight came they made a short scout, to satisfy themselves that no Indians were in the immediate vicinity.

Convinced upon this point, they permitted their ponies to feed upon the grass, while they themselves ate a breakfast of jerked beef, and then started their little herd of jaded steers once more toward the old range.

It was not their intention, however, to follow them far.

Knowing that if left alone they would not wander so far but that they could be readily found, and that in all probability they would strike straight back for their old range, and believing the Indians were too badly beaten and too much afraid of meeting with further punishment to return, they proposed leaving this bunch of recaptured steers, and making back to join the crowd that gathered from neighboring camps, they knew well was hot on the trail of the retreating savages ere this.

Accordingly they turned back along the way they had just come, and about noon struck the trail of the day before in the vicinity of the scrimmage of the previous evening, and were gratified and encouraged by evidences clear to the eye of a plainsman that a party of at least a score of cowboys, following the route of the retreating Indians, had passed the spot at an early hour of the morning.

At the point where the herd had been divided and at which they had made their successful effort to recapture a portion of it, they made a careful examination and decided that the Indians had divided into three bands and each taking a portion of the cattle had struck into the mountains by different routes and that their friends, the cowboys, had also divided and were in pursuit.

Judging from such indications as met their eyes they decided the number of their friends to be twenty, and that about an equal number, that is six or seven, had followed each of the trails made by the savages; and as they could not determine which would be most likely to be nearest, or most stand in need of their assistance, they concluded to follow the middle trail, thinking it probable that the other two trails would lead into this one after a time, and if not that they stood as good a chance of making themselves useful on this as on either of the others.

"I wish we may get the whole band corraled somewhere," remarked Sam as they rode along at a swinging gallop.

There was little danger to be feared in the rear of the party which had gone on in advance, and the two rode at as rapid a pace as they felt their ponies could stand, and without taking extra precaution, such as avoiding what appeared to be good places for ambush, or going out of the way to reconnoiter the trail from each eminence which they came to, as they would have done if in advance of the other party of whites. Riding so they felt confident of overtaking their friends by nightfall, if not before, and hoped to get up in time to take a hand in any fighting which might take place.

"Wish we may corral the whole mendacious lot of 'em," repeated Sam a little later on. "I'd be content to lie around among the rocks on some of these mountain sides and practice target shooting for a whole week if only the targets were Apache Indians."

"It appears to me," laughed Phil in return, "that for a fellow who less than two years ago was a tenderfoot taking his first lesson in riding a bucking pony you are grown mighty bloodthirsty."

Sam looked at his partner in a way which Phil did not fail to understand, and then answered:

"You and the rest of the fellows have had lots of fun over that little accident, and I know it was funny, though I couldn't well be expected to see the humorous side of it myself. Well, you are welcome to joke about it as much as you like ; I can afford to let you do it."

"You're mighty right you can, old fellow," and Phil, who was in the lead a few paces, held his pony up and reaching back grasped Sam's hand and wrung it hard and long.

"The boys never did take you for a softy exactly ; you know that, but they have to have their joke, and you were the last to pitch camp among us. Some time the time may come when I can show you how much I am obliged to you and Peters for happening to be at the shanty just the moment you were, and if it does come I'll try and make my feelings plain to be understood."

"Oh that's all right, pard, that's all right," answered Sam, wringing his hand in return. "I didn't mind it much, but I'm glad that I didn't flinch when the time came to prove what stuff I was made of ; it will make the loss of the steers come easier you see. But I shouldn't have been there only going over to borrow some coffee of Peters I met Peters coming over to borrow some coffee of us, and being as neither of us had any we decided to ride back to our camp for dinner and then go over to Simmons' ranch on the other fork and get some there ; and just as we came over the little divide on the other side of the creek we saw the reds coming down towards the cabin yelling and shooting like mad. We couldn't see you because of the corral, but we knew mighty well what it all meant, and you bet we made our ponies stretch themselves.

"We kept in line with that clump of cottonwoods until we reached the corral and then we were hid by the shanty itself, and I reckon the reds were a little surprised at our being there."

"Sam," said Phil, "you're a trump."

The two rode on in silence for a few moments, a silence that was broken by Phil.

"I'm mighty glad Peters' camp was out of coffee," he said.

CHAPTER VII.

FOLLOWING THE TRAIL—WATCHING FOR AN OPPORTU-
NITY TO ATTACK THE INDIAN CAMP.

The farther the trail was followed the rougher and more precipitous it became, and the slower the progress made, though they still rode principally at a gallop. There was no difficulty in following the trail, as now that they were well into the mountains there was but one way that a bunch of steers could be driven with any speed, and that was up some ravine, or along some bit of table land hedged in by cliffs too steep and rugged to make clambering over them a feasible thing; or if they came to a little valley across which the trail led, the lay of the country made clear to practiced eyes, such as Phil's were, the point at which the trail must leave it again, and thus enabled them to ride forward without paying much attention to the signs left by those whom they followed.

They knew that the Indians would have traveled all

FOLLOWING THE TRAIL.

EVIDENCES OF A SKIRMISH.

night—that in fact they would stop only when it became impossible to keep the steers from lying down from exhaustion—and they did not expect to overtake either them or the other pursuing party much, if any, before night.

About noon they halted for the purpose of giving their ponies a rest and a bite of grass, and each in turn threw himself upon the ground and slept a few moments. Neither had slept a wink the night before, and the hard riding and loss of sleep was now beginning to tell on them, and would have done so sooner but for their excitement and their anxiety to get on as fast as possible.

Pushing on again after an hour's rest they came, at about three o'clock, to a spot which exhibited indications of a halt on the part of the party which preceded them, and closer examination convinced them both that here a little brush between their friends and the Indians, or probably a few of the Indian scouts, had taken place.

They found where, in a ravine, the pursuing party had evidently left their ponies in charge of one of their number while the rest either reconnoitered on foot or made an attempt to crawl unperceived upon a hidden foe ; and in another place saw some dried blood, but whether the blood came from a man or a steer they could not determine.

Convinced, however, that nothing decisive had taken

place, they moved forward with greater caution, the way growing rougher and rougher, as they anticipated it would be.

The general direction of the trail was south. The savages were evidently making either for some fastness which they regarded as inaccessible to their pursuers, or were intending to keep on and, crossing the mountains, come out fifty or a hundred miles below Fort Stanton, and make for old Mexico, where they would be comparatively safe from pursuit.

Without stopping to make lengthy investigations the two men were able to tell where, here and there, a steer had made an attempt to leave the herd and been driven back by the watchful savages, and once they found the spot where a steer had been killed and dressed, evidently for the purpose of providing the captors with food and, in consequence, strength for other raids.

As the afternoon passed, too, they began to see evidences that they were gaining on those in advance, and near sundown they caught sight of a half dozen men riding around a mountain a mile or more in advance, and knew them to be their friends.

Halting their own ponies, they watched the little party in advance of them until convinced from the exceeding caution with which they were evidently moving that they believed themselves in the immediate vicinity of the Indians, and then hurried forward with all the speed consistent with their desire to keep out of the sight of any spies which the Indians might have out.

If possible they wished to join their friends before night set in, and so ascertain what plans, if any, had been decided on for the attack, and also to be there to take a hand in it if an attack was made.

They realized, too, that if they failed to overtake and make themselves known to their friends while it was still light, there was danger of each party mistaking the other for Indians, and accordingly they pushed forward with all the speed consistent with caution.

But darkness comes on quickly in the mountains after the sun goes down, and their efforts to connect with their friends before night came upon them were unavailing.

When they could no longer see to ride with safety they dismounted at the edge of a thick patch of chaparral, and leading their tired ponies into it tied them securely in such a way that they could lie down if they chose, and prepared to proceed on foot and endeavor to join their friends.

Before starting they again ate heartily of dried beef, as even in times of danger and excitement your frontiersman never neglects his stomach if he can help it, and especially is he careful not to leave his base of supplies, even if that base is only a small package tied to his saddle, without having eaten, if hungry; for when he does so he knows not whether he will be able to return to it, or, if so, how long it may be first; and it is a poor generalship to start on an expedition with an empty stomach.

When necessity compels, a cowboy may go without his food, but it is never a thing of his own choice.

After eating, the two men crept cautiously from the bunch of chaparral and began making their way forward.

The night was not dark, the moon being in its second quarter and the stars shining brightly.

They would have preferred that the night had been less bright, as with the moon shining they were much more likely to be discovered by the guards they knew the Indians would keep out, and they wished to avoid being seen at least until they could ascertain just how things were and get into communication with their friends.

That the Indians were in camp within a mile of them, and that their friends were in hiding somewhere in the vicinity, they felt confident, and they had little doubt that an opportunity for giving the Indians battle would be found or made before the sun rose again.

Keeping close together, they worked their way from point to point—now crawling on hands and knees to some point of elevation from which they hoped to be able to discover some indication of either friend or foe;

now crouching within the shadow of a rock or bush, and peering around for sight or sign ; again walking rapidly but with guarded footsteps in the deepest shade cast by an overhanging crag ; always with hands on their weapons and ready for whatever might come ; they at last reached a point which overlooked a little valley perhaps a quarter of a mile wide, hemmed in by the mountains on three sides.

Looking down into this bit of an oasis they could see animals, some feeding and some lying down, or what appeared to be such ; in the imperfect light and at the distance from which they were it was not very easy to distinguish between a bunch of weeds and a steer or pony, unless by seeing it move.

For some moments they lay flat on the ground, watching the valley below, and then Phil whispered :

"That's them."

"Where do you s'pose the boys are?" asked Sam after a moment of further looking.

"Don't know ; not far off, though."

Again they remained silent, watching for anything which might occur to indicate what course they had best pursue.

"You fellows think yourselves mighty sharp, don't you, now? Reckon you were just planning to go down and take that there camp of reds without any ceremony!" came a voice, in a guarded tone though loud enough t‹

be heard distinctly by them; and, glancing up, both men saw a head protruding from around a sage bush not more than ten feet away.

For a space of time sufficiently long to be noticeable neither said a word or moved more than a muscle. Then Phil replied, in the same cautious tone :

"I reckon you have the joke on us, Peters, and I suppose the only way to keep you from telling it to the boys and so get them to deviling us about it, is to put a bullet through you, and pretend we took you for a red. What d'ye say?"

Peters snickered.

"Wouldn't do it, if I was you; you need me to help you get those steers of yours back."

"Where's the rest of the boys?" This from Brown.

"'Round to the right there, 'bout eighty rods. See that big rock that sticks out on the other side of the canyon? They are on this side of the canyon just opposite that."

Neither of the three men had yet moved from their positions since Peters had surprised them by his unexpected speech, but now he began to let himself cautiously down, and in a moment was at their side.

"He, he!" he snickered. "You fellows are fine Indian trailers—let a man come onto you in this way!"

They could feel that he was shaking with laughter, but neither of them made any reply.

"Well, we had better be getting back to the boys," Peters said again.

"All right; strike out and we'll follow."

Neither of the partners was deceived by Peters' manner or words into supposing that there was no need of caution, nor did they feel annoyed by the joke he appeared to think he had played upon them.

Brown, being an Eastern man up to two years before, had never met Peters until he and Johnson had pitched camp and located their present range, but Phil and Peters had trailed Indians together three years before, and had herded together for more than a year, and were well acquainted and quite fond of each other.

Peters was a much older man than either Brown or Johnson, and had led a rough life as hunter and cowboy, but had, so he declared, been able to keep jolly all the same. He knew less of Brown than of Johnson, but the coolness and nerve displayed by him in the fight at the ranch had given him a high opinion of his courage and coolness, the very qualities which he knew Phil to possess in the highest degree; and it was because of this belief or knowledge that he had dared to venture on his little joke.

He had been delegated by the little band of six men

of whom he was the most experienced in Indian fighting, to scout about a little and learn just what the outlook for a successful attack on the camp was; and it was while doing so that he had chanced to catch a glimpse of Sam and Phil as they crawled carefully around a hummock where for an instant they were not in the shadow. Recognizing them at once, he had remained concealed behind the bush toward which they were making and within a few feet of which they took up their new post of observation.

It was when he saw them do this that the spirit of fun took possession of and prompted him to make his presence known in the manner stated.

Crawling on their bellies until out of danger of being seen from the Indian camp, the three men slowly raised to their feet and cautiously made their way from shadow to shadow and from point to point, until they reached the place where the others were waiting.

As was natural, this little company were greatly rejoiced at the addition to their numbers of Brown and Johnson.

Peters explained to them what he had discovered on the scout which he had made.

The Indians, he told them, were camped in the valley below, and were resting both the cattle and their ponies, and that besides guards on watch about the cattle, their scouts were posted at points which he indicated outside the valley, where they would be best able to detect the approach of an attacking party.

The question of what course to pursue under the circumstances was now discussed.

To return without making an attempt to recover the cattle and punish the thieves was not to be thought of, but at the same time the risk of making a night attack was very great, owing to the position of the Indian camp, and to the fact that the Indians were well aware of the presence of their pursuers in the neighborhood, their scouts having discovered and exchanged shots with them early in the day at the point where Phil and Sam had noticed the blood drops as already noted.

The blood in question was supposed to have come from a pony wounded by a shot from one of the party of whites, and not from a person, as none were believed to be hit.

It was finally decided not to risk a night attack, but instead to follow on after the Indians and watch for a chance to get back the cattle without running too great a risk of losing their lives in the operation, and to wait until that chance appeared, no matter whether they followed them one day or six.

That the chance would come all believed, and all were agreed to wait for it.

The little company of men now divided themselves

into two watches of four each, one half to watch while the other slept.

As Phil and Brown had no rest the night before, they were given the opportunity with two other men to go to sleep at once, and proceeded to stretch themselves out upon the ground without comment or delay, when a commotion of some kind in the Indian camp below was heard, and at once all thought of sleep vanished and every man listened and peered with all his might in an effort to ascertain the meaning of it.

Phil and Peters left the others and crawled away in the darkness. Those who remained lay perfectly still, but with every faculty alert and ready for attack or defense.

The commotion in the camp below continued for half an hour and then everything became quiet again, and in another hour Phil and Peters returned and reported that the band which they had been following all day had been joined by another band with other cattle; but whether the last comers were a portion of those who had raided the Brown-Johnson ranch or not, they could not tell. They thought not, however, and were of the opinion that the raid had been more general than was at first supposed, and that these last comers were a band who had been on a raid further up, and that this was in all probability the meeting point for all engaged in the raid, and that they might expect other bands to come in at any time.

Again Phil and three of the others threw themselves upon the ground and in a few moments were fast asleep. The rest kept watch and guard. Two only of the four sleepers were awakened after a couple of hours and took the place of two who had stood guard until that time. Knowing how greatly exhausted Phil and his partner must be, they were allowed to sleep undisturbed until events in the early morning light began to occur in the camp below, which required the consideration of every member of the little band of cowboys hidden in the chaparral on the mountain side.

―――――O―――――

CHAPTER VIII.

THE CLOUD BURST, AND THE FIGHT IN CAMP.

The matters transpiring in the Indian
which were of such interest to the little party
in the chaparral above were neither more no[r]
the arrival of first one and then another ban[d]
with live stock.

First came about one hundred head of
Johnson herd driven by a dozen or fifteen [Indians,]
before the yells with which their coming
had ceased there appeared at the lower end [of the]
valley still another and larger band with a lar[ger herd of]
cattle. These last were evidently stolen fr[om]
in the mountains close by, and had not bee[n driven]
far or so hard as the others, as they were stil[l giving]
a good deal of trouble to manage and ma[king]
dashes for liberty.

APACHE SCOUT.

There must have been at least three hundred steers in this bunch, and not less than fifty Indians in the band which brought them in.

The whole number of Indians already assembled were considerably more than a hundred, and it was probable that more might be expected at any moment. So far this was entirely satisfactory to the watchers from the chaparral. Nothing would have pleased them so well as to get the whole Apache tribe corraled in that little valley and wipe them all out at once. It was beginning to look as if Brown's wish that he might be furnished Apaches for target practice for the next week was to be gratified.

Of course the little party knew that behind every bunch of stolen stock would follow, sooner or later, a rescue party, and if the Indians were only foolish enough to remain where they were it would not be twenty-four hours before they would be surrounded by a sufficient force of cowboys to make the recapture of the cattle— if not the destruction of the entire band of savages—a certain thing.

The little party of whites therefore watched with interest quite as intense as that of the savages, and were nearly as ready to greet with cheers the arrival of any number of additional bands.

No others came, however, and very soon it was apparent that those already there were getting ready to move on, as they could be seen catching their ponies and galloping about gathering all the cattle into one bunch preparatory to taking them out of the valley.

Phil and Sam especially regretted this.

They would like to have seen all their steers that were in the hands of the Indians in one bunch so that they could the better judge of the chances for getting them back. However, they could do nothing in the matter, could not even make an immediate attempt at retaking those in sight and almost under their noses; for it would be folly for eight men to attack one hundred and fifty savages almost as well armed as themselves.

The result that would follow such a course would be that a part of the savages would engage them while the rest made off with the stock; and that when they were safely off with the cattle the others would slip away one at a time and rejoin them, without perhaps the loss of a man or a steer, leaving the whites in ignorance of whether an Indian was hidden behind each bush and rock in front of them or not.

Evidently the thing to do under the circumstances was to scout around and try and make connections with any other companies of whites which might be following on the trail of the marauders, and when the force so gathered together became sufficiently large attack openly or make a dash and endeavor to recapture the cattle and escape with them.

A SKIRMISH WITH APACHE SCOUTS.

Accordingly the little party remained in their concealment until the Indians had begun to move out of the valley with their stolen stock and then prepared to follow.

Emerging from the sheltering chaparral, they were about to remount their ponies when they were greeted with a shower of bullets fired at long range and perceived at once that their presence was known to the Indians and that they were in for a running fight; that is, that a part of the Indians would ambush them at every opportunity and endeavor to delay and hold them in check while the others continued their flight with the cattle.

This was by no means a pleasant predicament, but there was no way of getting out of it and they must do the best they could. Returning the ponies to the chaparral and leaving two of their number to guard them, the others crawled out of the bush upon their hands and knees and by different ways and began feeling for the savages.

By one device and another such as raising a hat on a ramrod and thrusting some portion of their clothing into view from around a rock, they succeeded in drawing the fire first of one and then another of the enemies, thus learning their exact hiding places, and occasionally getting in a return shot, though without being able to note the effect.

But this kind of fighting was by no means pleasing to the little party of cowboys, who were really quite as much interested in recapturing the stock as in punishing the thieves, and it chafed them greatly to be thus held at bay by a few reds while the stock was being driven beyond their reach, and they were meditating a dash for the purpose of dislodging the Indians, when the sound of other shots was heard, to which came answering shots from what appeared to be a half mile away, and to the left of where they were lying.

"That's the Wilson crowd, I reckon."

It was Peters who spoke, and by "the Wilson crowd" he meant another of the little parties which had followed a portion of Phil's and Sam's herd when the party had divided at the foot of the range and followed different divisions of the band that had stolen the sleek, tooth-tempting steers.

"I supposed they were somewhere in the vicinity," returned Phil. "Have been listening to hear the music of their Winchesters for an hour. I reckon we can crawl forward a little. These fellows in front have got onto the fact of their coming and have begun to light out."

While speaking, Phil had left the shelter of the rock behind which he was hiding and was making for another one some rods in advance when, with startling suddenness, "crack" came the report of a rifle and "zip" went a bullet close to his ear, causing him to drop instantly, and proceed to crawl instead of running to shelter.

"That Apache'll put your light out ef you ain't more keerful," snickered Peters; though whether he laughed at his own attempted pun or at the rapidity with which Phil changed his tactics one could not have told. Probably it was both, though he may not have known that he had been guilty of punning, in which case the reader will doubtless forgive him his offense.

Although Phil had come near paying with his life for his hardiness in taking too much for granted, yet the little company one by one followed his example, fully convinced that the Indians in front of them had retreated, or would do so speedily, to avoid being caught between two fires; and this surmise was soon proven correct.

No more shots came; and it was soon evident that the one who had fired at Phil was the last savage to retreat, and probably got in this shot just as he was on the point of doing so.

Neither were any other shots heard from the left, but a cautiously conducted scout in that direction discovered Wilson's crowd of six cowboys concealed behind as many different boulders, watching intently for the sight of an Indian along the line of retreat taken by the band.

None appeared, however; even those left behind had slipped away and were following on after their companions, and watching to prevent any company of possible pursuers from getting in between themselves and those in charge of the stolen cattle.

Communication was soon established between the two bodies of whites, and as soon as it was ascertained that the Indians had fled they came together, and after a few minutes' consultation returned for their ponies, which had been left behind when the skirmish with the Indians began, and together rode on after the retreating band.

All day they pursued, and every few hours they were greeted with the sound of rifle shots and whistling of bullets, though it was but seldom that one came very close to any of the party.

These Indian scouts were too much afraid of a close fight to even attempt an actual ambuscade, and contented themselves with firing occasional shots from long range— more, apparently, for the purpose of hindering the pursuing party by compelling them to proceed with caution than from any expectation of doing them injury. On this point the pursuers were the better content to submit to the harrowing delay from the expectations which they entertained of being joined by others from the vicinity of the ranches that had been raided in the valley above, as also by those of their own party which had branched off in pursuit of one of the parties into which the band had split up on entering the mountains.

A CHANGE IN TACTICS.

As night approached there arose the necessity of guarding against an attack in the darkness. The Indians having kept close watch of their movements during the day, might be inclined to make a night attack on them, thus turning the tables completely, and if successful, relieve themselves of further pursuit.

Taking this view of the situation, it was decided best not to follow too closely the retreating savages, and about the middle of the afternoon the party went into camp upon a bit of a plateau, which offered fair cropping for the ponies and at the same time afforded no very good opportunity for an enemy to approach them unperceived.

Here they waited until the afternoon was well spent, but were not joined by any other party of pursuers, and were forced to the conclusion that either none were to follow, or, if following, that they were long in getting started, and might not arrive in time to join in an immediate attack on the Indians. After much consultation it was decided, on the advice of Phil and Peters, to change the tactics.

Accordingly, a half hour before sundown, the whole party remounted and started back over the trail they had just come, as if having given up the pursuit. As soon as it became dark, however, twelve of the fourteen men dismounted, and taking with them only their arms and a blanket apiece, left th other two to make their way back to the settlement with the ponies, while the twelve struck off into the mountains and traveled all night on foot, in an effort to get in front of the entire band of Indians and be prepared to take advantage of such circumstances and conditions as might arise.

None of the party knew anything of the country they were traveling over further than its general trend, and something of the location of the different passes over the highest mountains, and the settlements on either side of the range, but this was sufficient to indicate to them the route which the Indians would be compelled to follow, and they felt confident of their ability to out-travel them and get to the front before they should have advanced far on the following day.

The lay of the country, not less than the desire to avoid being observed by any of the scouts which the Indians would certainly have out on all sides, compelled a wide detour, and a long, hard scramble over ravines and mountains, but all were used to hardship, and all stood the night's tramp without breaking down, though no one among them all but was badly stove up and greatly wearied when morning came.

With daylight the men halted, and after putting two of their number on guard, the rest lay down and slept. They were confident of being in advance of the Indians, and believed that all they could now do was to watch that they did not pass them unobserved. Therefore, while two watched the rest slept, and about ten o'clock the vigil of the watchers was rewarded by sight of an Indian scout, evidently in advance of the main body and about a half mile away.

A little later a small body of Indians, mounted on ponies, passed the same point, and behind them a quarter of a mile or so came the stolen cattle, accompanied by the main body of the savages. They were moving with caution, but with some leisure as compared to the day before, which caused the cowboys, who were watching them, to hope their scouts had reported that the pursuit had been abandoned.

After resting, the little company of cowboys again took up the trail.

Keeping outside of the limits which the Indian scouts would be likely to prescribe for themselves, in watching for possible or probable pursuers, they kept on at a pace which they believed would bring them up even with or a little ahead of the Indians by nightfall.

Their plan now was to keep as near the main body of Indians as possible and at the first opportunity make a night attack and endeavor to get off with a portion of, or if possible all, the ponies and cattle now in possession of the savages.

When night had fairly shut down Peters and Johnson went again upon a scout and found the Indians in camp in a deep gorge, inaccessible except from one point, and that strongly guarded. They therefore returned to their companions and reported that it would be unwise to attempt anything that night, and that they had better move on in advance of he Indians again and wait the coming of another night.

It was already past midnight and the party at once moved forward, traveling until noon the next day, having stopped only once and then only for an hour, to cook and eat a meal from the carcass of a deer which one of the party had shot. This was the first fire that had been built by any f the party since the pursuit began, and only the necessity of choosing between doing so and eating raw meat induced h m to build it now, though there was no great danger to be feared therefrom, as they were careful not to permit a column of smoke to rise from it.

Having roasted meat enough to last them the day out, they pushed ahead, and when the gain stopped it was at a point where they felt hat an atte. pt to recover the stolen cattle must be made if it wa to be made at all, and they had no intention of abandoning the pursuit without making one.

The spot in question was a point where three gulches or canyons converged, leaving a small strip of comparatively level ground in the center and between them, and through which flowed a stream of water that during heavy rain storms and for a few days or hours only, must have been very large, as it caught the flow from the sides of three eminences, either of which would send down a considerable body of water at such times.

This stream was now dried to a tiny rivulet, fed by a spring somewhere farther up in the mountains, but it was sufficient to supply water for the herd which the Indians were driving, while upon the ground, back a little on either side, was as good a growth of grass as was likely to be found at this elevation, and the necessity of allowing both the ponies and the stolen cattle an opportunity of getting a bite of feed would almost compel the camping of the whole herd at this point for at least a portion of the night.

After examining this bit of ground and the canyons converging to it as carefully as possible, without leaving too many signs of having been there, the little party of white men retired a distance up the mountain and concealed themselves to await the coming of the night and the Indians.

The two came together. It was the last of the sun's golden arrows, shot down the gorge from behind the mountain top, which showed to the men in hiding the head of the drove coming out into the open space from the lower side; and before the last steer—followed by a straggling line of ponies, each bearing his Indian master—had quenched his thirst at the little stream and begun to feed upon the grass on its banks, it was too dark to make it at all probable that the signs left by the white men would be observed by the enemy.

The Indians appeared to be less fearful of attack than on the night previous, and had probably come to the conclusion that their pursuers had dropped off and abandoned the chase. More than one attempt of cattle men and settlers to follow the Apaches to their fortresses and recover their stolen property had been abandoned, and this fact doubtless gave the rascals faith to believe that the present case would not prove an exception to their past experience, and had helped to make them a trifle less watchful than they would have been.

They were not without caution, however, for they built no fires, but contented themselves with eating raw steak from a steer which they had killed just before going into camp. The only preparation given it, to make it more fitting food, was to press the blood out of it between two flat stones.

They also put out guards both within the level ground and upon the heights above and at the mouths of each of the three canyons, so that the chances of surprising them or getting off with the herd, or any portion of it, were made extremely difficult, if not impossible.

All this the white men learned partly from observing the movements of the Indians, and in part, perhaps, by intuition or something approaching it. At any rate, they felt that every precaution against surprise had been taken by their enemies, and yet they were determined to make an attempt that night to surprise them and get back the cattle, Brown declaring that it was just a little more than a man could stand to see his cattle rounded up every night by a pack of thieves, and he was for making the attempt to get them back and take his chances on what might come of it.

Phil felt about the same way. This raid, if it resulted in the loss of so many of their cattle, knocked the life out of the plans he was building again with regard to that million of dollars, and he was ready to run any risk rather than let the cattle go.

Accordingly when the night was about half gone, the men left their hiding place, moving with more caution than they had done at any time since the chase began.

Making their way down the canyon, to within a short distance of its mouth, the little company divided into two parts, one of which, under the command of Brown, was to remain where it was for the present, while the other part, under the guide of Phil and Peters, was to get by the guard in some way, steal in among the ponies feeding below, cut their hopples and stampede as many of them as possible. This as a first step; further action to depend upon the success or failure of this attempt.

Brown and his companions were to act at such time and in such manner as would best aid the stampeding party when the trouble should begin.

Phil and Peters led their party carefully down the canyon and then left them, and together crawled away in the thick darkness. I say "thick darkness" for it is always thick darkness in a canyon in the night, unless the moon is shining squarely into it, and these men had been careful to select for their hiding that one of the three canyons leading into the open space into which the moon would penetrate the least at midnight; hence it would have been but little darker if there had been no moon at all.

The two men were gone a full half hour, and their companions, to whom it seemed much longer, were becoming uneasy, when suddenly there came a clap of thunder whose echoes, chasing each other from peak to peak, gave the impression of a field battery having been discharged. This was followed by other peals less sharp, but no less distinct, all giving indication of an approaching storm.

Immediately evidence of a commotion in the camp at the mouth of the canyon was distinguishable. It was apparent that the Indians were up and moving to get out of the way of the torrent, which would soon begin to pour through the open space from the three separate gulches.

An instant later Peters returned to the little group of waiting men and whispered to them to follow him. At the mouth of the canyon Phil joined them.

Had the lightning illumined their surroundings again at that moment it might have disclosed to their eyes the dead form of an Indian guard lying almost at their feet; but it did not and they passed hurriedly on in the wake of their leaders.

Already the rain was beginning to fall.

Guided by the commotion now plainly to be heard in front of them they hurried forward.

The Indians well understood the necessity of getting out of there and upon higher ground before the water came rushing down upon them, and they were whooping and yelling at the cattle, which were themselves becoming frightened and endeavoring to stampede.

The savages had secured a portion of the ponies, and in the intense darkness it was difficult for either the whites or the Indians themselves to find the others. In their search for them the little party of white men were repeatedly aware of the presence of Indians within a few feet of them, and once Peters brushed against one of their number, who in the darkness must have mistaken him for one of the band, for he gave utterance to something in his native tongue, of which Peters understood only enough to know that it was not a warwhoop, and that therefore the presence of whites in the camp had not been discovered.

But he had short space of time in which to congratulate himself on this fact.

First came a flash of lightning that lit up the mountains and made every bush and rock upon their rugged sides stand out as clear and sharp as if reflected in a glass; which showed every nook and cranny of the mighty canyon leading up and up toward the clouds and the mountain tops; which disclosed alike to whites and Indians the presence and position of their foes, and caused each to stand for a second dazed in the glare of light and the surprise of finding himself face to face with a mortal enemy.

Then darkness black, intense. Then the whole heavens rolled together with one mighty thunder peal, and breaking through this the war cry of two hundred savage throats, the beating of hoofs, the bellow of stampeding cattle, the snorting of frightened horses; and mingling with it and making itself felt rather than heard, the rush and roar of angry waters as the floods, released by the cloud burst upon the mountain tops, came seething and boiling down the canyons on either hand; and through all the sharp crack of rifle shots fired thick and fast and at random by whites and Indians alike in the midst of darkness so dense one might almost feel it, and rain falling in sheets.

CHAPTER IX.

A CHANGE IN THE PROGRAM—FOLLOWING AN ANCIENT AND HONORABLE CUSTOM, SAM BROWN WEDS.

A blind break in the darkness for safety, a wild scramble up steep and almost perpendicular mountain sides, mad bellowings of frightened steers, the snortings of stampeding horses, Indians trampled upon by hundreds of crazed brutes that a moment later are themselves swept away by the torrent of water—silence.

When a sense of that awful fate that awaited them if they were not speedily out of that burst upon their consciousness, the half dozen white men in the Indian camp made for the nearest mountain side with all possible speed.

It was Phil who gave the word to go, but there was little need of giving it, as a sense of their peril flashed upon all at the same instant.

A Letter from Brown

Luckily the men were near a point where the ledges were less steep than at some other places, and all succeeded in reaching a position of safety, though not all in getting so far up as to be able to move farther.

Phil and Peters found themselves lying on a ledge of rock above which the mountain appeared to rise in a perpendicular wall, and from which the boiling, foaming, seething torrent, now rushing along with a deafening roar beneath them, made it impossible to escape.

They could not see each other and for a time neither knew who the other was, or whether it was not an Indian instead of a white man ; but as their eyes became somewhat accustomed to the darkness, or more probably, as the clouds partially dispersed, their vision began to return to them a little, and Phil finally spoke but in a low tone and with his hand upon his revolver.

"Is that you, Peters?"

"I reckon so, Phil, though I'm not quite certain ; I may be an Indian, for I mistook you for one."

Nothing further was said for some time, as the roar of the waters made hearing difficult, and, besides that, an Indian might be within ten feet of them for all they could tell, and if so they knew the frightfulness of their situation would not prevent him from taking their lives, if it was in his power to do so.

They lay thus, flat on their bellies, for what seemed to them to be hours, listening to the roar of the floods, which gradually grew less and less and finally became so faint that they held a whispered conversation and decided to try and find a more comfortable position.

Rain had ceased some time before—in fact, none had fallen for more than thirty minutes.

They had been in the edge of the cloud which had burst a couple of miles farther up the mountain and thus exhausted, at one downpour, the ability of the heavens to supply moisture in drops.

They had not really been confined to the ledge of rock for more than an hour, for the volume of water, great as it was, could not have been that long in pouring through.

After descending a few feet, which they did by holding on to some brush and cautiously feeling their way, they worked along a little to the left, and finding the ledge less steep clambered up again, until they were two or three hundred feet above the bed of the canyon, and then crouched down and waited for daylight.

When daylight came they continued to ascend, but with caution, and after a time they began to search for their companions—still with great watchfulness for fear of skulking Indians.

After a few minutes' search they found one and another and finally all the four men who were with them in the Indian camp, when the cloud burst, and together they began working around toward the canyon, where they had left their companions the night before.

To reach this point they were compelled to cross the other two canyons, which they did with difficulty, and after going up the first one some distance to where the flow of water was less, for the flood had not yet all poured down, but only the larger portion of it, the ground having received and temporarily sucked in a large part, which it was now yielding up again to be carried down the canyon, through the bed of the little creek, and finally into the Pecos river by way of some of its tributaries, and so on to the gulf.

After crossing the two canyons they entered the third and followed it down to the point where they had parted from their friends the night before, but found no traces of them.

They therefore continued on and out through the mouth and into the open space on which the Indian camp had stood, and were rejoiced at seeing their friends cautiously skirting along on the opposite side, at a point not far from where they had themselves scaled the ledge in the storm and darkness but a few hours before.

Not considering it safe to halloo, they remained under cover of the rocks and watched until one of the others chanced to look in their direction, and then signaled him by a wave of the hand; and soon the little party was united again and congratulating each other on their miraculous escape from an awful death.

It appeared that the cloud burst had occurred at a distance of perhaps a couple of miles up the mountains, at which point the canyons diverged a considerable distance from each other. The cloud had burst over the canyon to the left of the one in which Brown and his party lay concealed, and awaiting the signal by which they should know whether or not the others had succeeded in stampeding the ponies belonging to the Indians.

He and those who were with him had followed on down, near to the mouth of the canyon, as agreed that they should do, and when the firing began made an attempt to rush forward to the assistance of their companions, but were met by a wall of water coming through the other gorge and retreated in haste to the mountain side in time to see a portion of the ponies, part of them with riders and others without, and followed by a bunch of a hundred steers or so, rush by and up the steeps. Some of the cattle fell back, but others made the ascent and were doubtless wandering about in the mountains.

An examination of the country on both sides of the

main canyon was now made but not a live Indian could be found.

A mile or more down the canyon the dead bodies of a score or more steers, drowned in the flood, were piled up against a ledge of rocks where the waters had left them, and mingled with these were the bodies of several ponies and three of the savages.

At several points evidences that numbers of cattle and ponies had clambered up the steep banks and escaped were discovered, and after consultation it was decided to put in a day in scouting about in search of any cattle or ponies that had remained in the vicinity.

No further fear of Indians was felt by any of the party ; or but very little.

Such as had escaped had undoubtedly fled to their strongholds and villages and would not return unless in search of missing comrades.

Indians are naturally superstitious, and although acquainted with the nature and devastating power of cloud bursts, they were yet likely to find in the awfulness of the storm, coupled as it was with an attack from enemies which they did not expect, some reason for believing the spot to be the abode of the spirit of evil, and to give it as wide a berth as possible in the future.

Two days were spent by the cowboys in searching for cattle and ponies in the vicinity.

Of the former they secured nearly 200 head and of the latter a good mount apiece and two or three extra.

Of the cattle only between sixty and seventy bore the brand of Brown and Johnson, but even this number was better than none, and the party made its way back by the trail it had come; and two weeks from the day of the raid on the ranch, Phil and his partner rounded up their herd and counted 187 head, instead of a few less than 400, which had walked out of the corral on the morning on which the raid had been made.

They had learned meantime that the men who had followed the third part of the band when it divided in the foot-hills, and each division took different routes, had been unsuccessful in their efforts to recapture any portion of the steers.

The Indians whom they followed had taken a trail that led into an almost inaccessible part of the mountains, and being joined by another and larger body of Indians, had been able to hold their pursuers in check and eventually to escape with their booty.

It was believed that they drove the steers as far as they could and then slaughtered the whole lot, and taking such portion as they could pack upon their ponies, left the rest to the wolves and made for their permanent camps, to which place few white men have ever been able to follow.

Naturally enough, both Brown and Johnson felt their loss quite severely. It was the knocking down in a very rude manner of all the fine castles which they had built in the air, and in which they had seen themselves living as cattle kings.

In fact, it was the putting them back at the place from which they had started two years before, causing all their time and labor to count for nothing.

However, there was no use crying over spilled milk. What was done could not be helped, and must therefore be put up with, and might as well be done cheerfully as complainingly.

Their herd was now too small to make it profitable to drive through of itself, and they therefore sold it—what was left of it—to a buyer on the spot ; 187 head at $25 per head, $4,675 ; just $75 more than the capital they started with.

They had in addition, however, their little band of ponies and their claim to the ranch, which were worth another thousand at least.

Before the raid took place the ranch alone would have sold for several times this sum, as good chances for grass and water were becoming extremely scarce and difficult to obtain ; but since the raid nobody wanted badly to buy or herd where the risks of having the stock stolen were so great ; hence, the ranch declined in value as greatly as their herd had declined in number.

After selling they must of course buy again, but before doing so Brown declared that he would pay a visit to his folks in the East ; so, after making arrangements with Peters to care for the little band of ponies and hold the ranch until they returned, the partners set out for Kansas.

They arrived at Caldwell after a journey without incidents worth relating. Here Phil was to remain until Brown returned from the East, which he promised should be within thirty days.

Instead, however, of his old partner back at the end of thirty days Phil received the following letter:

"NEW YORK, N. Y., Feb. 16, 188—.

DEAR PHIL:

I know you will feel like taking my scalp when you read this, but I can't help it. I only hope you will not think I meditated treating you in this way when we parted, for I honestly and truly had no such intentions.

The truth is, old Pard, I am married and am not going back West. Can't do it, you know. You will remember that I owned up to you once, one awfully lonely afternoon out there on the plains, that it was not so much a love for freedom that made me go West, as it was the inability to get just the party I wanted to own me and boss me around. In other words, I had quarreled with my girl and didn't care to stay around and see her married to a dude, such as the fellow was that I thought she was going to marry.

Well, all this time, that is, the time I put in with you whacking steers, riding bucking ponies, running down jack rabbits and fighting Indians, I couldn't quite get rid of a desire to know whether she really did marry that dude or not.

Well, when I got back here and met her on the street, the very first person that I did meet, and I knew she was glad to see me in spite of my being tanned almost as black as an Apache, I couldn't help being glad I had not lost my scalp on that raid.

Honestly, Phil, I couldn't help doing as I did.

I am awfully sorry for you, old boy, for I know you will be disappointed and lonesome, and that it may interfere with your plans very much for me not to return.

But you see I can't leave my wife, and I can't take her out there to be scalped or eaten, so what can I do? You are welcome to my share in the ranch and also to the ponies, and I hope you won't have any trouble in finding another partner with money enough to buy a big bunch of yearlings.

Write and let me know what you will do and how you are feeling. I know you will be disappointed, but I hope you won't feel hard at me, for really, Phil, I couldn't help it.

Your old friend and partner,   SAM BROWN."

Of course Phil felt disappointed.

Not to mention the pecuniary advantage which a partner with more capital than he himself had was to him, he had become attached to Brown during the two years which they had spent together, and regretted more than anything else the loss of his companionship.

He did not doubt that he could find another man to take his place, and quite probably one with more capital than Brown possessed, but some way he could not feel like doing so. The ranch without Brown appeared to his mental vision immeasurably lonely and far from human companionship.

He began to feel that he did not wish to return to it. He thought of Brown and the happy life he would lead in the future surrounded by friends, husband of the woman he loved, a quiet, happy home away from all danger and hardships. Such was the picture he kept imagining to himself whenever thoughts of his late partner came into his mind until presently the desire to have such a home began to grow in his own heart and to take form and shape, and he determined not to return to the ranch but to build him a home nearer civilization and in the midst of people of his own kind.

Caldwell was in those days the headquarters of the Oklahoma Boomers, as they were called, of whom Capt. Paine was the acknowledged head and leader up to the time of his death, some years ago, and it is probable that it was meeting with a member of the colony and hearing him discuss the plans of the "boomers" for building up a community and a state out of this beautiful strip of country that induced Phil to decide not to return to New Mexico, but instead to go to Oklahoma with the colonists and build him a home there, and cease forever his wanderings and his rough life.

He had enough to make a start with; would have a full thousand dollars after selling the partnership ranch and band of ponies, even after sending Brown his share, which he would do, not wishing to be under obligations in pecuniary matters even to him. With this sum to start with and a homestead claim on one of the little streams in the beautiful Oklahoma country he could surely make a home to his mind, after which, perhaps—

Just what he would do after the home was made he did not say even to himself, but thoughts of the quiet, happy life Brown was leading kept coming and going in his mind, and mingled with them were visions of the old ferry on the Wabash, and of the old folks, and of Nettie.

He even got so far along as to wonder, if he were to go back as Brown had done, whether or not the same thing that had happened to Brown would happen to him. He could not quite decide, but probably not, he told himself. Luck didn't seem to run to him, anyway. Probably Nettie had married long before this, and everybody had forgotten him. But if he ever did decide to make another attempt to find how things were back there it would be by going in person and not by writing; he was fixed in his mind on that point at least.

Meantime he would go to Oklahoma and get him 160 acres of land and make him a home. After that—well, after that he would see.

IN THE EMIGRANT TRAIN.

CHAPTER X.

OKLAHOMA.

As described in the several bills for its organization into a Territory now (June, 1886,) before Congress, Oklahoma comprises all that country "bounded on the west by the State of Texas and the Territory of New Mexico, on the north by the State of Colorado and the State of Kansas, on the east by the State of Missouri and the State of Kansas, and on the south by the State of Texas."

Oklahoma proper, however, or what has come to be popularly known as such, is comprised in a strip of land containing 1,887,100 acres, lying directly south of the eastern portion of what is called the Cherokee land strip, itself a body of 6,000,000 acres, just south of and adjoining the western half of the State of Kansas. Oklahoma is thus very nearly in the exact center of the Indian Territory.

Oklahoma formerly belonged to the Seminole Indians but was ceded to the United States government by that tribe under treaty of March 15, 1866, and was surveyed and section lines established by authority of the United States in 1873.

Its proximity to the Indian reservations about it, which were, as they still are to a considerable extent, the harboring places of outlaws from all portions of the country and all colors and nationalities, including Negroes and Mexicans, made it a location not desirable as a place in which to build a home and raise a family, unless it should be in company with a considerable number of other home builders; and it was in order to meet this necessity for neighbors and companions that it was proposed and finally decided to organize a colony for settlement in that beautiful country.

Having decided to join such a colony, Phil had first to provide himself an outfit.

A span of mules, a wagon, a plow and a few other agricultural implements, an ax and a hammer, a few earthen dishes and a tin bucket and cup—these comprise an outfit which is considered all-sufficient for the homesteader who is content to be the pioneer in a new country; and these Phil provided himself with.

He also retained the pony which he had ridden through from New Mexico, and of course laid in a good supply of ammunition, for until a crop could be raised the colonists would be compelled to rely for food very largely upon wild game, with which the country they were going to was reported to abound.

Immediately upon deciding not to return to New Mexico, Phil wrote to Peters asking him to sell the ranch and ponies which he and Brown had placed in his charge, or if he wished to do so to keep them himself, and pay for them at such time as he could, provided it was not too far in the future.

To this letter Peters replied, inclosing pay for the whole outfit at the very low cash price which Phil had fixed upon it, and saying that he had gone partners with another man, a stranger to Phil, and they were going to occupy the ranch and take their chances with the Indians.

This greatly pleased Phil, for he was anxious to have the matter finally settled, and he was also glad that Peters had raised a stake and got a start in life, even if it was one in which the risks were pretty large, for now that he was out of it himself, he felt that the herding of cattle for wages, and with no interest in the business beyond that of a hired hand, was not a calling calculated to bring out the best there is in one, and in proportion as he had a firm friendship for Peters, did he rejoice over his brightened prospects; and he wrote a warm letter of congratulation in reply, also telling his old friend about his own plans and prospects.

Then when all was ready, the little band of colonists took up their line of march toward the promised land.

There were about forty men in the company, some without families, but more with; all able-bodied and eager to reach the location selected in advance, and begin the work of home building, than which no man ever found sweeter employment for hand or brain.

A long string of covered wagons, each drawn by a pair of horses or mules, and in which were stored whatever of household goods the owner and his family possessed; a few cows driven in advance or following in the rear; from one to a half dozen faces of men and women and children peering out from under each white wagon cover; a dozen men and boys astride ponies; as many dogs trotting along contentedly by the side of as many wagons, or breaking away together in a mad chase after a jack rabbit, and all barking in chorus as they go —this is a scene familiar to all who have been upon the frontier, and such a one was presented by the colonists of whom Phil Johnson was one, on the morning of their departure for Oklahoma.

Only they who toil with their hands and who feel the fetters which the law, or that which is declared to be the law, places upon them in the acquisition of wealth and consequently upon their liberty of thought and action, can understand the glorious sense of freedom, of ability to conceive and execute which comes to those who, having once felt the fetters, stand freed upon the borders of a new, and to them undiscovered country.

To such, and at such times, there comes a sense of their own worth, of their own power and of a new courage which is sweeter than anything society or the world can give. It is a feeling which comes to men's hearts straight from the heart of God and lifts them up into a measure of the manhood which in its perfectness is worthy of being said to be in His image who is the Creator and Father of all.

Oh, the grandeur of liberty! Oh, the sweetness of being at peace! AT PEACE!

Peace with nature and with men; the peace which comes of the forgetting of jealousies, both great and small; of ambitions which the soul cries out upon as unworthy of the man; of hatreds born of greed and envy.

The peace which comes of faith in one's fellow man, itself born of renewed faith in one's own self, of one's own hatred of the bad, and love for and allegiance to that which is pure and good.

And oh! for a knowledge of the power which enables

us to dare and to do, to be brave and strong and good; which comes with a sense of freedom from the fetters which men in their selfishness and unwisdom throw about and over each other and themselves, whenever they do touch each other's elbows.

Phil was too much accustomed to this sense of freedom to feel any new inspiration when the little cavalcade left the town behind and swung out into the unbroken world beyond. Not having felt the fetters, he could not feel their falling away from him; but he sensed the beauty of the morning, the brightness of the sun, the softness of the air, the quietness and goodness of nature which lay around and about him.

He had, too, what he had never had before, a feeling that his wanderings were over, and that in front of him lay the materials from which, by his own labor, he was to build a home.

And a home meant—

Well, dear reader, what would not home mean to one whose heart held the memory of a fair young girl's face, a face not seen for years, but none the less fair for this reason, since not seeing it with the physical sense the mental eye had been left free to outline it as it chose.

So Phil would build a home.

As for the others, they were such men as are ever attracted to the frontier; such as have laid the foundations for whatever of liberty the people boast, whatever of wealth they have won, while civilization and the race have been crossing the continent.

They were men blown, by fate or circumstances, from far and near; men in whose hearts the love of home and liberty had been about equally implanted and nourished; men, perchance, who imagined that the bands which society and law placed upon their efforts to set metes and bounds to the approach of poverty had something of the feel of the slave chain; men who had been in debt, and to whom debt meant the curtailment of liberty in thought and action, and consequently degradation; men—but why ask me of these men? Shall not their own acts speak for them, and am not I their chronicler? Self-appointed, it is true, but none the less truthful to their thought as expressed in deeds.

Whatever they had felt themselves to be in the past, now they were free. Free to grow and expand to the full stature of the men they meant to be; free to build homes where no labor of theirs but should bear fruit for their own eating—theirs and those they loved.

Was ever brighter future in the distance seen by men?

And the children?

Bless me, how excited and happy the children in those covered wagons were; for were they not to see new scenes, to visit undiscovered countries, to ride for days and days through an ever-varying landscape, to sleep in tents and eat in the open air, to be free to fish in the streams, to catch rabbits and trap squirrels and prairie chickens and may be larger game, if they could?

And whenever did a child doubt its ability to do anything it wished to do and never had tried to do? Were they not to be free and happy and busily idle all the day long?

If you wish to know how happy were the children of those colonists on that morning when this journey began, just propose to your own children such a journey in your own and their mother's company; being first careful to talk for weeks and months of the beauty of the country to which you are going, and of the pleasures of such a trip, and from their faces and childish words and acts you can judge of the happiness of those other children, whose faces peer from the wagons just starting upon their journey on that sunny morning of which I write.

"And the women?

Why, the women had their husbands and children; what more has anybody thought necessary to woman's perfect happiness than that she have her husband and children?

You do but disclose your ignorance, my dear sir, of what the world, the old moss-covered, time-defying world, has decided is woman's sphere. My dear madam, you do but disclose your treason to old and time-honored theories, who question so of woman. Is it not enough, I say, that she had her husband and children? Knowing so much, what right have you to ask more or to say: "Is she happy?" "Is she filled with sweet content?" "Is she lifted up with great thoughts of great deeds—deeds the thought of which causes her soul to expand and reach upward?"

They had their husbands and children; what more would you have them have, or what have they ever had or left behind that you should ask of these women, who, going upon a hard, long journey, into a new country, to live lives of toil, have their husbands and children still with them? Is the world then wrong, and has woman longings, sometimes, for wider fields and greater things than she has yet been permitted to know?

Sun-bonneted women, who were the wives of these men, and the mothers of these children of whom I write, had all that any of their sisters anywhere have to make them happy, and they were happy as any; happier than most; for added to love of husband and child was the knowledge of the necessity of their own existence and labors to the comfort and happiness of those they loved.

It was a happy, joyous company, and the sun shone bright and the air was soft and the grass green as they drove away, and merry voices shouted one to another from out the wagons—voices of women and voices of children, while men grown suddenly self-reliant, strode by their side, or sitting in the front end of the wagon, spoke cheerily to their teams as they urged them forward along the trail over the broad prairies.

At noon they halted for a short hour while their horses fed upon the crisp buffalo grass, and they themselves ate cold lunches of bread and meat out of their provision boxes; then on again until the sun is low in the west, when they went into camp on the banks of a clear little stream which meandered through the prairie, and upon whose banks were growing scattered pecan and cottonwood trees, over which in places wild grape vines ran riot, and in whose branches birds sang and flitted back and forth, and told their tales of love to one another.

The stream was too small to contain fish of much size, but large minnows with sparkling silvery sides darted to and fro in the clear water; a sight which brought shouts from the throats of a score of children who came clambering down from the wagons, and skipping over the grass and swarmed upon the creek banks, making as many antics and "shines" as a troop of young monkeys.

Instantly a chorus of calls rang out, much after this fashion: "O ma! I want my fishing hook." "O pa! Get me my fish pole right away, quick, 'cause here's fish—lots of 'em—'n I want to catch some for supper."

What glorious music this was to the patriarchs of this modern Exodus!

Then one boy fell in the creek, which was perhaps two feet deep, and all the others set up a howl, the girls for fear he was drowned, and the boys because they feared he had frightened all the fish away.

And when he climbed out and declared that "The water was just right to go swimmin' in," half of them forgot their desire to fish and went scampering away down stream in search of a good place in which to undress and bathe, and only such as were called back and sent for wood to cook the supper were less than gloriously happy. Even these were so full of spirits a little hard work could not dampen their ardor except for a few minutes.

Indeed the rarity of getting wood for an outdoor fire was enough to make them happy of itself.

And so the women and the elder children gathered fuel and cooked supper, while the men unharnessed the horses, and having washed their sweaty shoulders in the creek staked them out to grass, and then all fell to for a meal which an epicure might well envy, provided the epicure had ridden all day in an emigrant wagon or walked by the side of one carrying his gun on the shoulder for the pleasure of a chance shot now and then at a prairie chicken or a mule-eared rabbit.

And then the stories told about the camp fire when pipes are lit, and a feeling of perfect peace and restfulness has taken possession of body and soul; stories of other days and other men (perchance their fathers) and their frontier lives; lives that closed but yesterday, yet were spent upon frontiers a thousand miles to the east, where now stand cities, and where the hum and bustle of commerce and trade, the whistle of the steam engine and the rattle of the loom, have driven the deer and the bear from the forests and transformed the forests themselves into fields of corn and barley and clover.

It may be that memories of their own old homes, the homes they have left and the friends they have loved, call up thoughts that are half sad and mournful, producing momentary regret that they have ventured upon this journey in search of new homes.

There is that in the flickering blaze of a camp fire by night, and in the blue columns of smoke rising up from burning brands as they fall away from the main body of the fire, the smoke that curls upward and is twisted and blown about by the faintest breath of air, that tends to excite almost any feeling which he who sits and watches it wills.

A veritable fairy is the fire, and a veritable wand in its hand is the blue smoke curling upward, and to see pictures either gay or somber, he who sits within the magic circle has but to wish, and lo, he shall seem to see that which he wishes for.

But mostly these men, these colonists bound for the promised land, talk of the country to which they are going.

Their leader, a man well worthy to lead such seekers for such homes, was called upon to tell again how broad were its prairies, how deep and clear its streams, how here the land lay like the waves of the sea when the wind, just touching it with its breath, compels it to lift and fall gently like the sweet breasts of women; and how in other places it was broken and rough, plowed deep in gulleys, and ledges of rock were thrust up through the soil and huge boulders lay scattered about as if the giants of other days had once held high carnival there, and vied with each other in giving tests of their strength before admiring audiences of the gods.

He told them, too, of the abundance of the game;

how deer and antelope fed upon the prairies and mated in the woodland; how wild turkeys stalked about beneath the shadows cast by the tall trees upon the river banks, and nested in the high grass at their roots; how, turn your footsteps which way you would, flocks of prairie chickens rose and went sailing away across the open country; how the grapevine clambered over the trees along the margins of the creeks, and the pecan and the walnut trees dropped their rich nuts in profusion upon the ground beneath, and the red and black haw and the persimmon trees stood in clusters.

And then these men, these home seekers, these men in rude costumes and faces all unshaven; these men of strong limbs and vivid imaginations, rose from off the ground where they had set listening, and stretched out their arms as if to clasp the future which they felt to be so great, and talked earnestly of the mighty state which they should found, and the homes they should build in this land of liberty, this promised land of corn and wine.

Wearied, at last, with the long day's drive, first one and then another began to slip away to his wagon and his blankets, noticing which the watch was called by the leader, and two men arose and went, rifle in hand, through and around the camp, and so continued watching, that nothing went wrong among the æthered animals, or about the smoldering camp fire, until two hours had passed, when they awoke two of their companions to take their places, and they lay down to rest.

Phil had no part in the watch that night, but he was long in finding sleep. This hearing men talk of homes and states to be builded had given him new thoughts, and awakened nobler ambitions than he had known before; had opened to him a new life—a life wherein he saw men as something better and higher than he had ever thought of them before; saw them aspiring to the great and mighty things; to be the forerunners of a great and wondrous civilization that should follow fast upon their heels, and add new honor and power to the nation, new dignity to the race of men.

To him these men seemed nobler and more grandly made than any men he had ever known before. He did not understand how men's grander impulses always bring to the surface their better selves; that the building, by honest toil, of homes dedicated to the domestic virtues, within a state dedicated to true liberty, is so high a mission that its light illuminates men's souls and makes them great, just to talk and plan of such.

Yet, so it is, and Phil was himself all unconsciously a living proof of it that moment; for he felt lifted up and made larger every way by the thoughts which came to him in consequence, as he lay awake and thinking that first night out with the little colony of which he was a member.

THE WITNESS.

CHAPTER XI.

IN WHICH THE SUN ENDEAVORS TO GET THERE IN ADVANCE OF THE BOOMERS.

Have you ever noticed, dear reader, that the sun gets up awful early in prairie countries? Well, he does, and he goes to bed late, too, which makes his early rising all the more inexcusable.

I suppose that a scientist—a scientist is one who knows everything that is not worth knowing and nothing that anybody else cares about—a scientist would tell you that the sun sets just as early in a prairie country, and gets up just as late as in a mountainous one; but then, too, a scientist will tell you—some of 'em will—that the sun does not set at all; which proves how little dependence there is to be put in a scientist.

Everybody who has ever worked in the harvest field on a big prairie can tell you that the sun gets up at least an hour earlier, and goes out of sight, and I suppose to bed, at least an hour later than he does when one works in a harvest field up in the valleys; and all the scientists in this, or any other country, can't make us believe anything else.

The sun got up early next morning, as he always does in a prairie country, but not early enough to catch all the emigrants, encamped on the creek bank, between blankets.

"There comes the sun," called one of them to another, whose head just then appeared at the front of his covered wagon.

"Well, let him come; I'm up," was the response, as the speaker crawled out over the end-board on to the wagon-tongue and then to the ground.

Then came others, from out wagons and from beneath them, and from under blankets stretched beneath the trees men came forth and shook themselves, and went to the creek's edge and washed the dust of sleep from their eyelids, and went and found their animals and staked them to fresh spots of grass.

And women, through the partially open canvas wagon covers, could be seen slipping their own or the children's frocks on, and a minute later descending to the ground to begin preparations for breakfast.

And presently the smell of coffee began to penetrate the camp and to float out upon the still air, until it reached the men as they worked with their horses or gathered in little groups, talking of the distance to the next water, or the time it would take them to reach their destination, and it brought them back to their several camp fires and families.

And then the odor of frying ham or bacon mingled with the smell of coffee boiling; and these men and women and children gathered about a rough box set upon the ground and ate of the hearty food and drank of the fragrant coffee, to which such as would added new milk freshly drawn from the cows belonging to this or that one of the colonists, and which was passed about with free hands to those who wished for it.

Then came the packing by the women of the few utensils used in cooking, while the men hitched the animals to the wagons.

A quick glance around to see that nothing of value was being left, and then a succession of sounds and sentences, snap of whip, "Get up," "Pull out, boys," "Keep to the left around the bend of the creek there," "Be careful with your guns, you youngsters," the creaking of wagons—and the emigrants are again upon their way, and the first night and morning of their journey have come and gone.

The first day and the second are the same, and those which follow are like unto them save as the succession of rolling and broken prairie, and wood and streams give variety to the scenery, and as with better acquaintance little friendships spring up between the women, resulting in visits from one to the other as the wagons move on and on along the trail made by herds of cattle, or by the men who carry the government mail.

Catching fish in the stream by which they camped, occasional dashes on horseback in pursuit of deer, sometimes, though not often, successful, frequent shooting into flocks of prairie chickens, killing so many that the whole camp ate of them, slipping away and following the banks of some wooded stream in a still hunt for turkeys or deer, until a hard ride to catch up, or if no horse is used, a long walk after the sun is down, and darkness covers the prairie with its mantle—these helped to form diversions and break the monotony of what might at other times have been a wearisome journey, and served to keep up the keen enjoyment with which all entered upon it.

And when finally, after two weeks of such travel and such life, the spot selected for the settlement was reached, though all were glad to be able to begin the building of homes, yet few there were who did not look back over the short journey with a half sigh at its hours and days of freedom from oppressive cares, and at thought of the labor to be performed ere homes could arise in which

LOCATING THE SETTLEMENT.

they might sit them down to rest and comfort without fear of want.

The location selected for the colony was a beautiful country lying along one of the forks of the Canadian river; the rich land, abundance of timber suited for building purposes and fuel, together with the climate, which is nowhere excelled for healthfulness or comfort, making it appear a paradise to these people, as indeed it well might be, or might be made to be.

Having decided upon a location, the next thing to be done was to ascertain the sectional lines, in order that each homesteader might select a quarter section for his own, as each head of a family is entitled under the law to do, from any unoccupied lands belonging to the government.

Accordingly a surveyor's chain and tripod belonging to one of the party, who had done a little surveying as assistant to a more experienced hand, were brought forth, and Phil and two or three others shouldered their guns and started out with them to find a corner post or mark of some kind which would locate a corner and give them a start.

After much wandering about and examination of trees and rocks, and tramping through the high grass, the party returned to dinner with a huge load of prairie chickens shot on the wing, but no more knowledge of the location of section lines than they had when they started.

After dinner they set out again, but at the suggestion of some of the older heads left their guns at the camp.

Again a weary tramp, and the scanning of everything which they fancied could by any possibility be a "witness," but still without success, until just as they were upon the point of retracing their footsteps again and abandoning the search for the day Phil stumbled against the stump of an old cottonwood tree, the body of which had fallen, and together with the stump was almost hidden in the tall grass. A moment later his companions heard his cheerful "halloo."

"Here she is, boys; I've found her."

They came hurrying toward him.

"This tree was standing when the survey was made, and here is where they blazed her; and here, see, there's the numbers, T. 12, R. 3 W., S. 28, plain as can be, though I'll be hanged if I know what it means exactly."

"That means town 12, range 3 west, section 28."

It was the surveyor who contributed this explanation.

"We are all right now" he continued; "we will come back here in the morning, and with this for a base, run out the quarters in this section and as many more as the boys want; no trouble to find the other corners, you know. Even if we should miss them a few feet we can't miss them so far but that we can find them easy enough."

"Kind of darned queer that this here stump should have happened to stand exactly on the corner of a section, aint it now?" queried another.

The surveyor smiled and scratched his head.

"The fact is," he said, "that this is not the exact corner; they simply made this the witness. That is, they marked it to show that there is a corner not far from here, and that the tree was nearer to it than any other prominent object; though for that matter they would have marked three trees if they had stood anywhere near and on different sides of the corner; in which case the corner would be found somewhere in the circle made by the three 'witnesses.'"

"Thunder! I thought you said we could come back here in the morning, and starting from this stump find any other corner we wanted to; and now it seems we aint found the corner at all."

"Oh, well, we can easily find it I reckon; it can't be far away now."

Search was at once begun, but again without result, and the party returned to camp to report progress, and get something to eat; particularly the latter.

The next day search was resumed, and after wallowing down the grass over a piece of ground nearly an acre in extent, a small stone with nearly square sides and about a foot long, bearing the marks of having been chipped into shape by use of an ax or hammer, was found set in the ground and protruding only a few inches above the sod, and the men knew that this time they had the exact corner and could begin the work of running quarter lines with this for a base.

The remainder of the day and the next day and the next were spent in running lines and fixing corner posts; and then every head of a family proceeded to locate his quarter section.

Some selected theirs in the open lands lying nearest the river banks, regarding such as the richest and hence the most valuable land.

Others chose the second bottom, as being less liable to possible overflow, or because they liked better the lay of the land to the south or the west, or for some one of the many reasons which cause men to differ in their judgment of what is desirable in a farm, but all striving to get some portion both of timber and prairie.

All were satisfied and delighted with the situation and prospects, and each began such improvements as are required by law to be made in evidence of the honesty of purpose on the part of the settler of occupying the land in person, and for the purpose of making it his or her permanent home.

For this purpose, as well as for their own convenience in living, a house of some kind must be erected, and to this task the colonists set themselves with right good will. That was their object in coming, and now that they were come, they were eager to begin the work.

"Changing work," that is, two or more parties forming a little company, and all working together first for one and then for another, enabled them to do their work easily and pleasantly.

The houses were of logs cut from the timber growing along the river bank, and hauled to the spot by the doubling up of teams, after having swung the larger end of the log by a chain under the hind axle of the wagon.

Phil worked with a man by the name of Jones, with whom and his wife he had messed ever since the journey began; having made arrangements with them to cook for him, in return for such service as he could render in the loan of his team or pony; Jones being poor and not well fixed so far as teams and implements were concerned.

Phil was to furnish his own provisions under their first agreement, but not finding this a convenient way of doing things, they fixed it up differently; Jones buying Phil's stock of provisions and paying him in board at so much a week.

For a time and until they got their houses up everybody lived in their wagons or in tents, with which a number of the colonists had provided themselves, and of course cooked their meals out of doors.

As for Phil, he was too used to camp life to wish for any better bed than the ground, unless it rained, and even then he could have stood it under his gum blanket without much complaining if there had been no shelter at hand. As it was, he slept on the ground when the ground was dry and in his wagon when it was not.

He could easily have cooked his own "grub," for that matter, and at first intended to do so, but having made the acquaintance of the Joneses, who were very nice people, he decided to accept their offer to eat with them, made without a desire to receive pay therefor, and to aid them in return as stated, thus making it a favor to them equally as much as to himself.

Both Mr. and Mrs. Jones were past middle life and without children, and Mrs. Jones was such a motherly woman, and together with her husband took so kindly an interest in Phil, that he grew confidential and told her of his having run away from home and of his life ever since. He wanted very much to tell her about Nettie, and ask her advice about ever going back to try and find out all about her, but he could not quite get up his courage to do so.

A site for the town, which everybody expected would grow into a city in a few years, was marked off on the high ground just back of the river, and here most of the colonists made their camps and cooked and ate and slept, what time they were getting their houses up, and indeed many of them were in no hurry to get their houses up, preferring to live in the wagons for a time until they could first break a bit of ground, and get something planted and growing upon which to live, without having to depend too entirely upon game and fish.

So a month, two months, passed by and many were still camping out, and still a dozen covered wagons stood in the "village" whose owners had not yet completed their houses.

But gradually one by one the wagons were drawn away to the different claims by their owners, until none remained, and the first town laid out in Oklahoma had become, for the time at least, a "deserted village."

But if the village was deserted the country about it was not.

Standing on the little eminence selected for the town site, one might see upon every quarter section for two or three miles on each side, bits of plowed land—black streaks upon a sea of green. These were the beginnings of fields which the colonists intended should grow into broad fields of grain in another year.

Some of these were already showing long thin rows of green peeping through the black earth, the evidence of springing corn which would ripen into golden ears yet this first season, and furnish food both to man and beast through the coming year.

In gardens about each cabin vegetables and vines were growing, having been planted and cared for in most instances by the hands of the women and children, while the husbands and fathers were busy turning broader acres for broader fields of grain.

Phil planted no garden of his own, but he aided Jones in breaking up and planting one about the latter's cabin, and afterward helped keep it clean; but for himself he had no use for one since he boarded with these friends of his.

With the exception of helping Mr. Jones, he devoted himself wholly to turning long straight lines of black across one entire end of his quarter section, and took a mighty interest in seeing this strip grow from day to day and week to week.

It was work which he was not used to—this holding the handles of a plow; something he had never done since he was a boy, and then only a little while at a time to satisfy his boyish ambition to do a man's work.

At first it seemed hard and slow work, tramping back and forth, turning one furrow at a time across a whole quarter-section. Used as he was to hard life, this work tired him. It made his legs ache and grow weary.

He compared it in his own mind to going up the trail with a herd of long-horn steers, and he felt inclined to give the preference to the herding. There was a bit of excitement there, or at least one did not know what moment there might be, but there was no probability of getting excited just following a pair of mules back and forth from day to day hanging on to the handles of a plow.

But then he was building a home.

Every furrow turned was a step in the direction in which lay the happiness he had begun to thirst for.

As furrow was added to furrow, and the black strip running across the east end of his claim widened, he began to take an interest in widening it still more. Every furrow turned was so much toward the home he was beginning to long for.

Each week he could see the long ribbon of black widen. At first a line which one could hardly follow with the eye across the claim, then a narrow trail, then a road, then a broad band of black reaching from side to side across the quarter-section lay ready to receive the seed.

And then came the seeding, the grain having been brought with them in wagons from Kansas.

The belts of black crossing the prairies on every claim would have been broader in most cases had the supply of seed been greater ; but, as it was, enough was sown to make certain of a sufficient crop to sustain the colonists and supply an abundance of seed for another year.

One thing the colonists saw plainly enough ; as soon as their grain came up they would be compelled to guard it against being ravished by cattle, of which there were large herds in the vicinity.

Occasionally the cowboys herding the cattle came to the settlement and chatted for a time with such of the colonists as they met or chose to visit at their houses.

Among the cabins in front of which their ponies were most frequently to be seen lariated were, naturally enough, those in which resided young women of marriageable ages ; for your cowboy is not unlike other men, and the quickest, if not the only, way in which to convert him from his attachment to his wild life is to introduce him to a number of prepossessing girls, and allow him to visit them at their homes, where he can get a glimpse, however small, of the comforts of domestic life.

Another cabin where cowboys were frequently seen was that of the Joneses.

Phil having retained sufficient interest in the old life to make him a pleasant companion to those who still followed it, friendly visits and an occasional meal eaten in company, either at the Jones cabin or at the camp of the herders, were natural and pleasant to all concerned.

Several times some of the cowboys hinted something to Phil to the effect that the settlement was not looked upon with friendly eyes by the owners of the large herds of cattle, but to this Phil gave very little thought or attention.

He understood easily enough how men with large herds would not be greatly pleased to see others coming in and appropriating any of the range they were accustomed to herd over, be it ever so little, but then he could not help that.

This was government land, and as such any citizen had a right to make a home upon it, and eventually to receive a deed to 160 acres which he should have improved.

He intended buying a few cattle himself as soon as he got his claim fairly opened. He had $700 yet on deposit in a bank back in Kansas, which he meant to invest in that way, and let them be growing into a fortune while he continued to work his claim. It would only take a few years—"just two or three," he told himself—to put him in good shape with a good farm and a nice bunch of cattle.

And so everybody worked and planned and hoped.

On Sundays and occasionally during week days, they met in a tent belonging to the leader of the colony, or in front of it, to hold religious exercises, or talk over their plans and prospects for the future.

They were as enthusiastic as ever over the situation.

The country was all they had pictured it; the climate delightful, the soil rich, and they, the pioneers, the men and women who, when the country became thickly settled—as it very speedily would be, now that a settlement was started—would be pointed out by everybody and honored as the first to come; in fact, the founders of a new State, one of the greatest in the Union.

One day, as a number of them sat thus, in and around "headquarters," as it was called, a long line of something—was it cattle or men?—was noticed in the distance.

"Reckon it's a fresh herd goin' up the trail," said one, and no further attention was paid to it for a moment. Herds going up the trail were no new sight to any person in that camp, and therefore did not provoke any special interest or comment.

"That's no drive," spoke up another, a few moments later.

"Look there, Cap! Hang me if I don't believe that's a company of regulars. Wonder, now, if there's goin' to be trouble with the Indians. If there is, we ought to be keepin' the women and children pretty close, and ourselves well armed, so 's to not let 'em get in on us unawares."

As it continued to approach, the fact that it was a company of mounted soldiers riding in ranks became apparent to all, and as they were evidently coming toward "headquarters," all were agape with curiosity to know the cause of their visit, and if there was really any danger to be apprehended from the Indians.

At last the soldiers arrived in front of the hut and halted.

"Where is the person in command of this party?" asked the officer at the head of the troops.

"Wall, now," responded one of the settlers who happened to stand nearest the officer, and was eyeing the company of regulars with considerable interest and attention. "Wall, now, thar aint exactly anybody in command here—leastwise, nobody entitled to boss anybody—but that there man over there is our leader what piloted us in here and is kind of a president or gineral manager like."

At this instant the "general manager" stepped to the front.

"Did you wish to see me?" he asked.

"Yes," returned the lieutenant, "and not only you, but all the members of your company. I have orders to arrest you for treason and conspiracy against the government, and to remove your families from out the territory."

Then, turning to his men :

"You, Sergeant and Corporal, take each twenty-five men and go and bring in the other members of the company, together with their families. I will remain here with the rest of the troops and guard these prisoners."

ARRESTED.

CHAPTER XII.

TAKEN TO PRISON.

"Arrested for **treason**? How? What? I **don't** understand!"

"Colony broken up!"

"Officer must be drunk!"

"Will they take us to prison?"

"What does it all mean, anyhow?"

"Must be trying to scare us for a joke!"

Such were the exclamations of one and another as they heard the order for the arrest "for treason and conspiracy" of every member of the colony.

But there was no joke about it.

It was a sober fact, as they very soon learned.

Those present at headquarters were not permitted to return to their homes and families, but were kept under close guard and threatened with being shot down if they made any attempt at escape.

The squads of soldiers sent out by the lieutenant

in command proceeded to the different claims, arrested such of the men as were not already under arrest, and peremptorily ordered them to hitch their teams to their wagons, and at the point of the bayonet compelled them to load up their household goods and drive to headquarters.

The women and children were either hustled in with the household goods, or were driven like so many sheep behind the wagons.

The cries and screams of the children and the tears and pleadings of the women were alike unheeded, while the curses and threats of the men were answered with orders to "dry up" or take what would follow noncompliance.

Phil was at work on his claim when the troops halted in front of the headquarters.

His claim was nearly a mile away, and he could see little of what was going on and had no idea of anything serious happening. But, chancing to glance that way, he saw there was a commotion of some kind. Recognizing the presence of a body of horsemen, he supposed it to be a company of cattlemen and cowboys on a hunt for horse thieves or estray cattle, and so gave it no further attention until he saw a squad of cavalry coming toward him.

"I wonder what's up now?" he queried mentally. "Cowboys and Indians been having some trouble, I suppose. Wonder if they think any of the settlers were mixed up in it any way."

He saw them halt in front of the Jones cabin and converse a moment apparently among themselves, and then a portion of them dismounted, while the others rode on in the direction of where Mr. Jones was at work plowing, not very far to the right of where Phil himself was at work.

A moment later he heard screams issuing from the cabin, and saw Jones drop his lines and run toward the house, and instantly he began stripping the harness from his own animals.

Springing upon the back of one of them, he dashed away across the plowed ground in the direction of the Jones cabin, leaving the other animal loose and running wild.

Phil had, as yet, no clear idea of what was happening, but hearing the screams and seeing Mr. Jones on the run, he knew, of course, that something was wrong, and was hastening to the assistance of his friends. He had a confused idea that the soldiers must be drunk, and might be committing he knew not what kind of an outrage upon the family. But these misgivings only accelerated his speed to the rescue.

Coming on at full speed, he rapidly neared the little cabin, and was within a few rods of it before the soldiers had noticed his approach. Then they leveled their weapons at the undaunted but astonished "boomer," and gave the order:

"Halt and surrender!"

He did not halt, however, but rode on and up to the cabin at a gallop. Springing from his animal, he was instantly seized by as many soldiers as could lay hands upon him.

Phil's first impulse was to resist, and indeed he had already nerved himself for a struggle, when, seeing both Mrs. and Mr. Jones standing together just within the cabin door apparently unharmed, he refrained from struggling.

"What is the meaning of this outrage?" he fiercely demanded. "What are you doing here? I will report you to your superior officers and have you all court-martialed."

Phil thought the soldiers were drunk and engaged in plundering, and he was wildly indignant.

But they laughed at his threats, and began pitching the household goods out of the cabin.

For a moment or two Phil looked on, with fast-rising anger, at what he regarded as wanton destruction of his own and his friends' property.

Mrs. Jones stood with her face buried upon her husband's shoulder, weeping, only raising her head as, every few seconds, some piece of household furniture came tumbling out of the cabin, propelled by the hands of the men in uniform within.

At last Phil turned to the Sergeant, who appeared to be in command, and asked, as calmly as he could, for an explanation of this strange affair.

"It means," replied the Sergeant, "that we have orders to arrest every member of the colony and to take them out of Oklahoma. That's all I know about it, and that's all I can tell you."

"But what for? What have we done? I do not understand it," persisted Phil.

The Sergeant retorted, none too good-naturedly: "I tell you I know nothing more about it than I have just told you. If you want to know any more, ask some one who is better informed."

And with that Phil was forced, for the time, to content himself.

He was ordered to catch his other mule, and then to go to the field for his harness, which he did, being accompanied by two of the soldiers, who told him that he might take his plow if he liked. But this Phil chose not to do, and left it standing in the furrow. He could not believe the affair was anything else than a monstrous blunder on the part of somebody, but he had not the faintest idea of the identity of the blunderer.

When he had returned to the cabin with his mules and harness Phil was ordered to hitch to his wagon, that stood nearby, and then was sent, together with Mr. and Mrs. Jones and their wagon, into which had been tossed their household goods, under guard to the headquarters.

Arriving there, they found that already many others of the settlers had been run in, together with their families and household treasures, and that more were arriving constantly.

When all were assembled, there was a scene worthy the brush of a master artist.

From some of the wagons the canvas covers had been removed, while upon others they remained as they were when the colony arrived at the settlement, and into these had been piled household goods of every description owned by the settlers. Cook stoves, beds and bedding, chairs, boxes and trunks—any thing and every thing thrown in as they came to hand, without regard to order, economy of space or possible damage to the goods.

Seated upon these piles of goods, or standing about the wagons in groups, were the women and children— the former crying and talking in one breath, and all together; the children clinging to their mothers' skirts and asking to know what it all meant; the women asking the same question of one another, and each of all.

Silent and sullen, some of the men stood with hard-clenched fists, and eyes which had a dangerous light in them, while others were moving about among comrades, uttering denunciations of what they termed an unparalleled outrage by the army of the United States on peaceful citizens, and demanding that they be at once set at liberty.

Finally the leader of the colonists obtained permission from the officer in command of the soldiers to talk to the settlers. Mounting a wagon and calling them about him, he explained, as well as he could, the situation.

"You have all been arrested for trespass," he said, "and in addition charges of treason and conspiracy are made against myself and a few others. This much I have learned from the officer here in command of the troops."

"Who's a traitor?"

"Who's trespassing?"

"I spent four long years helping to put down treason against the government."

"What right has the regular army to arrest peaceful citizens, anyway, I'd like to know?"

Such were the expressions that came in reply from one and another of the excited and angry men, as with upturned faces they pushed and crowded close about the wagon from which their leader was striving to address them.

"No one has committed any trespass in settling here, and no one, I am sure, is guilty of treason or conspiracy against the government. On the contrary, many among us gave some of the best years of our lives to upholding the old flag and putting down rebellion, and it is an outrage almost beyond endurance that we be accused of treason against the government we fought so long and so hard to maintain. It is an outrage, too, that we are being driven from our homes; but I can not think it is other than the result of a blunder, and that it will not be made right in time.

"From what I can learn from the officer here, it has been represented to the government at Washington that we are upon land belonging to the Indians—therefore, trespassers. If such were really the case, it would be the duty of the government to protect the Indians in their rights; but such, we know, is not the case, and hence we can only conclude that somebody has made a most grievous blunder.

"That this somebody ought to be held responsible for the blunder is true, of course, and no doubt he will be; but the fact that we know them to be mistaken in supposing us to be trespassers will not excuse these officers and soldiers from obeying their orders, which are to convey us all out of the Territory. We must, therefore, submit quietly to the orders of the government, trusting and believing that when the truth comes to be made known at Washington we shall be exonerated from all blame, and reparation for our trouble and losses made to us.

"I urge, therefore, that each of you bear this hardship as courageously and uncomplainingly as possible, and that you be not down-hearted. Every thing can, perhaps, be explained and set right as soon as we reach Fort Reno, whither, I am told, we are to be conveyed. If not, then we will appeal direct to the government at Washington."

He further told them that the officers would permit them to unload and repack their goods in their wagons, so as to prevent unnecessary breakage or serious damage of any kind, and enable them to make such arrangements as were possible for the comfort of the women and children on the journey, and closed his remarks by expressing the hope that thirty days hence would see them all back again working upon their claims.

A cheer went up when he said this. And, thus pacified and encouraged, they became, in a measure, reconciled, and began at once the work of repacking their wagons and making such arrangements for the comfort of their families as the circumstances would admit.

There were still to be heard mutterings of anger and threats of revenge to be taken upon the author of their woes, whoever he might prove to be, when they should have discovered who he was ; but the deportees no longer felt any particular resentment toward the soldiers, whom they regarded as being but tools in the hands of others, compelled by military law to obey orders without asking any question as to the right or wrong involved in the matter. After having gotten their goods in proper shape for hauling and eaten a meal prepared on the spot by the women with such facilities as they could muster, they even began to feel cheerful and to crack jokes about the matter.

"Here, you Johnny Reb!" called one to another— an old army comrade. "You climb down out of that wagon and let that chuck be. Bein' as you're a rebel and a prisoner, we will have to put you on short rations, I reckon."

"Glad you did n't mention the matter earlier," the other replied. "I've just got away with a pound of jerked venison and three big potatoes, so I can stand short rations for a spell—till next meal, any way."

> "How the sweet potatoes even
> Started from the ground—
> As we went marching through Georgia."

Thus sang one—evidently in memory of old army times. Then a half-dozen struck in on the chorus:

> "Hurrah! Hurrah! We bring the jubilee.
> Hurrah! Hurrah for the flag that makes you free!
> So we sang the chorus from Atlanta to the sea—
> As we went marching through Georgia."

"H—ll of a jubilee we 've got," called out one more surly than the rest, yet himself beginning to feel the mellowing influences about him.

"Wonder how the Cap'n will look with a rope about

his neck, any way. Be kind of a surprise to the old
man to be hanged for treason, I reckon." This was
ventured by a man between bites, as he stood with a
piece of corn bread in one hand and some cold meat in
the other. And then others chimed in:

"'Spect they'll turn Cap loose with four rods start,
and then run him down and lasso him."

"Bet he leads 'em a good long race if they do. The
Cap's mighty lively on his pins."

"You fellows better be sayin' prayers for your own
selves. You're just as likely to be called on to furnish
the entertainment at a foot race or a hanging bee as the
Cap is."

"And how about yourself?"

"Oh, they'll let me off on account of my good
looks. They wouldn't hang the best-looking man in the
Territory, no way it could be fixed—so I am perfectly
safe, you see."

This last, from the champion homely man in the col-
ony, was regarded as a good joke by everybody, and all
laughed heartily. This raised the spirits of even the
surliest several degrees, and a feeling of comparative
cheerfulness took possession of the little company.

The cavalcade had now formed in line, and the "ex-
traordinary march was begun."

The Lieutenant led the way with a portion of the
troops, while the rear was brought up by the others of

his company of deporters, under the command of an orderly.

The colonists were not permitted to carry their arms, which were all stacked into one of the wagons and then guarded by two of the regulars, who tied their horses behind the wagon, while they themselves rode inside with the property in their charge.

Thus guarded, the company proceeded on its way in the direction of Fort Reno, and at dusk camped upon the open prairie and spent the night in their wagons or upon the ground, guarded by sentries regularly stationed about the camp, and as regularly changed every two hours.

Fort Reno lay west and a little north of the settlement and just within the edge of the Cheyenne and Arapahoe Reservation, and a weary-dreary way the unhappy colonists found it. Especially did the women and children suffer, as they were allowed few privileges, and rode hour after hour all the days through, cramped up in their seats in the wagons, by the side of which the men were sometimes allowed to march, while their wives or some of the older children drove, but from which they were not allowed to stray, for any purpose whatever, beyond the reach of the carbines of the ever watchful guards.

Arrived at Fort Reno, they were turned over by the Lieutenant who had been in command of the company which arrested them to the authorities at the fort, the commandant of which proceeded to question the leading men among them as to their purpose in settling within the borders of Oklahoma.

They, each and all, replied that their purpose was to make for themselves homes upon land belonging to the government of the United States, in accordance with the law giving to each head of a family who would settle upon and improve it 160 acres of land. They were told in reply that the land in question—that is, Oklahoma—belonged to the Indians, and had been leased by them to certain men for grazing purposes, and that, while the government had no interest in the lessors, it was bound to protect the Indians in their rights, and that it was for this purpose that the settlers had been sought out and placed under arrest.

Replying for them, their leader denied that the land in dispute belonged to the Indians, and offered to show that it was the property of the United States under a treaty which had been made in 1866, but he was not permitted to do so.

He then demanded an immediate trial for himself and his companions; but this, too, was denied them. Capt. Paine and four others—of whom Phil Johnson was one—were confined in cells connected with the barracks, while the rest of the men, together with the women and children, were held under guard outside.

The five men were kept thus confined for five days, and were then released. They and those who had been kept under guard outside were ordered to hitch their teams to their wagons. When this was done, the women and children were told to "climb in," and the whole company, still under guard, moved off in the direction of the Kansas State line.

Another weary jaunt of nearly four days, and then they were halted on Kansas soil, drawn up in line and told that they were at liberty, but that they must not return to Oklahoma on pain of more severe treatment the next time, if they did so.

* * *

"What shall we do, men?"

The leader of the Oklahoma colonists was the querist, and his words were addressed to the members of the colony as they stood where the regulars had left them —gazing first at the retreating troops and then up at the faces of their wives and children, peering from beneath their wagon covers with looks of mingled hope and anxiety.

"What shall we do, men?"

For some seconds there was no response, and then a

voice from down near the end of the line called out with a ringing clearness :

"Move we strike straight back for Oklahoma and our claims."

Phil Johnson had spoken. Instantly came back the response from the other end of the line :

"I second the motion."

An enthusiast sang out :

"That's the way to talk it! I'm with you every time. Hip, hip! Hurrah! Hurrah! Hurrah! Phil Johnson's all right!"

This was taken up by others, and for several minutes the prairie rang with the cheers of the men, with which were mingled the shriller voices of the more courageous of the women and the piping tones of several brave children.

But, with the sober second thought came a sense of what they had lost, and how illy they were prepared to make the return journey at once and without recruiting their stock of provisions.

What little store they had on hand when the army swooped down upon them had been eaten or destroyed since that time. If they returned now without providing themselves with more, it would be necessary for them to depend entirely upon game for subsistence, not only during the journey, but for an indefinite period after they reached their claims. Their growing crops would most likely be found trampled down and destroyed by the herds of the big cattle men.

All things considered as they were, the advisability of delay was at least debatable.

Finally they decided to go into camp on the spot and talk the matter over after supper.

THE COUNCIL.

CHAPTER XIII.

GATHERED ABOUT THE COUNCIL FIRE TO PLAN FOR THE FUTURE—AN UNEXPECTED MEETING.

After supper the men gathered around the camp fire of their leader, prepared to discuss the situation and decide upon their future course.

Some sat on the ground and some on chunks of wood; some made seats of their feed boxes; two or three leaned against the nearest wagon, while still others threw themselves at full length upon the ground. Nearly all lit pipes and smoked as they talked or listened to what the others had to say.

And as they talked one grew angry at the wrong done them, and raised his voice in wrathful denunciation of all who were in any way responsible for the outrage perpetrated upon them.

Then the women came and formed a circle back of the men and watched and listened. And the children came and clung to their mothers' skirts and listened and watched also.

The camp fire flared with the night breeze. Back and forth it waved—red one moment and the next took on a bluish tint. Long, pointed tongues of flame leapt up and lapped out, as if in search of something to feed upon, and, finding only the darkness, bit at it and sank down again.

Some one drew forth a brand and tossed it farther into the flame, causing a shower of sparks to rise; these snapped and crackled and darted hither and yon for an instant, and then went out.

A wolf away out on the prairie sent forth a dismal howl, and another wolf answered from the opposite side of the camp.

Then one man arose and passed out through the circle, and went to see if any of the tethered animals had become tangled in their ropes. Finding none such, he returned and resumed his former place.

Meanwhile the women and children kept their positions at the back of the circle, and the men talked and planned.

But these were not men of many words and slow to reach a conclusion. A little thought, a little exchange of opinion, and their course was decided upon. They would halt for a few days where they were. There were water and feed at hand, and they would camp at that spot. Leaving their families with proper protection, a portion would go to the nearest settlement and procure needed supplies, while their leader, with one or two others, should make an effort to place the whole matter —the fact of their right to make homes upon the spot which they had selected, and the wrong and indignity which had been done them—before the proper authority, so that they might not be again disturbed; and then they would return and begin anew the work of improving their claims.

Accordingly, the next morning certain of the wagons were unloaded of household goods, and the owners put their teams to them and started out for the purpose of purchasing supplies. The leader, with Phil Johnson and one other, mounted and rode away to perform the mission assigned them.

The next day, about noon, the three appeared before the judge of a court in one of the border counties, and wrote out and made oath to the facts in the case as they believed them to exist.

First calling attention to the fact that the law permitted, and was supposed to encourage, the settlement of unoccupied government lands for the purposes of cultivation and occupancy, they cited the treaty under which Oklahoma had been ceded by the Indians to the government of the United States, and followed this with a detailed account of the manner in which they had been evicted from the claims which they were occupying in good faith under the law.

Having made this statement in duplicate, they next attached their signatures and made oath to the truth of the facts therein set forth, and mailed one copy of it to the President of the United States and the other to the Secretary of the Interior, at Washington.

This done, they remounted their horses and started upon their return journey.

Late in the afternoon, while riding at their usual gait —a long, swinging gallop or lope—they overtook and were passing a number of emigrant wagons, when from one of the wagons there came an inquiry regarding the distance to be traveled before reaching water and good camping ground. Reining in their horses, they gave full answer to the question. Other questions naturally followed, and finally one of the emigrants was asked:

"What part of the country might you come from, strangers?"

"Indiana."

"What part of Indiana?" queried Phil, who until now had taken no part in the conversation.

"From down on the Wabash—south half of the State."

Phil spurred his nag and reined him close up to the emigrant's wagon. Leaning eagerly forward, he peered into the face of the man who was driving. He was an oldish man and covered with the dust of a [...] yet Phil knew him now, and wondered that [he should?] know him the instant he saw him.

There was just the faintest suspicion of a [tremor in] Phil's voice when he spoke again. He said:

"Mr. McKinley. I reckon you don't rec[ollect me.] I am Phil Johnson, and my folks used to live [next] to you years ago, when I was a boy."

Mr. McKinley—for he it was, and no mist[ake—for an] instant looked at him without speaking. Th[en, turning] half-way around in his seat, he called to som[e one] in the wagon:

"Here, Net! And you, Marm! Here's [Phil John]son—him they used to call the three P's. [Don't you] remember him, both of ye."

And then Phil—whose heart was making [strenuous] efforts to escape from his body, first by way of [his mouth,] and, failing in that, by knocking a hole in [his ribs—] heard a rustling within the covered wagon, [a head was] thrust out and the flap of the wagon cover [lifted, and he] heard a voice saying:

"Is it really you, Philip? Well, who 'd [have thought] of running against you, 'way out here in th[is wil]derness?"

Such was Mrs. McKinley's greeting.

Phil wished Nettie had been the speaker. [Surely] she would speak now, so he might know he[r voice.]

to her, for suddenly he felt that he did not know how to address her unless she first spoke to him.

But in spite of the awful throbbing of his heart, Phil managed to reply to Mrs. McKinley, telling her it was he and no other, and also to mumble something about being glad to see them.

And still Nettie had not spoken.

Through the opening made by the upturned flap, he saw a portion of her dress, but that was all. Mrs. McKinley filled the opening with her own person pretty completely, as she leaned forward and talked to him.

Mrs. McKinley was a good talker when she wished to be. And just now, for some reason, she did wish to be.

Phil's parents, so she told him, were still living on the old place, and were well when she left there—some three weeks ago last Thursday.

"They thought you must be dead, Philip—not getting any answer to their letter."

"Did they write?" asked Phil. "Did they get my letter?"

"They got the one you sent from down in Texas somewhere—the one in which you said you were going to Kansas with a drove of cattle for somebody. That's the only letter they ever got. They answered that one right off, for they were awful anxious for you to come home. And they told you about every thing and every body—so your mother told me—and urged you to come

right home as soon as you got their letter. And then
they waited and waited, but heard nothing from you;
then they writ again several times, but they never heard
any thing more. They thought you might a-been killed
or something, 'cause they never heard from you again.
But Nettie—she *did* say she knowed you was n't dead,
and that you 'd come back some time, shore."

"Is—is that Nettie in there?" asked Phil, with some
trepidation, when Mrs. McKinley had paused to take
breath.

"Why, Lor'—yes. Nettie, you have n't spoken to
Philip yet. You have n't forgotten him, have you?
Crawl over here and take a look at him; he 's growed
powerful."

And Mrs. McKinley took her daughter by the shoulder
and drew her forward, where she could both see and be
seen. She said:

"How do you do, Mr. Johnson?"

To save his soul, Phil could only answer:

"I 'm pretty well. How do *you* do?"

He would have given his pony—and Phil thought a
great deal of that pony—to be able to say something
more and to say it better, but he could not. He had been
thinking what to say to Nettie all the time her mother
was talking to him, trying to decide whether to be dignified and lift his hat and say, formally, "I am pleased to
meet you again, Miss McKinley," or to say "Hello, Net-

tie," and take her hand and squeeze it a little, and thus re-establish their familiar relations at once.

And here he had only said: "I'm pretty well. How do *you* do?"

It seemed so ridiculously idiotic, he told himself a minute afterward, that if his pony was only warranted to kick on proper occasions, instead of improper ones, he would get right down then and there and ask to be duly kicked.

And Nettie said never another word, but after a few moments drew back from the opening, and left Phil with only the sight of her skirts to console him—the same as before she had spoken.

But what Nettie lacked in conversational powers on that occasion her mother made up for. The moment Nettie withdrew her head from the opening in the wagon cover her mother's filled the space, and she resumed her narrative, giving him items of news from the old neighborhood mingled with incidents concerning their own family, and telling why they had left the old home to come "out West."

"The ferry is still there," she told him, "but mostly it is n't used any more, as a bridge has been built across the river only a half mile below.

"That was the reason we came West—one of the reasons, anyway—though Nettie was always urging us to come."

Here Phil pricked up his ears and listened with all his might.

"You see, Nettie has n't run the ferry for ever so long. She was up to Terre Haute to school three winters; taught in the old school house in the summers to get money to pay board and schooling with.

"But she did n't like teaching there, where every one knew her. The children were harder to manage, seemed like, 'cause they all knew her so well, and so she wanted to come West and teach. But Mr. McKinley would n't move till it got so the ferry did n't pay us any more, because of the bridge. Then we decided that we would come.

"We 're going to pre-empt some land somewheres, and as soon as we get settled like we 're going to try and get a school as nearby as we can for her to teach. The other girls can do the work, you see. They are now in Mr. Sommers' wagon, on ahead there. The boys are in some of the others' wagons, too.

"But you have n't told us any thing about yourself yet—where you 're living and what you 're up to. Driving cattle yet?"

Phil told her that he had been in New Mexico for two years, and since that he had been in Oklahoma, where he had a "claim," and that he was about to return there.

He also told her that he had failed to get his dear

mother's letter, and had not known what to think at not hearing from home; that he feared his parents were either dead or had moved away, and that had he known they were living and anxious to have him go home he would have done so.

He was desirous of talking more about Oklahoma. He wanted to suggest that Mr. McKinley's family join the colony and go there too, but he some way could not. He thrilled through and through at thoughts of having Nettie near him again; of being able to re-establish the old familiar relations, and of what that might lead to— later on.

But the meeting had been so sudden and unexpected, and Nettie had seemed so cool and formal, that he could say nothing except in reply to questions from Nettie's mother.

He kept trying hard to think of something to say to Nettie, but he could not—or, rather, he could not muster the courage to voice his thoughts. His failure to say any thing better than "I 'm pretty well; how do *you* do?" when she spoke to him first, discouraged him from making another attempt.

"She must think me a fool, or else the most bashful man alive," was his mental comment. "Confound it all! If she had only called me Phil, now, instead of 'Mr. Johnson!' It was calling me 'Mr. Johnson' that took me off my feet—it was so confoundedly formal."

MR. M'KINLEY HAS AN IDEA.

While Mrs. McKinley was thus entertaining Phil her husband was talking with Phil's companions, who, without exactly knowing it, were doing all that could be done to induce Mr. McKinley to regard Oklahoma and the spot selected by the colonists as the most desirable place in the world for him to locate in.

Nettie's father listened attentively to the description given of the extent and fertility of the prairies, the abundance of timber and the salubrity of the climate. He evinced considerable interest in the statements made with regard to the abundance of game, but it was at the mention of fish that he became thoroughly alive—alive all over.

Fish meant a river; abundance of fish must mean a pretty large river, and a large river meant——

* * *

"Going to lay out a town there?" queried the ex-ferryman.

"Yes. Town already laid out. All we lack now is the people."

"Going to be a pretty good-sized town, I s'pose? Lots of travel back and forth across the river?"

"Not a doubt of it. Just as soon as it becomes known that there is an abundance of government land there people will rush in by the thousand, and the country will settle up rapidly."

"Be a pretty good place for a ferry, won't it?"

Phil failed to catch the reply, but a few minutes later, when the wagons halted for the night, Mr. McKinley was overheard saying to his wife:

"Marthy, I believe Oklahoma is just the place we were looking for."

This was music to Phil's ears. He said to himself: "The leader is headed right."

NETTIE.

CHAPTER XIV.

PHIL FEASTS HIS EYES—THE M'KINLEYS CONCLUDE TO
LOCATE IN OKLAHOMA.

Phil and his companions went into camp that night with the emigrants from Indiana.

To have induced Phil to do otherwise would have required greater persuasive powers than his companions possessed, even had they cared to exercise such powers, which they did not; though before overtaking the travelers they had intended to go five miles farther before camping. They had delayed a little in chatting with the emigrants, and it was now fairly late, and here were water and fuel and all things needful for their purposes; besides which there was a prospect of inducing these people to join their colony, which of itself furnished inducement for the other two to remain in communication with the emigrants.

As for Phil? Well, if asked to go on, the odds would

have been a thousand to one that he would have declared his pony was lame, sore-backed and generally done for— in fact, could not travel a mile farther.

Maybe a suspicion that Phil would prove obstinate in the matter helped to move his companions to decide it would be best to go into camp with the emigrant party. This is not known. Be this as it may, they swung themselves from their saddles the moment the wagons came to a halt, and prepared to stake their horses out and to care for them.

Phil's pony seemed to realize that his master was in a hurry to get him taken care of that night, for the moment Phil's foot was out of the stirrup the pony made an effort to remove his own saddle by dropping on the ground and rolling. And when he was compelled to get up and allow it to be taken off in the usual way, the animal refused to be rubbed down in a manner so emphatic that Phil accepted it as evidence that he ought not to fool away any time on that kind of a job. Accordingly, he tethered him out without rubbing him down, and then hurried around to where the McKinleys were preparing supper.

Nettie was stooping over a fire just started when he approached, but arose on hearing his coming footsteps.

Then it was that Phil noticed how tall and graceful she had grown to be. He had not seen her fully before —not even her face, which had been half concealed by the wagon cover—but now he saw both face and form fully by the light of the camp fire, and he felt that even his imagination had utterly failed to do full justice to her beauty.

And Nettie McKinley *was* beautiful. She possessed the beauty of youth and innocence—yes, and intelligence.

To her natural strength of mind, inherited from her mother, she had added education. Her education was not extensive and broad, it is true, but was such as the schools of an ambitious and thriving little city, anxious to keep pace with the world in educational as well as other matters, could furnish.

From her father she had inherited the dignity which at times sat upon him as an ill-fitting garment, but which rested on her with a naturalness that added to her face and form an expression of womanliness and goodness which might well have charmed another than a frontiersman like Phil, who had known little of women and less of women possessed of grace both of body and mind.

True, Nettie exhibited little of either grace or dignity in her first meeting with her girlhood's sweetheart, after their long separation; but the fact must be borne in mind that an emigrant wagon, where one is compelled for lack of room to sit in a position that is more or less cramped, is not the most favorable place for the exhibition of grace and dignity. Besides, the meeting was so entirely unexpected, and Phil was—as Mrs. McKinley expressed it—"growed powerful," and in his cowboy costume, to which he still clung, with a Winchester rifle lying across his lap, looked so much like the brigands of whom she had read and so little like the boy in patched clothes and straw hat who used to help her run the ferry that there is small wonder if she failed of making as good an appearance as under other circumstances she might have done.

But now she was upon the ground, where graceful dignity was possible, and she had recovered from her first surprised start at the meeting. When, on rising from her stooping position in front of the little camp fire, she saw Phil approaching she was the personification of grace and dignity. With much cordiality she said:

"I am glad you and your friends are to camp with us, Mr. Johnson. We want very much to hear about your adventures since you left the old neighborhood; and we can, I am sure, tell you much that will interest you about your father's family and others whom you used to know."

Phil would have given worlds to feel that he could answer with equal dignity and self-poise, but his life and vocation had not been such as to give him confidence in the presence of such a woman as he felt Nettie to be; and, besides, there kept coming up thoughts of that last trip which they had made together on the ferry boat the afternoon before the night in which he ran away from home, to begin a life of perilous wandering, and he could not feel at ease because of it.

Yet Phil Johnson was naturally self-confident and manly; and now he gathered his mental forces and answered, with some stiffness of manner, that he could not think of going on without first learning all they could tell him of every one he had ever known back there.

The ice thus broken, they fell into a conversation which soon put them on as familiar a footing as could be under the circumstances.

Mrs. McKinley soon joined them, and with her came the younger members of the family—boys and girls, most of whom were but toddlers when Phil and Nettie were quite well-grown children. But now these were big boys and girls—almost men and women.

After all the rest came Mr. McKinley, who shook hands with Phil, now that shaking hands was not such a difficult matter as when one was in the saddle and the other was sitting on the spring seat of an emigrant wagon.

There was a good bit of cordiality in his manner, notwithstanding the sense of dignity which he felt belonged to the man who was commissioned by two States to run a ferry had not all left him with his leaving the interstate business.

When all preparations for such a meal as they could get under the circumstances were about completed, Mrs.

McKinley suggested to her husband, who had been too busily engaged talking to think of it, that he find Phil's companions and invite them to supper—a suggestion to which he responded with alacrity, although Phil assured them that it was not necessary, as they had provided themselves with food before leaving town, and had it safely store away at the backs of their saddles.

Nevertheless, Mr. McKinley hunted them up, but he found them already eating with some of the other emigrants, and so he returned to his own camp fire without them.

After supper Phil's companions sought him out, and they were introduced by name to Mr. McKinley and his family.

Then others of the emigrants gathered around, and they asked questions about Oklahoma, about the trouble which the colonists had with the military authorities and about other portions of the country with which their new acquaintances were familiar—through all of which Phil waited and watched for an opportunity to speak with Nettie out of hearing of the others, though knowing all the time that if such a chance were to occur he would be no more capable of saying any but the most commonplace things than he was of flying. He was not even quite sure that he would be able to say any thing, but none the less he wished that they might be alone, if only for a minute.

To be alone with Nettie would, he felt, bring her, in some way, close to him ; give him a kind of possessorship, as it were ; a possessorship such as he had when as boy and girl they ran the ferry boat together and were recognized by everybody in the little village as being partners in every thing and as having a perfect right to be together.

But no opportunity of speaking with Nettie apart from others occurred, nor indeed of addressing her at all except as he included her with others of the family in some questions relating to those he had known or events which had occurred in the vicinity of his old home.

Occasionally Nettie answered, being best able to do so from her better knowledge of those earlier companions of whom he wished to know, and that was all. And when the little crowd began to disperse, and when Phil finally felt compelled to say good-night, he knew that he had received no sign to tell him whether Nettie remembered him as he wished to be remembered.

But he was miserably happy—never had been so much so in his life. He rolled himself up in his blankets by the side of his comrades, but if he slept or not is only known to the sentinel stars that "kept their watch in the sky."

Only this much is known : After tossing restlessly for an indefinite period, Phil thought of his pony, which had refused to be rubbed down when unsaddled, and he got up and went to him and curried him, where he stood with his legs spread out and his nose almost touching the ground—asleep.

The sleeping pony awoke with a little snort when his master spoke his name, and then quietly submitted to having his sweat-dried coat rubbed clean with a handful of grass and a smooth stick, which Phil managed to find by feeling around on the ground in the darkness.

After rubbing down his pony Phil returned to his sleeping comrades. But instead of lying down on his blankets, as they lay, he gathered them up and went and spread them at the roots of a tree a little way off, where he lay down again, and there remained until morning.

So soon as he saw that the family was astir the next morning Phil took his stock of provisions over to the McKinley wagon. He had not forgotten that in the other days he had always a friend in Mrs. McKinley, and he was shrewd enough to guess that she was still his friend.

Phil had now had a little time to think matters over, and he felt that, having been received kindly, he would have only himself to blame if he did not drop at once into the old-time relationship with the family.

In this reckoning of the family he did not include Nettie, however. If he won Nettie for his wife he must first prove himself worthy of her. He felt sure of that. Even if she remembered him as he hoped she did, he knew now that she would not acknowledge her love until he had proven to her that he was capable of some higher calling than that of trailing Indians or herding long-horn steers.

What Philip sighed for now was an opportunity to prove to her that, though unlearned in books, he was yet the equal of most other men in ability and in moral and physical courage. He meant to make himself the equal of the best. He could do so with her to help him—so he told himself; and he meant to learn what she would prefer him to be—what her standard of manhood was, and to make that his standard.

Not that he had not strong convictions of what was just and right, as between man and man, for he had. It had been said of him more than once, and by men who knew him intimately, that there was no squarer man on the range than Phil Johnson.

But of many things he was ignorant—just how very ignorant he did not know, but he meant to find out. He meant to learn by watching Nettie, if possible for him to be near her, and to be in all things what she would have him be.

And, now that he had come to himself, he knew that the way to begin was to accept to the fullest the friendly interest shown him by the family and do as nearly as possible as he would have done when a boy helping Nettie row the ferry, and that was to go to a meal with them as if one of their own family, if so it happened that he was necessarily present at meal time.

It was, therefore, the result of well-digested thought that brought him to the McKinley wagon with his pack of provisions and tin cup for coffee that morning.

"Mrs. McKinley," he said, "I supposed you would expect me to breakfast, so here I am. I 've brought along my own stock of provisions, so if you happen to be short I 'll not rob the family. I expect you remember something about my appetite, and probably noticed last night that it has grown no less since I ate at your table when I was a boy."

That Mrs. McKinley was pleased with his frankness and desire to resume his old relations with the family even modest Phil thought he could see. At any rate, she treated him exactly as she used to do—with a kind of motherly solicitude—which made it very easy for him to feel at ease, and so appear to the best advantage.

And Phil was as good-looking and as manly-looking a fellow as one meets in a day's travel. Standing 5 feet 10 in his boots, well formed and muscular, with a good head set firmly upon his shoulders, mustache of brown inclining to red, with brown hair and blue eyes, Phil approached the ideal man. It is doubtful if Nettie had ever seen a more manly form than the sun-burnt and sombrero-topped young fellow who came and took the bucket of water out of her hand as she was coming up the creek bank, and there must have been something in her face which showed that she was conscious of this fact, for Phil suddenly felt himself to be more of a man than ever before and more worthy to be her husband.

Together they walked back to the wagon, chatting easily and freely, both of the past and the present. At breakfast Phil managed to secure a seat upon the same log with Nettie, and close by her side. And Phil was not conscious of what they had for breakfast, and can not tell to this day.

The talk while eating was principally of Oklahoma and the advisability of the McKinley family joining the colonists.

Phil told them, as nearly as he could, the facts about the country and the prospects for its early settlement. He knew enough of the ways of the owners of large herds of cattle, and of the necessity of their keeping control of great tracts of land for herding purposes, to understand something of the danger which the colonists were in from that quarter, but he could not conceive it possible that, when the facts were known to the authorities at Washington, any one would be allowed to interfere with those citizens who were seeking to make homes upon the public lands, and he therefore felt safe so far as fear of further trouble with the military forces of the government was concerned.

Naturally, he was intensely anxious to have McKinley's family join the colonists, for only in this way could he hope to keep Nettie by him.

True, he would have given up his claim and selected another in the vicinity of any spot where the McKinleys might have chosen to pre-empt, in Kansas or one of the territories, but to do so would be to indirectly declare his hope with regard to Nettie, and to do it in a way which he felt would hardly be manly under the circumstances.

Such a move would be too clear a declaration of his desire to be in her society not to be accompanied with a direct offer of marriage, and he felt that the time to do that had not come. Therefore, he must either persuade them to go to Oklahoma or submit to being separated from Nettie almost as soon as he had found her, and depend for success in winning her upon correspondence by letter.

He was sure she would not refuse him permission to write to her, but he was not accustomed to writing, and he doubted his ability to show to advantage in a correspondence such as that would be. Yet, above all other things, he disliked to be separated from her, now that they had met again.

Nettie took but little part in the discussion of the proposition to go to Oklahoma. Beyond asking Phil if he thought the country would settle up rapidly, so that good schools would follow, she said nothing.

Her father once asked her squarely whether she was in favor of the family going or not, but her mother very dextrously parried the question for her, and she was not obliged to answer it.

In the end it was decided to go. Mr. McKinley was in favor of it, because he believed that as soon as a territorial government was formed he could procure a charter for running a ferry boat across the river; the boys favored it, because there was plenty of game and the trip promised excitement ; and Mrs. McKinley favored it because—well, if the truth must be known, because she thought her eldest daughter's happiness would be made secure by it, without injuring in any way the prospects of the younger children.

Mothers, be it known, are acquainted with the ways and the hearts of girls, and quick to understand and sympathize with them in their heart troubles and joys. If Nettie loved Phil, had loved him and clung to his memory all these years, it is reasonably certain that her mother knew it.

Mrs. McKinley was wise in her unlearned way, and was a good judge of character. She knew Phil when a boy, and she knew his parents and from whom they were descended. She had confidence in Phil—in his integrity of character and in his ability to make his way in life. Therefore, she was not inclined to do that which would needlessly separate the young people, now that they had been brought together again, until they had full opportunity to know whether the feeling of their childhood remained to them in their manhood and womanhood. For thoroughly sound good sense and womanly wisdom, give me the mother whose life has not been all it might have been of ease and comfort ; give me the mothers of the Wabash and other agricultural districts.

To say that Phil was rejoiced at the decision arrived at by the McKinleys would be a waste of both time and words.

He wanted to look at Nettie and see how she received the decision of her parents when it was finally made known, but he could not muster sufficient courage for a moment, and when he did look at her she had turned away, and appeared to be mighty busy at that particular moment.

He felt pretty certain, however, that she was not sorry, and so he was content.

Before they broke camp that morning, Phil wrote a long and loving letter home, in which he told of his joyful meeting with the McKinleys, of his failure to get the letters addressed to him, and promised faithfully that as soon as he got his claim fairly in shape he would pay a visit to the old place "down home." He promised, further, to spend several weeks at least with those so dear to him.

Mrs. McKinley also wrote to Phil's mother. Just

what she wrote in that letter only two persons were supposed ever to know. But it is safe to say nothing was written that would make Mrs. Johnson feel ashamed of her son.

∙ ∙ ∙

Only two families from the half dozen who composed the company of emigrants with whom Phil and his friends camped that night decided to go to Oklahoma, and of them one was Mr. McKinley's. The others continued their journey westward, and settled near Garfield, in Pawnee county, Kansas. Beyond this mention their fate bears no relation to this narrative.

After giving directions as to the route to follow in order to reach the camp of the colonists, Phil and his companions left them and galloped on ahead.

Gladly would Phil have remained behind and piloted

them through, except that there was really no need of it and he felt that it would be wisest not to run any risk of seeming to force his company upon the family.

The three horsemen arrived at the camp of the colonists a little afternoon of the same day, and the wagons bringing the new accessions to their numbers reached there just at sundown.

So Phil had the pleasure of seeing Nettie again before he slept that night.

A Strange Betrothal.

CHAPTER XV.

BACK TO THE CANADIAN—HAVING BUILT A NEW HOUSE, PHIL CONCLUDES TO DEDICATE IT.

The journey back to the settlement on the Canadian was made without incident, so far as the company at large was concerned.

To Phil and Nettie every day, and almost every hour, was filled with incidents—the incidents of their hourly meetings and partings, of his riding by the side of her father's wagon as they journeyed along, of a spoken word, a glance, a simple flower which he stooped from his saddle to pluck and hand to her.

And then the evenings spent about the camp fires, in which memories of the trifling incidents that made up the days and years of their childhood were recalled and lived over again in all their sweetness. All these were mere passing incidents of a flitting evening, unnoticed and uncared for by others, but to these two young people they were things to be thought over and dwelt upon after they had retired for the night and before the morning risings.

Phil professed still to board with Mr. and Mrs. Jones. But his real status as a boarder with the Joneses was about like this: Having reinstated himself with the McKinley family on something like the old down-home basis, he did as he had been wont to do when a boy. He ate with them about as often as anywhere else.

The two McKinley boys were now approaching manhood, and one of them was beginning to watch with impatience for the appearance of down upon his upper lip. Both these boys at once "took to" Phil, as the saying is, being caught by his evident knowledge of frontier life and by his splendid accomplishments as a horseman and rifle shot.

As much as possible they put themselves in his company, and to them he gave lessons in frontier craft—the "signs" of the different kinds of game with which the country abounded and the best method of securing it.

His rifle was always at their service, and also his pony, and many were the attempts made by one or the other of them to bag a deer or antelope, droves of which were often seen, as the line of wagons, one following the other, moved away across the prairie. And, unskilled as they were, they were not always without reward for

HOME AGAIN.

their efforts. At least, their success was sufficient to sustain their interest and excitement in the sport. Of course, when the boys failed to keep good the supply of game, Phil and others succeeded, so that fresh meat in variety was always abundant in the train.

Phil was now happily miserable—happy in the belief that he was regarded with favor by his sweetheart, and miserable because he could not be in her presence more than about half of their waking moments. But he managed some way to continue to exist, and even to avoid being called crazy by anybody in the company, though just how he did it he could not have told. Certainly he said and did some things which only a crazy man or one madly in love would have perpetrated.

* * *

A cheer broke from the lips of the colonists when first they neared, once more, the spot from which they had been so ruthlessly driven—the spot whereon they had begun to make themselves homes.

It was at the close of a day long and warm, and they

were grown weary of the journey and eager to get back and be at rest and at work upon their claims.

This forced journey had not been to them like the one by which they had first come to this spot.

Then they were filled with joyous anticipations of the future, with which were mingled feelings of love for, and pride in, their country as the possessor of such unbounded resources and so glorious a Constitution—a Constitution which guaranteed to every citizen, no matter how humble, a right to life and liberty and a home upon the soil, provided only that he was willing to fashion that home with his own hands. There was a sense of security, a mantle of peace, resting upon them then—a feeling that peace instead of war and love in place of hatred constituted the normal condition of men, and that within that condition of peace and good will they could embrace all races of men.

Such is ever the feeling produced by conditions in which hope of a good time to come is founded upon the belief that justice is enthroned and rules over all, and that labor will receive its perfect reward.

But now?

Now they were returning to homes from which they had been driven by the very power which they revered more than all other earthly powers—by the government of which they had been so proud; in spite of the Constitution in which they had placed such implicit trust.

True, they did not believe the wrong to have been an intentional one on the part of the government. It was a blunder, doubtless; it had arisen out of a misunderstanding of what and who they were, and of the exact locality in which they had located their claims.

But, nevertheless, the annoying and costly wrong had been done them, and the instrument by which it had been accomplished was a company of government troops which had been stationed on the frontier professedly for the protection of just such as they—the protection of citizens seeking to make homes for themselves and build up great States on the unoccupied lands of the smiling West.

This fact hurt, in spite of themselves.

The knowledge of the source of their wrongs took from them the feeling of absolute security, and left in its place the smart of injustice, which, however much they compelled themselves to make excuses for it, still rankled in their hearts and made the sun seem a little less bright, their hopes for the future a little less gay, their confidence in themselves a little less perfect.

The colonists were anxious, too, to know how much damage, if any, had been done to their crops, planted and up before they were dragged away; to know whether their rude cabins had been destroyed or not.

These lovers of peace and domesticity longed to be in possession, full and complete, of their homes and their claims, and to continue the work which they had begun with such enthusiasm only a few short months before; and they greeted with a cheer the first sight of the belt of timber fringing the river, beyond which their cabins lay, and, touching up their now somewhat jaded animals, they pushed forward with a more lively step.

And then some one—some woman—began singing "Home, Sweet Home."

Clear and low the music and the words floated out upon the evening air, and mingled with the scent of the flowers and the grass, upon which the dew was beginning to fall and the harvest moon to shed its soft rays as, like a ball of silver, it arose above the horizon.

Oh, how thrilling and ennobling is the music of a woman's voice, whose notes express the yearnings of a pure heart!

Thus ran the old song—the great American home song:

> "'Mid pleasures and palaces though we may roam,
> Be it ever so humble, there's no place like home.
> A charm from the skies seems to hallow us there,
> Which, seek thro' the world, is not met with elsewhere."

A child's voice, piping and clear, like the notes of a robin, joined that of the woman in the middle of the stanza, and when the chorus was reached other voices of both men and women joined in, and added to the volume of the music and sent it flying across the prairie to be broken into echoes against the line of timber upon the river bank.

> "Home, home—sweet, sweet home!
> There's no place like home!
> There's no place like home!"

Uncultivated voices these, did you say?

Granted.

But they were voices strong, clear and sweet; voices filled with a pathos born of deep feeling and strong emotions; the voices of men and women who longed for the sweets of home as the roe panteth for the clear waters.

They forded the river with the full light of the moon shining down upon them, passed through the strip of timber upon its farther bank, where the shadows were black, and only here and there a ray of silver found its way through thick foliage to the damp ground; made the little rise upon the other side, where the timber gave way to the prairie, and emerged upon the site of the town which they had laid out with such high hopes when they first came, and near to where the cabins of two of their number had stood.

But the cabins were not there!

The spot where they had stood was a bit of bare, black earth, and that was all. Even the ashes to which they had been reduced had been blown away by the winds.

The whole party camped there that night. As one

and another of the canvas-covered wagons emerged from the shadows and moved on and up into the prairie and the moonlight they halted, and their drivers got down from their seats and unhitched their teams and picketed them, with scarcely a word spoken to wife or child or comrade.

None felt it worth while to drive their wearied teams farther in any faint hope that their own cabins might have been spared, for they knew perfectly well the motive which had prompted the destruction of the two cabins which had stood on the spot near where they now were, and that it existed equally for the destruction of each and all the rest, and that in all probability all were destroyed. Nevertheless, when their animals had been cared for, one and another of their number slipped away on foot and visited their separate claims, but only to find their worst fears proven true. Their homes were gone. The earth where their cabins had stood was bare and black and desolate.

But did these men weep and wring their hands, and weakly moan over the desolation wrought—over cabins burned, over crops trampled into the ground by the hoofs of thousands of half-wild cattle?

Not so!

Some angry words, some oaths, some threats of what they would do if the perpetrators of these new outrages should be incautious enough to fall into their hands—

and that was all. There was no crying over spilled milk, but no more milk was to be spilled.

They built other cabins as they had builded those destroyed by the selfish greed of the cattle kings. The ground where the growing corn had been trampled and devoured they sowed to wheat.

The corner stakes which marked the boundary lines of their separate claims they re-established where they had been removed. They foreswore the pleasures of the chase, or hunted only as they had need of procuring food, and worked steadily and hard.

They spoke not over much of the past at first, and then less and still less, and then not at all, but only of the future and of the good time coming.

As for Phil, the loss of his cabin was not a heavy affliction, and he was not suffering greatly for the want of it. The burning of a dozen or a hundred cabins all belonging to him, if he had possessed so many, would not have made him unhappy just then.

His corn was trampled and destroyed, of course. This was a much greater loss than his cabin, which had not been a very valuable one, and had not cost a very great amount of labor.

Being without a family and boarding with a neighbor, he had considered it necessary to build only such a house as would meet the requirements of the law. A few logs put up without much hewing or nice care and roofed over with poles and long grass—a house in which, in fact, he kept his plow and whatever other implements of tillage he had, and allowed Mr. Jones to store his also, but in which he slept occasionally, that he might comply with the letter of the law, the spirit of which he was complying with in breaking the sod, and in whatever way he made clear his intentions honestly to make it his permanent home—this was the kind of a house Phil had owned, and such another he could build, if he wished, in a week's time, with a little help from some of the neighbors in putting the logs in position.

But Phil did not hurry to rebuild. Instead, he gave assistance in rebuilding to Mr. Jones, and to others who had families, and were in more immediate need of home shelter.

The McKinleys were strong handed of themselves. True, the old gentleman was not over fond of work, as a rule, but now he awoke to the spirit of the occasion and of those with whom he was associated. With the help of his two sons, he soon had a very comfortable double cabin erected on the claim which they had fixed upon. This claim abutted upon the river at a point where it would be easy to establish a ferry, when he should have secured a license to do so from the Territorial Legislature which was to be.

To erect a ferry without a license, probably, did not occur to him as possible, or if it did he did not care to do so. The owning of a ferry without a charter signed and sealed in due form with the big seal of the State and with a ribbon attached to it would carry no dignity with it. It was recognition by the Commonwealth as a person fit to be intrusted with the responsibility of the high position which Mr. McKinley coveted, and not the work or profits of the business.

Heretofore, at least, Mr. McKinley had worried himself very little over the problem of how to make a living for the family. That was a duty which he felt belonged by right to his wife, and with which he never interfered to any great extent. He probably reasoned that, as it was the generally accepted theory and one everywhere reduced to practice that the wife should cook the food for the family, and as in order for her to do this the food must first be procured, it followed naturally that whoever did the cooking should also procure that which was to be cooked.

Mr. McKinley indorsed and adopted the recipe which opens with the admonition:

"First catch your hare."

Thus Mr. McKinley's recipe for all manner of cooking was:

"First get something to cook."

Having furnished this recipe, he felt that his duty, so far as it related to providing food and raiment for his household, was fully performed. All that yet remained for him to do was to properly sustain the dignity of the family, which in his opinion could best be done by securing recognition from the State in the shape of a charter or license of some kind, such appearing in his mind to be in the nature of a certificate of character, a formal acknowledgment from those in authority that the person certified to was one worthy of being held in high esteem by them, and hence by all.

He had insisted on maintaining the ferry across the Wabash long after it had ceased to pay for the trouble of tending it, and had only consented to leave the town when his charter expired and he learned that he could not get it renewed because of the fact that a ferry at that point was no longer needed by any considerable number of people; and now his anxiety for the rapid settlement of Oklahoma arose apparently from a desire to see the Territory organized and a Legislature elected, which would be endowed with authority to grant him a certificate of respectability—or, in other words, a charter to establish a ferry across the Canadian River at the point where he had located his claim.

This little weakness of Mr. McKinley did not, however, interfere to make either himself or family inhospitable or unsociable. Indeed, its members were more than ordinarily sociable, both among themselves and with others.

Mrs. McKinley was a woman of much natural ability

and good sense, though entirely without education, and was quite capable, as a general thing, of both catching and cooking her own hare, and she respected, and taught her children to respect, this fear which their father had of compromising his dignity, and to treat him with a mild species of formality quite sufficient to satisfy his idea of what was right and proper, and so prevented any rasping of tempers on anybody's part, and made theirs one of the pleasantest of families in which to remain, either for a short or long period of time.

Phil soon found that he was not alone in his admiration for the beautiful eldest daughter. Neither was he the only one who was a frequent and apparently welcome visitor at the spacious and inviting double cabin on the river bank.

Meantime he kept industriously at work on the improvement of his claim.

Phil had found his plow in the furrow where he left it when he was arrested by the soldiery, and had again hitched to it, and resumed his plowing when he had rendered such assistance in the erection of new cabins as he felt was necessary to those who had families. He kept this plow bright by constant use until the time for seeding was over.

Then he began the work of erecting a new house, which he meant should be a little better than the most of those built near him.

He felt under no need of making great haste, for he still boarded with Mr. Jones and his wife, and he had not reached a formal understanding with Nettie. In truth, Phil was a little jealous, at times, of some of the other young men of the colony. Generally, however, he was hopeful, and even confident; and, as he had to erect a house of some kind in order to keep good his claim under the law, he decided that it should be one as nearly worthy of Nettie as could well be, considering the circumstances. So he hewed all the logs of which it was to be built in such a way that the walls would be smooth both inside and out, and notched and laid them up with care. Then he carefully chinked and plastered them as best he could.

He also made a wide shed or porch at the rear of the house.

This was done by allowing the third log from the top, in the body of the house, to extend over at the back some eight or ten feet. Then by putting posts under these at the end and a girder across from one to the other, and extending the rafters upon that side clear down to the girder, it was ready to be roofed over with "shakes," rough shingles, split or rived from straight-grained trees —the same as those with which the main body of the house was covered.

The autumn was far advanced when Phil's house was completed. He felt a little proud of it, as it was the best one in the settlement. At least, this was the owner's estimate of his handiwork.

And now if Nettie would consent to become his wife his happiness would be complete, and he felt that he could not much longer delay asking the question, upon her answer to which his future happiness or misery solely depended.

He thought over the matter a great deal—thought of it all the time, in fact. But, like many another lover, he was loath to

"Put his chances to the touch,
And win or lose it all."

Here, again, was procrastination the thief of time. Poor Phil! He waited for some word or look from Nettie which should give him better courage and a basis for hope.

And so, waiting and hoping, the days went by, and a week had elapsed since his house was finished. Still he had not asked Nettie to share it with him.

Finally one of the young men with whom he associated said to him:

"I say, Phil! Why don't you have a dance and a party over at your new house? Dedicate it, you know? Joe Anderson will fiddle for us, and we can have a way-up time. Say you'll do it."

Phil jumped at the idea, and wondered he had not thought of it before.

He would invite everybody—which would, of course, include Nettie. Maybe, when once she was over there, actually within his own house, he could find some way of telling her how much he loved her, and how he had built the house with the hope that she would share it with him.

He told the friend who had suggested the party that it would be all right, and together they fixed upon a time for it to come off. Then Phil told him to invite every-body he saw, and to tell them to invite everybody they saw, so that no one in the settlement might be missed.

This preliminary arranged, Phil set out for McKinley's cabin to invite Nettie and the rest of the family.

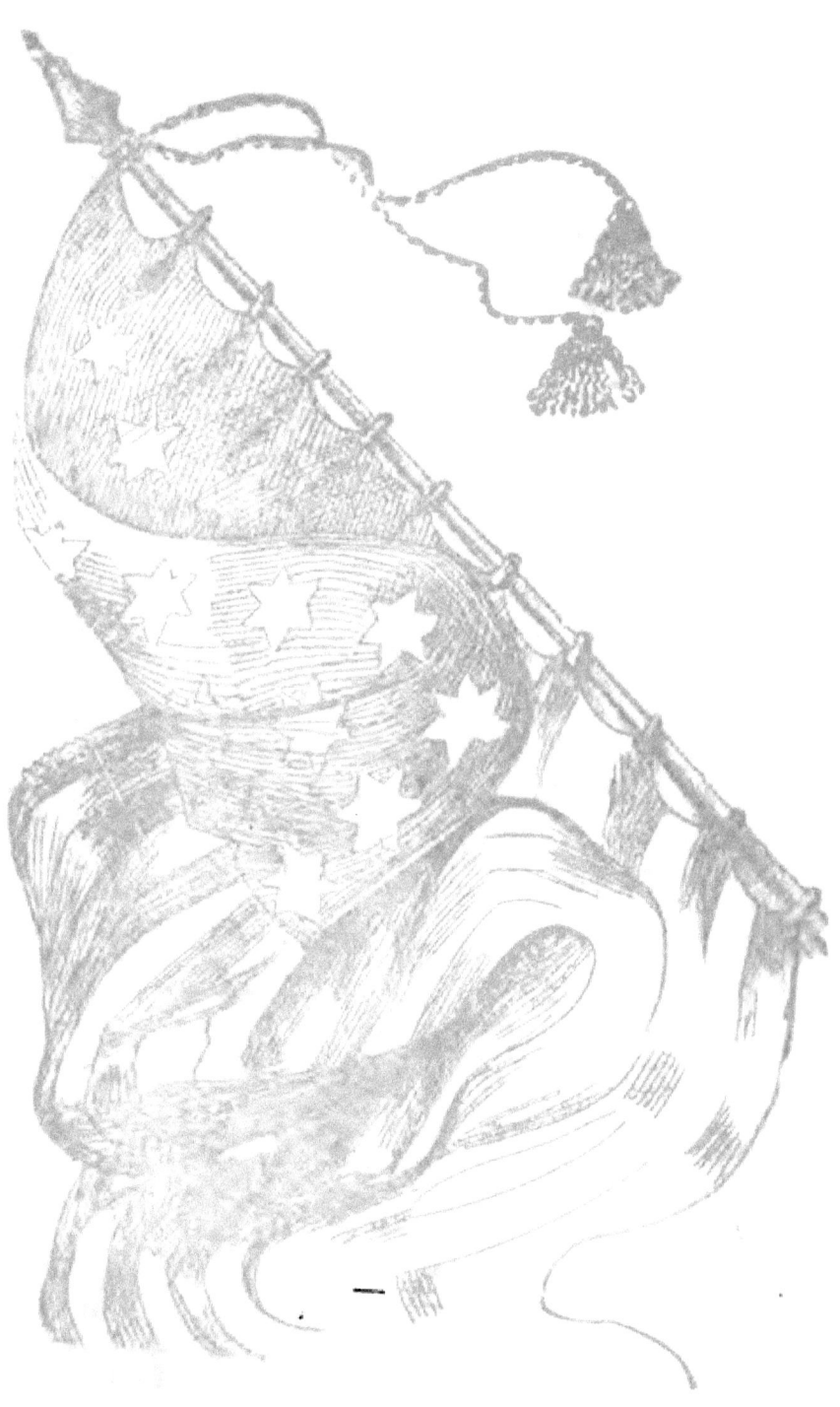

PHIL IN HIS FIRST CABIN.

CHAPTER XVI.

A RATHER STRANGE BETROTHAL—FOLLOWED BY HASTY PREPARATIONS FOR A FIGHT.

"Nettie and the other girls are gone over to a neighbor's," Mrs. McKinley told Phil when he inquired for her at her father's cabin. Then he started out to find them and escort them home.

He found them at the house to which their mother had directed him, and with them he ate supper there. Then they all started to walk home.

As they walked the younger girls went on before, but Phil and Nettie lingered.

At first their conversation was on the things of which they had been talking while at the neighbor's where they were visiting. These were some trifles—the newest happenings among the families constituting the colony; the contents of a letter some one had received from friends in the East; then of their own friends, and of things which had happened when they were children; of the old home in the older times.

Then Phil told her of how his house was finished and ready for occupancy, and of how they were all going to have a frolic there some evening soon, and that he wanted her to let him come for her and see her home again afterward.

To all this Nettie assented with so sweet a grace that Phil grew bold.

He told her, with much stammering, how he longed to make her his wife, to have her love him and share his home; how he always had meant to have returned some time to the old home and to her; how, not hearing from home, he feared to go, lest he had been forgotten or lest he find her married to another; how, since he had met her that afternoon in the emigrant train, he had thought of nothing else save how to win her and to be worthy of her afterward.

To Phil's impassioned story Nettie made no reply, but instead walked by his side with her head turned from him, and gazed away off across the prairie and the river, as if looking at some distant object.

Seeing that she turned away from him, Phil thought Nettie was indifferent to his suit. This made him desperate, and he pleaded the harder. He told her that for all his imperfections—his lack of education and polish— he would try to even up with a fuller measure of love;

told her how, with every blow struck upon his new house, he had sent up a fervent prayer that she might share it with him and make it bright and cheery with her presence.

But still Nettie walked with head averted and made no answer.

Phil cast his eyes in the direction she was looking. He saw that which caused him to stop in his walk suddenly and his cheek to pale, though the tan upon it was as thick as the sun and wind could make it.

Nettie stopped also, and for a few minutes they stood side by side, gazing away across the river, where could be seen approaching a body of horsemen in uniform, and riding at a sharp trot. Then Nettie turned to Phil, and, putting her two hands in his, she looked him in the face and said:

"Phil, I love you. I have always loved you and believed in you, and always will; and I am ready to be your wife and share your home. But not you nor any of us will have a home tomorrow."

And Phil answered not a word, for he knew she spoke the truth. He, too, had recognized the approaching horsemen as United States cavalry, and he knew they could have but one errand there; that they had come a second time to evict the settlers from their homes. And he released Nettie's hands without even offering to seal their betrothal with a kiss.

"A strange betrothal," did you say?

Well—perhaps.

Strange conditions environed them.

Those are strange conditions which induce—yes, compel—men whose souls are tall and strong and white to leave the settled portions of the country, those locations where the genius of the race has achieved its grandest triumphs over the forces of nature, and where wealth is a thing of so little value that it is heaped up in stacks and measured by millions, and go out into the wilderness, where there is absolutely no wealth, in order that they may obtain shelter and food for themselves and their families.

And yet more strange is it when they have done this and are peacefully seeking by their own labor, upon God's own land, to build homes for themselves and those they love, that there should come bands of armed men bearing aloft the ensign of the country of which these home builders are citizens, and burn their houses and drive them from the country.

Strange, indeed, are these things—so strange that one scarce can believe them true. But when one knows them to be true, there is nothing that can follow which can appear strange, or which can not follow naturally.

The apple blossom without fragrance, the fruit all withered upon the boughs, the tree dead and bare in the midst of green fields and soft waters—even these anomalies cease to appear strange when it is known that those other things can be, and are.

Nor is Oklahoma the only spot where the joyfulness of young lovers has been stolen from them in the very moment of betrothal; where mothers have given birth to infants whose gestation was not yet complete; where men have clasped the hand of Death and have gone with him from the sight of those who loved them and whom they loved, because of these things which are here narrated.

There are ruins of coliseums and palaces, of principalities and of states, to be seen in Greece, Italy and many other countries—ruins which appear strange and unaccountable until we remember that there, too, armed men drove forth those who, in obedience to the divine law, sought to make themselves homes and fortunes by the tilling of the soil.

* * *

The thoughts which were now burning themselves through Phil's brain as he stood there after letting go his sweetheart's proffered hands were plainly written on his face, and Nettie read them as from an open book.

She saw the great veins upon his forehead swell, the

fire of determination and hate kindle and flash from his eyes, the lips draw together, the hands clinch, and the right hand lift as if to draw a weapon from the belt, and she was frightened—not at what the fast approaching soldiers might do, but what Phil might do in defense or retaliation.

Quickly Nettie's small hands crept back into Phil's larger ones, and her fingers twined themselves about his, as if she would hold him back from the desperate deeds on which he seemed to meditate.

Then he stooped and kissed her upon the lips— kissed her cheeks and hair, put his arms about her and spoke lovingly, albeit solemnly.

"Nettie," said he, "I know what your fear is, and I will do no rash thing. For your sake I will be careful, and will hold my life and the lives of our enemies of more value than the pleasure of resistance to a mighty wrong. It is an awful thing, this feeling that we are being wronged so deeply without power of resistance; this being compelled to receive insult and injury without giving a fitting answer. But it must be so. Those soldiers come in the name of the law, and we must respect the law; though if it were not for you, I think—I don't know—I—I don't understand why we may not be left in peace here—why the government permits us to be so wronged."

Nettie, sobbing upon his shoulder, begged him to be

patient. She assured him all would come right in the end; and that maybe, after all, the soldiers were not come to drive them away.

But Phil knew better than to think this. He well knew there was nothing else to bring them into that vicinity in such force, and he felt that the worst might be anticipated.

He guessed that the explanation which he and others had sent to Washington had not been properly directed, or in some way had not reached its destination, and that the military were acting under their previous orders to keep the colonists out, and not upon orders which were newly received.

For a few moments yet the lovers stood exchanging pledges of continued love and fealty, and might have remained thus longer but for the sound of approaching horsemen. So, after a parting kiss, they hastened toward Nettie's home.

A moment later several men on horseback, with rifles in their hands and revolvers in their belts, came flying across the prairie, headed in the direction of the ford.

These men were neighbors, members of the colony, who had observed the approach of the soldiers and were hurrying to meet them. They called to Phil, as they flew past, to get his rifle and come on.

Looking to the right and left, Phil and Nettie could see others of the colonists, some afoot and others astride horses or mules from which the harness had been hastily stripped, riding and running and gathering on the bank of the river. And they, too, hurried as fast as they could, even running the last part of the way, and soon reached the ford, at which the people—men, women and children—were now gathering.

Few of the men but had brought their arms, and all those who had not were being urged to return to their cabins for them.

Threats that the soldiers should never cross the river were heard from some, while others proposed that each man return to his own cabin, barricade his door, and refuse to be arrested or evicted under any circumstances.

Some of the women were wringing their hands and weeping; others were following their husbands or sons about, pleading with them to do nothing rash. Infants were carried in arms, and children crying with excitement clung to their agonized mothers.

The leader or president of the colony was not present, he having, as it chanced, gone out for an afternoon hunt across the prairie, from which he had not as yet returned; and when Phil entered the excited group quite a number turned to him for counsel and advice, for he had come to have influence among them.

Gathering about him, they asked: "What shall we do? They are coming to arrest us again, and if they do the cattlemen will burn our houses as soon as we are out of the way. Our crops will be destroyed and our settlement broken up."

"Fight 'em—that's my advice!" called out one who had just reached the group.

"They're nigger troops, anyway!" shouted one of the men.

This announcement caused fresh tremors to extend through the crowd.

"I fought four years to free the niggers," shouted a colonist, "and I'll be d——d if any crowd of niggers is going to oust me when I'm minding my own business and disturbing nobody."

That this sentiment was generally approved was evidenced quickly.

"I'm with you, old comrade."

"Your head's level there."

"That's the way to talk it."

These exclamations came indiscriminately from the crowd of excited men and weeping women and children gathered upon the river bank, watching the approach of the colored troops sent to evict them a second time from their homes.

Phil felt his whole soul respond to this warlike spirit of the more reckless of the crowd.

He had spent so much of his life among those whose hands are for ever playing with the butts of their revolvers, had seen so much of force and so little of any thing else, as a governing power, that he hardly knew there was any other way of opposing the wrong or protecting the right except with fire-arms.

The slave bred and born in slavery feels but slightly the weight of his chain as compared with him whose limbs it chafes for the first time, and while in the full possession of health and strength and with a knowledge of freedom's worth.

Phil's whole soul cried out in wrathful protest against the indignity and wrong now threatening them. His hand clinched involuntarily, and the fire of mighty anger flashed from his eyes. But before he had given expression to the thoughts and feelings which were burning for utterance a small, soft hand from out the crowd touched his. Looking down, he saw Nettie's anxious eyes and tear-stained face turned up to his, and at once his anger cooled, and instead of urging his companions to prepare for fight he pleaded with them to be patient and keep cool, and so do nothing rashly.

At first his voice was hoarse and his words came with an effort, but as his anger died out it took a smoother tone, and then became soft and flexible, with a strange power to sway the excited feelings of his fellow backwoodsmen.

Phil felt a mild surprise at this. He was surprised, first, that he could speak after this fashion, and then that his words should have such power over his companions. He had not suspected himself of possessing such oratorical ability, and he knew nothing of the power that lies in the word, if strongly asserted, to compel obedience; and he was, therefore, as much surprised at the effect of his speaking as he had time to be.

Having calmed the excitement in a measure and having brought order out of confusion, he was on the point of proposing that a committee be selected to ride forward and meet the approaching soldiers, when the leader of the colony arrived, and to him Phil resigned the authority with which circumstances and his own recognized fitness had momentarily invested him.

This man whom the colonists called their leader was not one having any autocratic authority over them. He was the one who presided at their meetings held for the purpose of deciding upon business of interest to the colony, at which each head of a family was entitled to a voice and a vote.

He was their guide and spokesman. He was their leader in the sense of one who goes ahead. But he was not one who had autocratic power to compel others to follow. If they followed, they did so because they were pleased to follow, confident that they were being led in the way they themselves had decided to go, and not because they were ordered to do so.

But this man was a natural leader of men as well. He had that quick perception of what is necessary and best to do on occasion, and also an air of knowing that he knew, which showed itself in every word and movement, and inspired that confidence in others which in times of unusual happenings gave him a power that was autocratic so long as exercised within limits which permitted those over whom it was exercised to retain their self-respect unimpaired.

This man did not await the appointing of a committee. He took command as by right, and with one word produced quiet. Then he said, in a voice that betrayed no trace of excitement or fear :

"If the rest of you will remain here, Mr. Johnson and I will ride forward and see what the troops want. We will report to you as soon as we ascertain the situation."

To Phil he said :

"Come with me. If you have no horse here, one of the men will lend you his."

With this Capt. Paine turned away and rode down the bank into the river.

Phil borrowed a horse and joined him before gaining the opposite shore, and together their animals clambered up the bank and cantered away, side by side, to meet the troops, now only a few hundred rods distant.

When they had approached quite near, the Lieutenant in command of the troops, who were part of a black regiment that for some months past had been stationed on the frontier, rode forward accompanied by an orderly, and both sides saluted with proper courtesy.

Then, wheeling their horses, the two colonists fell in line with the Lieutenant and orderly, and rode back a little in advance of the company of regulars, whose nags had dropped to a walk.

The Lieutenant was the first to speak. His manner was not lacking in politeness, but his words carried an awful meaning.

"You see that we 've come for you again."

"I supposed that was your purpose," replied the leader of the colonists, "as I could not think of any other errand you could have down this way. I hoped the explanation that we made and forwarded to Washington on the other occasion would prove sufficient to save us further trouble, but it appears to have failed, in some manner."

"Who gave the order for driving us out of the country?" asked Phil.

"Orders to me came from my superior officers," answered the Lieutenant, "and that is all I am supposed to know. However, I learned that they originated in Washington; indeed, they could not well originate anywhere else."

"Do you mean to say," asked Phil, a little excitedly, "that the government—that is, the President—ordered that we be taken out, after the explanation we made under oath the other time?" Though not so intended, Phil's words nettled the officer.

"I don't mean to say anything about it," replied the officer, hotly. "All I care to know is, that I have orders from those whom I am bound to obey to take you out of here, and that you are going."

The words and the manner of the officer rasped both men, but they managed to contain themselves, although Phil was compelled to call up Nettie's words and looks before he could choke back the hot retort that sprang to his lips.

His companion, more accustomed to self-command, answered without apparent feeling that he regretted that such orders had been issued. "Could there be found," he asked, "some way by which the matter can be held in abeyance for a time, so the colonists can be left in possession of their homes until communication can be held with the President of the United States, who certainly is laboring under a misapprehension regarding the matter, and an effort made to secure the revocation of the order?"

"I have no orders of that kind," replied the Lieutenant.

"But could you delay a little? I will send to the nearest telegraph office a man mounted on the swiftest horse in the settlement, or will go myself, and there telegraph a full account of the nature of our claims, and who we are and just where we are located, to the President, and ask him if it is with his approval that we are to be evicted. If he says it is, we will leave peaceably; if he says not, and countermands the order, then you will be relieved of its execution."

"Can't do it," answered the Lieutenant. "I tell you I have my orders to take you and your families—everybody—out of here, and to take you to Fort Reno. And these orders I must obey, without waiting three or four days or weeks, trying to get the President to countermand the order."

* * *

By this time they had reached the ford on the Canadian River.

Plunging in, the troops crossed the river, and came up the opposite bank a few rods below where the crowd of colonists stood.

CHAPTER XVII.

THE LEADER AND MR. M'KINLEY MAKE SPEECHES—TIED TO THEIR WAGONS WITH ROPES.

After talking still further with the Lieutenant, without receiving any encouragement from him, or promise that time would be given, or delay made in the execution of his orders, the two men returned to their waiting companions, and sorrowfully reported the state of affairs to them.

"We are," said their leader, "again arrested, and the officer declares he has orders to again take us to Fort Reno, beyond which he has no authority, and no knowledge of what is intended.

"My friends, I know with what feelings of grief and indignation you learn this. I am myself overwhelmed with grief and indignation for you and for myself. Why government permits it is something difficult to under-

THE LEADER SPEAKING

stand, but doubtless it is because it has not had full and complete knowledge upon the subject. It can not be possible that it is the settled policy of the administration to turn over this whole Territory, containing about all there is remaining of valuable agricultural land, to a few foreign cattle companies and Eastern capitalists ; and it must be, therefore, that when the facts are known at Washington we will be reinstated in possession of our claims, and full reparation made us for all the losses we have suffered or may suffer.

"I have not forgotten that I said this same thing before, when we were arrested, and I thought we had taken the steps necessary to at least prevent our again being disturbed. But it seems now that we were not thorough enough ; that we should have done more, in some way, to make plain the fact that we are not violaters of the law, but peaceful citizens, claiming protection from it.

"If we can not induce the officer in command of these troops to delay, then there is but the one thing left us. We must again submit to being conveyed out of the Territory.

"We make no promise not to return, and we never will make such promise. On the contrary, we proclaim our unalterable determination to come back, to hold on to our claims and to assert our right, and the right of all citizens who desire to do so, to come here and take up a claim and improve it, and live upon it.

"I beg of you to be patient. All will yet be well. We will yet live to see our wrongs righted, and see our Oklahoma one of the finest States in the Union, and you who have borne the heat and burden of the contest shall be honored and rewarded as you deserve.

"I shall be glad now if some of you, say a committee of five, will go to the officer who is in command of the troops, and see if it is possible to make a compromise by which ourselves and families may be benefited. In doing so, any committee which you appoint will have but two things to bear in mind:

"First—That we, having an inalienable legal right to the claims which we have pre-empted, need not feel ashamed at being arrested, nor at any thing which may follow.

"Second—That the officer in command is under orders from his superior, and to violate them may cause him to be court-martialed and dismissed the service."

While Capt. Paine was thus speaking, many of the men crowded about him. They listened to his address attentively and without interruption, but some there were who held back and were evidently little disposed to submit quietly to being again driven from their claims.

This contingent would have been better pleased had their leader counseled resistance to the death. Even as it was, they might have stood out against eviction, but for the pleadings of the women, who, for the moment, lost sight of every thing else in the fear that their loved ones might be killed, and with tears and pleadings held them back from the desperate deeds they might otherwise have done.

The committee of five suggested by the leader was selected, and repaired at once to where the officers were awaiting the arrival of their camp equipage, the wagons containing which had not yet come up.

As no one of the others upon the committee felt any great confidence in his ability as a spokesman, Mr. McKinley, who was one of them, assumed the responsibility of that position. He felt confident that he could salute the officer with proper decorum and state lucidly their mission.

Being, like his father before him, an old line Democrat, with a genealogical tree which was fondly believed to have first taken root somewhere in the sacred soil of Kentucky, he felt with especial keenness the threatened indignity of being arrested and evicted by colored troops. He felt that, if the committee should be unable to preserve the rights of the colony, he could at least preserve its dignity; and there was a little more than the usual amount of stiffness in his manner as he addressed the officer, after saluting him.

With a dignified wave of his hand in the direction of the people on the river bank, he said:

"We have come, Sir, Mr. Officer, as the representa-

tives of those people, Sir. Yes, Sir, their re[latives]
tives, Sir—authorized, as you may say, to [speak for]
them. And we come a-axin' for justice; ye[s,]
justice.

"We are here, Sir, Mr. Officer, a-claimin' [as]
citizens—as citizens, Sir—which has always [done its]
duty to their country and been loyal to their fl[ag,]
Sir.

"Some of us has been honored by the [great]
wealth in which we have lived in the past; yes,
honored by the Commonwealth. If you don['t believe]
it, just you come down to my cabin, and I'll [show you]
a document sealed with the seal of the grea[t State of]
Indiana and the great State of Illinois, in w[hich is set]
forth the fact—yes, Sir, the fact—that some [of us are]
known to be worthy of the confidence and este[em]
—of everybody, Sir; which, I reckon, makes [the case]
of a nigger soldier, if not of them as comin[g]
And we intend, as soon as the country about [here gits]
settled up—which will be as soon as it gits [settled]
around that this here is gov'ment land—fer [a]
ferry across the river here. Yes, Sir, a ferry [and we]
are a-goin' to build a town up there on that t[ract]
of ground there; yes, Sir. We are a-goin' to [fix things]
up as they ought to be done, and to cause t[he wilder-]
ness to blossom as the hollyhock—yes, Sir, as [the holly-]
hock.

"Now, Sir, Mr. Officer, do you suppose that we are such rantankerous villains as to go and vi'late the law, if we did n't know that we had a right to settle here? No, Sir—not by a large majority. We are truly loyal citizens, Sir—all on us—and we want you to reckonize that fact and take your nigger soldiers out of here, Sir—yes, Sir, out of here—and leave us in peace to set under our own vine and fig tree."

Considerably to Mr. McKinley's surprise, this peroration failed to have any particular effect upon the officer, except that his face assumed an expression of weariness and contempt.

Nor did any of the other members of the committee appear any more able to move him to delay action or to retire without accomplishing the purpose for which he had been sent.

He, however, consented to allow the colonists to return to their homes for the night, the members of the committee being told to consider themselves under arrest and to report at the officer's quarters on the following morning.

Such was the report which the committee was forced to make.

The evening was now becoming dark—too dark even to see each other's face distinctly at a few paces distance —and the little crowd slowly and with heavy hearts dispersed. Some went directly to their homes, but others lingered by the way and stopped to talk over the situation with this or that one of their neighbors. All took with them the feeling that nothing could be done to avert the calamity which had befallen them, and many began at once to pack their household goods into shape for loading into the wagons preparatory to the orders to move out, which they expected would be issued early on the morrow.

However, they were not ordered to move the next day, nor the next, nor yet the next.

When the committee of the day previous, together with Phil Johnson and Capt. Paine, who had also been ordered to report as under arrest, did so, a guard was at once placed over them.

These men were kept thus for ten days, while all the remainder of the colonists were allowed to come and go as they chose, but always with the understanding that they were to be ordered to move the next day.

Whether the object had in view was to induce them to leave secretly, and so save the trouble of conducting them out, is not known. The unexplained delay is a fact of history.

On the morning of the tenth day after the arrival of the troops the order to move was actually given, and the whole array pulled across the river and headed for Fort Reno.

And now the indignity of being tied with ropes to the

hind end of their wagons and compelled to march in the dust and dirt, between guards with loaded carbines, was inflicted upon all who were recognized as in any degree leaders among the colonists, while the women were treated, if not with open indignity, yet with a lack of the courtesy commonly recognized as due them.

Crowded into the wagons with their household goods and compelled to sit all the day through, they and their children, without opportunity to move about or stretch their weary limbs, sometimes without water to quench their thirst, and surrounded by brutal soldiers whose color, if it did not prevent them from being good soldiers, certainly added nothing toward inspiring confidence in the breasts of these women who were now their prisoners—such were the conditions and surroundings under which they were taken back along the trail which they had once before traversed to Fort Reno.

Phil Johnson was among those tied to the tail end of a wagon, and again Nettie's pleading eyes and voice prevented the enactment of a tragedy.

But the eyes and voice which were so effective in preventing her lover from rushing upon death in defense of his bodily freedom, or in revenge for the exasperating indignity done to him, had no effect upon the officer in command to induce him to countermand his order to tie the men to the wagons.

The sagacious Lieutenant had been careful to see

that all those who were to be humiliated had first been deprived of their knives and revolvers before the order to tie them was given.

And thus like cattle were they driven away across the prairie, along the beautiful table lands and by the clear streams, until they reached Fort Reno, where such of the men as were supposed to have influence with their fellow colonists and would be likely to use it to induce them to return to their claims if released were again consigned to military prison.

During the period of their incarceration they were compelled to sleep on the floor, without blankets or bedding of any kind, and without being permitted to talk with their friends outside or to send letters or telegrams, or in any way communicate with the government at Washington or with the civil authorities of the State of Kansas.

As for the remainder of the colonists, they were simply held in camp by guards, and were fed on rations that were issued from the commissary department of the army at the fort.

After five days had elapsed, the larger portion of the colonists, including the women and children, were again put upon the march, and were conducted to the Kansas State line and then turned loose, much as on the former occasion, and without any formal charge of any kind being made against them.

After these had been gotten fairly off, those who had been kept in confinement were brought out, mounted on their own horses, put in charge of a squad of soldiers and conveyed the long journey of nearly 150 miles to the Red River, which forms the boundary line between the Indian Territory and the State of Texas, and driven into the river by their guards, who from the bank watched them half-way across and then turned and rode away in the direction of the fort from which they had come.

Without crossing to the other side, or so much as setting foot on Texas soil, these men turned about, when they saw the soldiers retire, and returned to the Territory side of the river, where they camped for the night.

The next morning they took up the trail of their guards, followed it as long as it lay in nearly a direct line with their Oklahoma claims, and then leaving it, they branched off to the right, and two days later reached the deserted settlement, where they slept one night in the McKinley cabin on the bank of the river.

They had entertained a faint hope that a portion of the colonists might have returned there, but it was only a faint one, and they were not greatly disappointed at finding none of them had done so, as they knew that, even if so disposed, there had probably been scant time for them to return from the Kansas State line, whither they guessed them to have been taken.

Early the next morning the party began their own

ride to the State line, in search of their lost families and friends.

Just where to look for them they did not know, but, believing them to be somewhere in Kansas, they struck out for Caldwell, at which place they were enabled to learn at what point the troops having them in charge had entered the State.

Again mounting their animals, after a night spent at Caldwell, they rode west along the border line between the State and Territory a distance of nearly fifty miles, and there found those for whom they were searching, or a portion of them.

Not all the colonists brought out by the troops had remained together.

A portion were disheartened. They were out of both money and provisions and utterly incapable of making an immediate attempt to again enter Oklahoma and take possession of their claims, and had moved on up into the State in search of temporary employment for themselves and their teams, or had started to make their way back to the neighborhoods from which they had originally emigrated.

A considerable number, however, had remained together, and among them were the McKinleys.

Mr. McKinley and Phil found them in camp, and in possession, with others, of an old shed, which they had been given the use of by a farmer for whom the McKin-

NETTIE'S RESOLVE. 267

ley boys and several others of the company were at work shucking corn.

* * *

Not knowing what had become of those left behind when they were themselves conveyed north from Fort Reno, they had decided to wait where they were until they heard from them, or, failing to hear from them soon, to take steps toward their liberation.

Nettie had declared that she would go to Washington and present the case to the President or to Congress, or to somebody who had authority, if her father and lover were not soon released from prison and permitted to rejoin them.

In this resolve the brave young woman was rather encouraged than discouraged by her mother, and it is probable that she would have made the attempt had they not arrived within a day or two from the date of their appearance.

As it was, the family had acted upon the knowledge that if the two men were released soon they would seek for them somewhere not far from the same territorial line across which they had been driven, and the young men having sought for and found employment, at wages that would keep the family from want, they had accepted the offer of the use of the shed in which they were, and which, with the wagons to sleep in, enabled them to be tolerably comfortable for the time being.

"HERE THEY ALL ARE."

CHAPTER XVIII.

PHIL AND NETTIE REUNITED—MR. M'KINLEY ILLUSTRATES THE DIGNITY OF LABOR.

The meeting between Phil and Nettie on the return of the former from his enforced trip to the Red River was not very different from the meeting of other lovers, and the scene may well be intrusted to the imagination or to memory.

Nettie was at work in the shed, occupied in common by four or five families to cook and eat under, they sleeping at night in their wagons.

It was neither more nor less than a shed intended as shelter for cattle from the fury of the blizzards which occasionally sweep over the prairies in winter, and without which cattle are apt to drift away, and at times to become severely frozen.

This shed stood in a corn field eighty or one hundred

acres in extent, and was far enough from the road to render it difficult to see any one that might be approaching until he was quite opposite to the people standing in the shed. Therefore, the approach of Phil Johnson and his party was unobserved until they had entered the corn field and, riding through the tall corn, were but a few rods distant.

Then, hearing an unusual rustling among the dried corn blades, some member looked out, and at once the cry went up:

"Here they come!"
"Here's Phil Johnson!"
"Here's our leader!"
"Here's Mr. McKinley!"
"Here they all are!"

Then wives bounded forward, children came running, men sprang from their saddles and everybody gathered about them. Those who were husbands and fathers kissed their wives and took their little ones in their arms and hugged them and set them upon their horses or on their own shoulders, and all asked questions and all answered at once, and many laughed and some cried, and all were for the moment supremely happy.

In the midst of it all, Phil whispered to Nettie to come and help him stake out his pony, and as soon as they had put two rows of corn between themselves and the others he took her hand and held it close, and together they led the pony around on the other side of the shed and made him fast. Nettie patted the pony's neck and rubbed his nose, and finally kissed him, at which Phil made motions signifying that he was as good as the pony, and then Nettie ———

But what does the reader expect? Has he not been warned that this narrative will not go into the details of Phil and Nettie's courtship?

When Phil reappeared and mingled with the others at meal time, he tried to, and possibly did, look as innocent of having kissed anybody as his pony, munching his corn stalks around on the other side of the shed, and no one should be accused without evidence.

Neither is it known how Nettie managed to get back to her family and the little crowd in and about the front of the shed without attracting attention to her coming.

It is thought, however, that she went, first, to her father's wagon and got therefrom some article that may or may not have been needed for use in the shed, and returned there with it, and with a look of knowing as little of any thing having occurred at the back of the shed as Phil Johnson or his pony; and if she had been asked about it there is no doubt she would have feigned as much ignorance of the matter as either of them.

That night, after such of the colonists as had found work in the neighborhood had returned to their families, an informal talk regarding the future was held, and it was decided not to make an effort to return to Oklahoma until the following spring.

Their claims would not lapse by reason of an absence of any thing less than six months, and they could remain in Kansas during the winter, working at whatever they could find to do to make a living for their families, and perchance get a little stock of provisions ahead with which to start life again upon their claims when they should return to them.

They had learned that they could get employment with their teams upon a new railroad which was being built farther up in the State. To that point most of the stranded boomers repaired, and among them Phil and the McKinleys.

Before going it was agreed that they should meet at Caldwell at a certain time, prepared to again enter Oklahoma, with as many added colonists as they could induce to join them.

There was no talk of not returning by any one.

It was only a question of when they could gather together enough upon which to subsist until a crop could be raised.

They were beginning to be suspicious that their being driven out of the country was not wholly the result of a mistake; that there were those higher in authority than they had first supposed who were interested in preventing the settlement of Oklahoma and the Cherokee Strip, and in keeping them as herding grounds for cattle, until some way could be found or made for making permanent in the cattle kings the title to these immense tracts, thus laying the foundations for a landed aristocracy in the West which would fraternize with and sustain the stock and bond holding aristocracy of the East.

This suspicion did not have the effect of influencing them to abandon their attempts to settle there, and so redeem the country from the clutch of the cattle companies. On the contrary, it aroused them to a feeling that they had a solemn duty to perform in connection with the matter.

If, indeed, it were true that the conspirators expected to found there an aristocracy based on large land holdings, and if it had progressed so far and had become so powerful that it could compel the use of the standing army to drive from their homes those who were there by full permission of the written law, then it was their duty to do and to suffer whatever must be in defense of their right to settle upon this land, since they were thus made the representatives of all the people, and to them was assigned the solemn duty of preserving the rights and the liberties of all.

Neither could it matter to them if the civil courts or the heads of the departments, or if their representatives in Congress, had been drawn into the conspiracy or been packed or suborned into unholy support of the awful wrong which the regular army was being used to perpetrate upon them.

On the contrary, this only made it the more imperatively their duty to contend for their claims, since only by contending for them could they attract public attention to the matter and compel an investigation by the people into the facts of the case.

It was resolved, therefore, to return; and if evicted again to again return, and to continue this, and increase their numbers, if possible, until their persistency should provoke the desired investigation.

Even Mr. McKinley was aroused and active in his efforts to hold the colonists together, and to sustain them in their determination to return to their claims in the spring.

Tying him with a rope to the tail end of a wagon, and compelling him to march there between two files of colored soldiers, had aroused the lion in his nature. He was not less dignified than before, but he displayed more activity.

Mr. McKinley had been heard to say: "I'll see if a citizen who has been honored by the people of two great States can be deprived of his right to settle on the public domain by a mob of nigger soldiers, commanded by a dude in a lieutenant's uniform."

For two weeks those who had gone into camp at the corn fields remained there, employed in shucking corn for neighborhood farmers, and then the whole company moved farther up in the State. Here the men began working upon the railroad, getting wages sufficient to keep their families and lay by a bit for the coming season's need.

The great difficulty was to obtain shelter—houses in which their families could be kept comfortable—and so some were obliged to put up cheap shanties and live in them.

Nettie had been fortunate in getting a position as a teacher in a country school at fair pay, and consequently was not at home, except occasionally for a day.

This change in the status of affairs was not at all to Phil's liking. He desired to be married at once, or at least that Nettie should remain at home, where he could see her every day. But she reminded him that at the time she had promised to share his home she had not promised to marry him until he had one. Seeing that he looked a little bit hurt, she put her arms about his neck and her cheek against his, and so comforted him. After this she pointed out how much better it would be for them—for all—that she should teach during the winter, and thus add something to the general fund with which the family and he should return to Oklahoma in the spring to resume the work of making a home, than it would be to marry, and be under the necessity of spending a portion of what Phil still had in building a cheap and comfortless cabin, or by remaining with her father and mother in the dug-out that circumstances had forced them to occupy.

And so Nettie went to her school, ten miles away, and Phil hitched his mules to a road scraper and scraped dirt for the construction company, or to his wagon and hauled it. He continued to board with Mr. and Mrs. Jones, who had secured the occupancy of a pretty comfortable sod-house, from which a settler of several years before had moved into a new frame house recently completed.

But as regularly as Sunday came, the Johnson pony might have been seen heading in the direction of the Bronson settlement, in which locality Nettie taught the young idea how to shoot.

And as no one ever saw him when he returned, and he was always promptly on hand with his mule team on Monday morning, it is fair to conclude that he lingered at Nettie's boarding place until rather a late hour each Sunday night.

Meantime every member of the colony, wherever he stopped, was making efforts to induce others to join the colonists that were to locate homes in Oklahoma in the spring.

Especially was the leader busy in this direction, and also in seeking to make known to the general government and to the public at large the true condition of things, and the facts as they existed with relation to the title of the lands on which the colonists had laid their claims.

He found, though, that it was far more difficult to do this than he had thought.

The Captain and all those associated with him were already branded by the reports of the military authorities at whose hands they had suffered arrest, as well as by those interested in preventing the truth from becoming known, as men seeking to deprive a peaceful nation of Indians of the rights solemnly guaranteed to them by the government of the United States.

As a result, when he sought the use of the columns of the influential and widely circulated newspapers for the purpose of relating the facts he was refused, or, if granted the use of one, his statements were denied in another column upon authority that appeared to be beyond impeachment.

He appealed to the civil courts for protection from the military and for a decision as to his right and also the right of those acting with him to settle in Oklahoma under the homestead law, and was refused.

He appealed to the Secretary of the Interior, and he could get no satisfaction.

He appealed to a United States Senator from Kansas, but got no reply.

Discouraged with his efforts to thus bring the matter

before the public, and convinced that men high up in authority were interested in overthrowing the law, and that it was through the influence which they wielded in government circles that the army was being used to overawe himself and his companions, and render non-effective the law whereby the people had sought to make the public lands secure to those who desired to make homes upon them, there appeared to him but one way remaining by which they could protect their rights to the claims which they had made and call public attention to the situation to an extent that would compel the relinquishment, by the cattle syndicates, of the grip that they had upon the country, and so save this beautiful Territory to the people.

This one remaining way was to raise a still larger colony, and by persistently returning as often as driven out, finally compel the public to take such interest in the question as would eventually bring the entire matter before Congress for settlement, through the introduction of a bill providing for the organization of that district under territorial law.

Accordingly, he put forth renewed efforts to induce others to join the colony.

He rode, wrote and talked constantly.

He got one man interested in a neighborhood and induced him to work upon his neighbors to enlist them.

He secured the meeting of a half dozen neighbors in

the house of one of their number for the purpose of having a talk about Oklahoma, and in another place he got the entire neighborhood interested and rode fifty miles on horseback to tell them about Oklahoma.

Possessed of considerable property when the idea of settling in the beautiful country first took possession of him, he spent it freely in scattering a knowledge of its beauty and fertility among the people as far and as fast as it was possible for him to go personally or transmit information.

He reckoned as of no value time, money and his own comfort, so he made known the facts about Oklahoma, and opened the eyes of the people to efforts being made to prevent its settlement by any except the cattle syndicates already there—the kings already in possession, and using the army to enable them to retain possession, of the last and most beautiful of all the free lands of the Grand Republic.

With his own efforts and those of Phil Johnson, Mr. McKinley and others—all, in fact, that had been of the colony before—the approach of spring saw a company many times larger than the old one assembling upon the border of Kansas, preparatory to entrance into Oklahoma.

From many States and from long distances the additions had come.

Those who had returned the fall before to their old

homes had told the tale of the advantages which nature had showered upon this beautiful spot to make of it the fairest of lands and the most desirable of homes for all who wanted to make homes upon a virgin soil.

They had told, too, all the facts regarding the efforts being made to shut the people out of their heritage, and in this way they had aroused the spirit of hatred of oppression, the love of liberty, the pride in country and the determination that here, at least, in America, shall there be fair play.

By the appointed time there had started westward a long line of canvas-covered wagons, that centered upon the border of the Indian Territory, and whose owners announced themselves ready to take the risk of eviction, imprisonment—yes, even death—in support of the inalienable right of the children of the Republic to homes upon the public lands.

For some weeks before the day set for starting they began to arrive.

First came a single wagon, containing the members of one small family—a man and his wife. Then arrived two others and went into camp with the first. Another and another followed, and then came a score of wagons, when the camp looked like a village of tents and prairie schooners.

Among the later comers were the colonists who had been at work for the construction company during the winter. Their apparent dilatoriness was understood by the others.

Understanding the necessity which might arise, they were anxious to lay in as large a supply of provisions, and that which could buy provisions, as possible, and so remained close at work until within four days of the time set for leaving the Kansas border, en route for their old claims and homes in Oklahoma, and then drove direct and without an hour's unnecessary delay to the place of rendezvous.

With this party came the McKinleys and Phil Johnson and the people he boarded with.

Nettie had finished her school and received her pay. At the request of her mother and brothers, she had put the greater portion of it in a bank, where it might prove helpful later on.

She would have passed it all over to swell the family fund, but they were resolved that she should not, seeing that it would not be long before she would have need of it in a home of her own.

Nettie and Phil intended to be married in the fall, unless they were again driven out of Oklahoma; and even if they were again deported, it was not impossible that they would still be married. They did not know for sure; the happy event must depend somewhat upon circumstances.

For the present they were happy, being where they

could be together every day, and with the knowledge that they were to be near each other all summer in camp and in their Oklahoma homes.

And so they had gone to the place appointed for the meeting of the colony, preparatory to the start for the land of their dreams, and along with them had gone a dozen other families from among the new friends whom they had made during the months they had passed in the Sunflower State.

Some of these new recruits were men who had been employed on the same railroad with Phil and the other colonists. Some were families who had come West the fall before, and had not yet bought homes, or who, having small homes, had sold them to join the expedition to Oklahoma.

These last Mr. McKinley claimed as his especial followers, he having been the principal factor in inducing them to join the colony.

Owing to the willingness of his family, both sons and daughters, to support him in his efforts to maintain the dignity which he felt belonged to him, as one who had been honored with a commission to run a ferry boat, he had not been compelled to work on the railroad, and had put in most of the time talking up Oklahoma and the interests of the colony.

While thus engaged, he gradually came to consider himself more and more in the light of the real leader of

DECIDES ON THE LEGISLATURE. 283

the company and organizer of the enterprise, and to assume a yet more dignified manner.

'About this time the idea possessed him that it would be better and more in accord with the natural fitness of things for him to become a member of the Territorial Legislature which was to be, when Oklahoma was settled, than to apply for a license to establish a ferry across the Canadian River, as he had for several months intended.

In the former event he would be in a better position to secure the charter for the ferry in the name of one of his sons, and so cause two generations of McKinleys to be honored, while in case he applied for it for himself, the honors done to the family would die out with his passing.

Not that the old gentleman had any thoughts of his dying, except as something too far away to be regarded as a matter of any present importance beyond the preparation to meet the Day of Judgment by occasionally, like the rest of us, repenting of sin long enough to be tolerably certain that we have repented of it, in order that we may keep on sinning in a comfortable state of mind.

Never before this had he felt himself to be an active leader of men or molder of public opinion. Heretofore he had waited until his opinion had been asked for, and then answered in that dignified tone of exaltation which belongs by right to the judge.

But now he forced his opinions upon people.

He spoke as one having authority to compel men to hear the truth about Oklahoma and the injustice done to the colonists by the army, with the sanction of the government at Washington—or, at least, without being reprimanded or its action overruled.

From talking the beauties of Oklahoma and the competence to be speedily won there by labor on the virgin soil, he finally got to talking of the honorableness and dignity of labor in the abstract, even going so far as to shovel sand on the railroad one whole day to prove that labor was compatible with dignity of person.

A FRIENDLY COWBOY.

CHAPTER XIX.

BACK TO OKLAHOMA AGAIN—LIFE **AT THE** SETTLEMENT —A COWBOY IMPARTS **STARTLING NEWS.**

But now, just as the colony, **thus largely** augmented, was on the point of starting, came tidings of the arrest, by a United States Marshal, of their leader, as he was on his way to join them from some point farther east, where he had been attending to some business for the colony.

This news threw a damper over the spirits of all the colonists, and caused a few of the new members to waver in their determination to enter Oklahoma, and two families actually turned about and sought for homes in other and undisputed territory.

The majority, however, remained firm. They even felt that the arrest might bring the whole matter before the courts, and result in great good by settling at once and forever the question of their right to pre-empt land in Oklahoma, and in the whole country under dispute, which was now understood to extend to what is known as the Cherokee Strip, containing six million acres, and also to the Public Land Strip, a body of land lying north of Texas and west of the Indian Territory, and containing, as roughly estimated, something over three million acres.

With hope to buoy them up, the old colonists—they who had been among those evicted from their claims on two previous occasions—were in no way cast down by the fact of the arrest.

They loved their leader as a brother, and regretted exceedingly the suffering, both of body and mind, which he might be compelled to undergo, but still they felt that good was likely to come out of it, and so they could not regret the marshal's action, feeling that they should be glad instead.

Upon the question of whether they should await the action of the court, and the release of their imprisoned leader, or move at once under the leadership of some other member, there was some difference of opinion at first.

A number of the more timid ones advised staying, while others asked :

"How can we wait?

"What shall we do in the meantime, if we decide to

wait and have all the points involved settled before we move?"

"It may be six months or a year," they said, "before a decision can be obtained in the courts. Such delays have often been, and may be again, and if we consent to wait they may keep us waiting indefinitely.

"Should we wait, we must either consume the stock of provisions that we have on hand, and which ought to sustain us until a crop is raised on our claims, or we must separate and search for work, in which case we can not get together again without trouble, and probably will never all get together again."

And, besides, they knew that the time was already at hand when they should be planting, for this season's crop, the ground broken the season before, and also be preparing new ground for later seeding.

Evidently, if they separated now, they could not enter Oklahoma before fall, and this delay they were not willing to submit to.

They felt that their right to go was perfect—absolutely unclouded by the shadow of a doubt which had its origin either in the written law or in the spirit of the Constitution.

Firmly imbued with this feeling, they determined to start at once, and leave their leader to follow when he should have vindicated himself and them in the courts, and before the country.

They knew that if he were where he could give them advice he would say: "Go." They believed that in going, and thus proving their faith in their right to go and making more difficult of execution the purpose of their enemies to keep the matter from reaching the public ear, they would be doing both their leader and themselves a service which, perhaps, could not be done so effectively in any other manner.

Therefore, they called a meeting in the camp, and formally voted to start without further delay; and somebody had just made a motion that Phil Johnson act as president and leader for the journey back to the settlement on the Canadian River, when, to the surprise and joy of everybody, their old leader rode into camp, and dismounted in their midst.

Then went up a cheer which caused all the women and children in the camp to clamber down from their wagons or rush out of their tents, and come running to see what it all meant.

The chairman of the meeting jumped down from the wagon in which, as presiding officer, he was stationed, and from which, with a kingbolt for a gavel and a dry goods box for a desk, he had been preserving order, and rushed to welcome the returned chieftain, about whom all were gathering, shaking hands and asking questions as to how he managed to get off, and whether he had had his trial yet.

And when he told them that he had been tried before the United States District Court at Topeka, the capital of the State of Kansas, and declared "not guilty of any criminal offense," they threw up their hats and cheered and cheered again, shouting themselves hoarse in their efforts to express the intensity of their joy.

For now they could go forward with confidence—the perfect assurance that they would not be disturbed or interfered with by the military authorities. For is not the civil above the military in this Republic of ours? And had not this leader, as their representative, just been tried by the civil authorities upon a charge of illegally entering and taking possession of land in Oklahoma, and had he not been declared innocent of any criminal offense in so doing?

Certainly he had, and that settled it—*must* settle it; for such was the law of the land, and such the natural justice of the case.

Such was the course of reasoning followed by the colonists, and that night they held a grand jubilee in the camp, at which speeches were made and songs were sung, and the glories of the Republic, and of the civil law, which meted out even-handed justice to rich and poor alike, were proclaimed in impassioned language. Pride of country and love for the old flag were rekindled and made to glow with a brighter flame.

Then all retired to rest. Each member awoke fresh

and joyous in the morning, to begin the journey toward the Promised Land.

They broke camp in the cool of the morning with song and quip and calls back and forth, and with high hopes and bright faces.

Phil had been made train master, and upon him had devolved the duty of seeing that everybody connected with the colony was made as comfortable as could be, and that the route followed was such as to lead them through a portion of the country where water and grass were abundant.

He was also to fix upon the camping ground at night, and to give the word of command for breaking camp and resuming the journey each morning.

One of the McKinley boys agreed to drive Phil's wagon and mules, thus leaving him free to attend to the duties of his position, of which he was proud.

Nettie was proud of him.

After his selection for the place at the meeting held the night before starting, Nettie slipped away from the circle about the camp fire, and when she returned she brought with her a red sash which she had made once on a time for use at one of her school exhibitions.

Coming up slyly to Phil, she threw the sash over his shoulder, and, blushing and laughing, tied it under his arms, telling him it was his insignia of office, and that he must wear it worthily as became a brave knight.

She then darted away before Phil, whose happiness was showing itself in every lineament of his face despite his efforts to look as though that was only an every-day occurrence, could find words in which to fitly express his thanks.

Now, in truth, Nettie had some reasons to be proud of her lover, who, as he cantered back and forth, getting the wagons into line that first morning, and making sure that nothing was forgotten or left undone, sat his pony like a very centaur, and was a lover in whom any girl might well feel a pride.

Under Phil's direction, the long train of more than eighty canvas-covered wagons drew out upon the prairie and wound its way along.

They traveled almost directly south the first day, following the line of the proposed extension of the Atchison, Topeka and Santa Fe Railroad, and camped that night on the banks of the Osage Creek, a branch of the Big Salt, itself a branch of Arkansas River.

Traveling south again, on the second day at noon they crossed the Big Salt by fording, and, still following the line of the proposed railroad, late at night of the third day out, went into camp at Buffalo Springs, on or near the line between the Cherokee Strip and Oklahoma, having for the last two and one-half days traveled continuously across lands held, and generally fenced with barbed wire, by these four cattle companies: Williamson, Blair & Co., Snow & Rannalls, Cobb & Hutton and Hewins & Titus.

Resuming their journey on the morning of the fourth day, they passed into Oklahoma through lands held by Hewins & Titus and by Williams Brothers, crossed the Cimmaron River and, still upon lands held by the Williams Brothers, turned to the southeast along the old Chisholm cattle trail, and, a half day's journey farther on, entered upon the still larger tract of land held by the Wyeth Cattle Company.

Thus they continued their journey, making twenty to twenty-five miles each day, camping at night on the banks of some beautiful stream, sleeping the sweet sleep which comes of abundant exercise in an atmosphere in which there is no malaria, and as a result of high hopes and consciences unburdened with any sense of wrongdoing.

Traveling by day and resting by night, they came, in time, in sight of the river flowing by the spot that was to be their future home—the spot already memorable to a portion of their members, and one doubly dear to them because of those memories.

And these old memories started a cheer at sight of the spot—a cheer which the newer colonists were quick to take up when they understood its meaning—and once again the echoes came back from the timber growing upon the river's banks, and once again all felt that joy which abides only within the home. It was natural that some one should start the song, and again the welkin rang with "Home, Sweet Home."

* * *

The same "assistant" surveyor who had run out the previously taken claims was called upon to do more of the same kind of work, and other claims were laid and their boundaries marked off.

Again new cabins began to rise, not only upon those claims where twice before had cabins been built, but new ones on new claims.

The Vandals had again done their work. Not one house was found standing.

There were soon to be seen cabins of logs, of sods cut in the shape of bricks and about two feet long and laid up as bricks are laid, and others made by digging into the side of some little rise in the ground—"dug-outs," as they are called.

In front or at the side of each cabin might be seen a

covered wagon, or if not the wagon then the cover only, still stretched over its bows of ash or hickory, and serving now as a depository for implements of one kind and another for which there was no room in the cabin. Occasionally the children used them as play houses.

New patches and ribbons of black earth began again to appear in the midst of the wide stretches of green, the old ones having already been worked over and planted, making the third time that these older colonists had sowed and cultivated without being permitted to reap a harvest.

And so the time passed.

The men worked at turning the sod and preparing for a future harvest of grain, taking only an occasional day off for hunting, that there might never be a scarcity of meat in the larder.

The women looked to household affairs and to the bright bits of gardens about their dooryards.

The children fished in the river, hunted for flowers in the prairie grass along the borders of the wood, and while so occupied grew strong and healthy and as black as Indians from the sun and tan.

By-and-by the corn, which for a time had turned to green again the patches and ribbons of black, changed them to brown and gold instead. The first harvest of the colonists is nearly ready for the gathering.

It is not a large one, but it is the first fruits which

have ripened beneath their care, and they are proud of it—happy because of it, and because of the promise that it contains of other and broader harvests yet to spring from the rich soil of this most beautiful valley in this fairest of lands, when they shall have had time to turn some wider furrows across the prairie's rich soil.

The McKinleys, like all the rest, have been busy, and their claim has some narrow bands of gold and brown, and some wider ones of black across it, where the young men have been plowing and planting.

Mr. McKinley's interest in life, as in the prosperity of the colony, has increased rather than diminished with the passing weeks, and he has been as busy as the very busiest—though just what he has done is not so clear, except that he has helped to imbue the colonists anew with faith in the dignity of labor and with lofty aspirations for the future of Oklahoma, and has selected, at least in his own mind, the exact site for the new Territorial State House, which the first Legislature, of which he will be a member, will order erected.

Immediately after getting into their own cabins, the colonists had erected a school house on the site of the city which is to be, and in this Nettie has been following her vocation as teacher to the children.

They made a pretty large school, and a pretty difficult one to manage well, but Nettie has had experience with such, and manages them nicely.

The younger ones are kept in only just long enough to be heard say their A B C lesson or read an a-b ab lesson and then sent out to play, while their teacher gives her attention to the larger scholars, to whom she is a companion as well as teacher.

On Sunday afternoons, and usually on one or two evenings during the week, she gives private lessons to a young man by the na.ne of Johnson, familiarly called Phil, in matters not set forth in the school books.

Phil has his new house under way again now, and is building the same sweet hopes in with the other material that he put into the one which he built a year ago, and which was destroyed by order of the cattle kings during his enforced absence.

Nettie comes over with him on Sunday afternoons, and together they lay their plans for the future, which is to begin so soon now—just so soon, in fact, as the house is finished, and that will be but a little while, only a few weeks.

A printing press has been purchased and brought out by the president of the colony, and a little paper devoted to the interests of the members and to the settlement of the country about them has been started. Weekly editions of it are struck off and sent here and there and everywhere, to friends of the colonists and to any who can be induced to take an interest in this new country and the development of its resources.

The colony, quite plainly, is already assuming the airs of an old settlement.

It has faith in itself and in its future, and it has room in which to grow.

One Saturday afternoon, as the weekly paper, the Oklahoma Bee, was being distributed to a group of colonists who had come for it, a stranger appeared, dressed in the garb of a cowboy.

He was mounted on a cow pony, as the little Mexican horses used so largely by the cattle men are called. He wore the usual complement of revolvers and carried the customary Winchester rifle lying across his lap behind the pommel of his saddle.

Halting in front of the little group gathered about the board shanty in which the newspaper was printed, he leaned forward in his saddle and looked the crowd over leisurely without speaking.

Naturally all eyes were turned toward him, and one or two of the younger men pitched some half joking remark in his direction, to which he made no response, but continued coolly running his eye from one to another with a look of quizzical curiosity.

At last he said:

"I was wondering, as I rode along, what kind of stuff you fellows are made of. You don't *look*, now, like a set that would show the white feather without first finding out what the other fellows had for exchange."

For a moment no one answered. Then one asked, angrily: "What do you mean?"

"Oh, not much," replied the other, with an air of carelessness.

Then the mysterious visitor glanced away across the country, and after a moment added:

"Got some pretty good claims here, I should say Pretty good claims. Nice town site, school house and printing office—every thing getting fixed up just about right. I should think you fellows would kind of hate to pull out of here. I should, for a fact."

"Say, pardner, if you 've got any information that 's of value to this crowd, this is just as good an opportunity to dispose of it as you will ever get. Suppose you speak right out now, and have it over with at once."

It was Phil Johnson who spoke, and as he did so he left the place where he was standing in the door of the printing office, and came close up to the horseman, who eyed him closely, and then said:

"Your observation is correct, pard. You 've hit the bull's-eye dead center, first pop.

"Now, what I 've got to say I can say mighty quick. So here goes.

"If you fellows mean to hang on to your claims, you 've got to fight for 'em.

"Do I make myself understood?"

"No! Speak out plainly about the matter."

"What do you mean, anyhow?"

"Who's going to jump our claims?"

Everybody spoke at once, and all crowded forward and formed a circle about Phil Johnson and the strange horseman.

The stranger had the appearance of enjoying the sensation which he was creating.

He again surveyed the crowd with a look of careless indifference which one could not help seeing was partially, if not wholly, assumed.

The man was doubtless a natural lover of the tragical, and almost unconsciously sought to gratify his love of it by the manner in which he imparted the information he had to give.

"Well," he said, still with an air of nonchalance, "you fellows can see who I am—tell that by the set of my clothes.

"I'm a cow puncher, and I herd for one of the companies that own cattle and a range not very far from this locality. That is, they own the cattle and claim to own the range—leased it, you know, from some other fellow, who leased it from the Indians.

"Well, I accidentally overheard a little conversation between a couple of partners—cattle kings, they are called—the other night, and they were remarking that your corn fields would make right good picking for their steers this winter, after the soldiers had run you fellows out of the country again. Then they chuckled, and appeared to like the arrangement."

This choice bit of cattle king pleasantry excited general indignation, and one of the colonists replied :

"But they can't run us out. We have a decision of the court in our favor."

"Oh, well! Just as you fellows think; this aint my chuck wagon, of course," returned the stranger. "But maybe you don't know who's back of this thing as well as some other folks. Maybe the military have n't been informed of the decision of the court, and maybe it would make no difference if they had. Maybe those who are back of this thing don't care what the law says, anyway.

"But if you know more about it than I do, why, then I can't see that you need any more information from me."

He straightened himself in his saddle and lifted the bridle from the neck of his pony, as if about to ride off, but they called to him to "hold on," and urged that he tell them all he knew about the matter, and whether he was certain that a descent upon them by the troops from any of the forts in the Territory was positively decided upon.

They could not believe such a thing possible, and yet they were quick to take alarm, being made suspicious by previous experiences.

But the good-hearted cowboy, although anxious to warn them, had told about all he knew.

He had overheard a conversation from which he had gathered that a movement was on foot to again drive the colonists out of the country, but when the attempt to do so was to be made he had not learned.

He was of the opinion that the date was near at hand —it might be any day, or it might not be for a month. He could not tell.

But he was confident of two facts—that the troops were to be again ordered to remove the settlers out of the Territory, and that the orders came straight from Washington.

While an excited talk, which this announcement created, was taking place among the colonists, Phil put his hand upon the neck of the stranger's pony, and then walked a few paces by his side.

"Pard," he said, "you have done us a good turn, I reckon, though I can't say as it's pleasant news you 've brought. Come, spend the night with me, and rest both yourself and pony."

"Can't do it. Would if I could, but it is better not. I told the boss when I left camp that I was just going for a little canter after some antelope, and I 'll tell the boys when I get back that I had a long chase of it.

"I reckon the looks of my pony will bear out that last statement, if I get in much before midnight."

"It will be a sad thing for the members of the colony, if what you think is in store for us proves true," said Phil.

First satisfying himself that no one but Phil would hear what he had to say, the cow puncher remarked with emphasis:

"And if you fellows have the sand to make a fight, and so bring the question of who owns this country before the world, it will be a sad day for the cattle companies. There 'll be 'weeping and gnashing of teeth,' sure."

Putting spurs to his pony, he was soon out of sight in the gathering darkness.

Fight Between Citizens And Soldiers.

CHAPTER XX.

A ROUGH-AND-TUMBLE FIGHT—MR. M'KINLEY ASSISTS IN
SAVING THE COUNTRY.

The rumor that troops were to be again sent to take away the settlers spread rapidly, and produced the wildest excitement.

Instead of diminishing, the crowd about the printing office constantly augmented, and at midnight was many times greater than at sundown.

A bonfire had been built early in the evening, which, flashing out across the prairie, attracted the attention of one and another of the settlers.

Every one who saw it wondered what it could mean, and while wondering grew uneasy in his mind regarding it and hastened over to his neighbor's house to ask if he knew what its meaning was. Then the two looked, and saw the flames leap up and flare out, and a shower of sparks arise as some one threw on fresh fuel; saw the group of men standing by, **and wondered yet** more what it could mean.

Wondering **and speculating,** they heard the hallo of a third **neighbor, calling to them** from the road, asking if they **were going up to see what** the bonfire meant.

They joined him, **and all three went** together; and so, from **every** direction, **men, singly and** in groups of **three or four** and a dozen, began to **come in** and swell **the crowd about** the fire, **and,** hearing **the** rumors, to talk loudly **of** resistance or to keep silent **and to** finger their weapons.

The bale-fires built by old-time Scottish chiefs to call the clans together, **the** blast by Roderick Dhu on lone Benledi's **side,** were scarce **more** magical in their effects than was this bonfire built upon a little eminence away out on the prairies of Oklahoma, albeit there was no previous understanding that it should be the signal for the rallying of any clan.

And never did bolder men gather **at** any bugle blast or bale-fire's gleam than gathered there that night and discussed the probability of the story told by the cowboy being true.

Some asked what could be done; others told what they would do in case eviction was attempted.

What they *would* do?

What *could* they do?

"Can **we** again **submit** quietly to being **driven from** our claims, insulted, imprisoned, **robbed ? Can we lift hands against the** authority of the government **to** which we owe allegiance ?   Against men who wear the uniform and carry the flag of our country ?"

"What can we do ?"

"Can we see our families rendered homeless, subject to indignities—God knows what—and **make no resistance ?** Shall we lift no strong **hand to defend them or** avenge **them** ?"

"Can we leave this fair land, **and with it all** our bright visions of comfort and happiness, because a syndicate of rich men, many of them aliens to **the** government and enemies of the Republic, **want it for** herding grounds for their cattle ?"

Such were the questions they asked themselves and each other, standing **about** the bonfire that night in early December.   This is the conclusion they came to:

"Rather than **be** driven off again, we will fight."

And yet **to do so was to array** themselves against the old flag.

Could they do that ?

In their desperation they **said** they could.

They said the flag had ceased to represent liberty and **justice ; that** the government **no** longer protected the weak against the strong ; that it was no longer worthy of respect and reverence.

Yet, within their hearts, the echo of their own terrible words caused sharp pangs, and their awful meaning caused them to hesitate and grow silent.

Could they fight?
What would they do?
What could they do?

* * *

It was not until two weeks later that the troops came—a detachment from Fort Reno, headed by Lieutenant Knight, acting under orders of his superior officer.

In regular line of battle the troops advanced, and they were met by the colonists—armed and ready for the contest.

The latter had decided that they could not submit to being again driven from their homes without making armed resistance.

They had the law, justice and the decision of a District Court on their side. So they felt, and they would fight.

Marching his troops up to within short rifle range of the colonists, who had thrown up some slight breastworks in front of the printing office and school house and were waiting to receive them, Lieutenant Knight sent an orderly with a demand for an immediate surrender. This demand was refused. Surrender could not be even thought of.

"Go tell your master to turn his dogs loose!"

Such was the answer sent back by the leader of the colonists in response to the demand for immediate surrender.

Turning to the colonists, he added:

"Prepare to defend yourselves."

This was not just what the Lieutenant expected, and it put a new and not entirely pleasant face upon the situation.

The commanding officer found his force of less than one hundred opposed by at least an equal number of determined men, all of them good shots and well armed, and protected in some degree by the redoubt which they had thrown up.

An order to his troops to fire would surely be met by a volley from the settlers, which might wipe out his little company of regulars at the first round, and would surely do so before the firing ceased.

His own life would not be worth a rush, once he gave the order to begin the attack.

Therefore, the Lieutenant concluded that discretion is the better part of valor, and he decided upon using strategy. He asked for a parley, which was granted.

The leader, Phil Johnson, Mr. McKinley, Mr. Jones and Tom Price went out between the lines and met the

Lieutenant, who was accompanied by an escort befitting the occasion.

The pour-parlers held a long consultation. The Lieutenant tried to convince them of the uselessness of their offering resistance. The pioneers answered that, since nothing else was left them, they were compelled to fight. Only by resistance could they bring the question of their right to settle in those parts before the country, and so arouse a public sentiment which would save the whole of Oklahoma, the Cherokee Strip and the Public Land Strip to the people, which else would remain for ever in the grip of the syndicates and cattle kings.

After more than an hour spent in this kind of argument, the parties separated and the soldiers went into camp on the spot.

The colonists, not believing an attack would be ventured upon and not intending to begin an attack but only to act in defense of their lives and their property, simply lounged about, chatting and smoking. But they stayed close by their arms and kept a watchful lookout on the camp of the soldiers.

By-and-by the Lieutenant came strolling over to the settlers' camp, accompanied by an orderly. A little later a Corporal and three privates strolled over, and after a bit a few more soldiers.

Discipline appeared to be pretty loose, considering that they were regulars, but as they left their arms be-

and nothing was thought of it by the unsuspecting colonists.

The settlers understood as well as did the Lieutenant that only as the very last resort was blood to be shed, or such a course pursued as to compel the country to take recognition of what was going on.

No John Brown affair was to be made of this thing—no martyr blood shed if it was possible to avoid it; but a quiet removal of the settlers, the imprisonment of the leaders for a time and their discharge without trial after their followers had scattered. This would raise no storm. This would never be heard of by the country. This was the thing intended.

Well knowing this, the settlers thought nothing very strange when—the attempt to frighten them into leaving having apparently been abandoned—the soldiers lounged about without arms, and so strolled over to the opposite camp, only a few rods away.

The unarmed soldiers mingled freely in the camp of the settlers and chatted with some degree of friendliness, for the soldiers had personally no enmity against the colonists and the colonists understood that the soldiers were but obeying orders.

At sundown the soldiers were recalled to their camp, and the settlers slept upon their arms, after eating such food as was brought to them from their several homes or as they cooked around their camp fire.

Both parties put out pickets—the regulars only for purposes of discipline, for they knew they would not be attacked.

The settlers did not know that the regulars would not attack them, though they did not expect it, knowing that a more quiet plan would be devised if the commandant could arrange it.

Next day the soldiers and citizens fraternized in the camp of the latter, and mingled more freely than on the day before. That is to say, there were more soldiers—in fact, about all the soldiers except the guards, who paced back and forth in front of the Lieutenant's tent and the commissary wagon. They appeared to have come over for a friendly talk and smoke with the backwoodsmen.

Lieut. Knight came with them, and after chatting pleasantly awhile with the president he proposed that he call together eight or ten of the more influential settlers, and hold another conference. He said he hoped to convince them of the folly of continued resistance, and so end the matter.

The president replied that he had no objection to the Lieutenant talking to as many of the settlers as he chose. He was assured, in advance, that nothing which he could say would change things. If he got them out of Oklahoma this time he must do it by force, as they were now determined to make a stand for their rights.

ODD ARMY TACTICS. 311

However, he called Phil Johnson, Mr. McKinley and a dozen other colonists into the printing office, and told the Lieutenant to go ahead with his entertainment.

As those inside talked, those outside gathered about the doors and windows of the little frame shanty, and listened.

At first those gathered around seemed to be about equally citizens and soldiers, but after a bit there were more soldiers and fewer citizens, and gradually these few were crowded back until a cordon of soldiers surrounded the building, and a number had entered it.

Phil Johnson noticed this disposition on the part of the soldiers to crowd forward, and he grew suspicious. It was not customary for privates in the regular army to attend a conference with the officers, even where the meeting was in a way informal and in their midst, as was this one.

He felt sure that an attempt was to be made to capture those in the shanty, thinking that by securing them without bloodshed or the use of arms the others would capitulate without a fight.

Nor was he wrong in his conclusions, for suddenly, at a signal from the Lieutenant, the soldiers pressed forward and attempted to seize upon the persons of the settlers, two or three reaching for one man.

The officer expected to secure them almost before his intentions were understood.

But his calculations for the coup were far too optimistic.

Phil Johnson, at least, was prepared, and at the first move indicating treachery his fist went straight out from his shoulder, and a man in uniform went sprawling over the floor in front of his companions, causing several to stumble and fall.

This prompt action on Phil's part gave his comrades time to realize the situation.

And now began one of the oddest rough-and-tumble fights on record—a fight with fists between soldiers of the regular army, led by a commissioned officer, and a body of frontiersmen cooped up in a shanty.

Nor was the fighting confined to those inside, for the settlers outside the printing office heard the sounds of the melee and attempted to push their way inside.

Being resisted by the soldiers about the door and windows, who were acting under orders of a Sergeant and two Corporals, blows fell thick and fast, and in a few moments a free fight was going on that would have done credit to Donnybrook Fair in its palmiest days.

Inside the shanty, a half-dozen settlers, crowded into one corner by twice or thrice their number, were making the best fight their cramped condition would permit. Blows, the force of which was greatly lessened by the nearness of the combatants to each other, but which started noses to bleeding and caused black eyes to suddenly appear and bumps to start forth in profusion upon heads were being given and taken on both sides.

At the other end of the shanty the combatants had overturned the cases of type. Some had stumbled over these and others had been knocked over them, and the soldiers and settlers were mixed up in an indistinguishable mass.

It was a bad mess of printer's "pi."

Among those entangled were the Captain, McKinley, Jones and the Lieutenant, though to have picked out any one of them and separated him from the others would have appeared quite an impossibility, as nothing was to be seen except an indiscriminate pile of legs, arms and heads.

Beginning at the bottom, there appeared, as nearly as could be seen, first a couple of cases of type, then a man in uniform, then Mr. McKinley and the ink keg, then another soldier and more cases of type, then Lieutenant Knight and old man Jones, then more soldiers and the leader of the colony with more cases of type and more men, both in uniform and without it.

After this fashion the battle raged, and for a time victory appeared loath to decide between these unscientific combatants.

Within the shanty the settlers were getting the worst of it, so far as could be judged from appearances. As they were hemmed in and fighting two or three times their own numbers, they were at a disadvantage and had barely held their own.

Outside the shanty the citizens were in the majority, and they were crowding the soldiers and rolling them in the dirt. Here and there, on the outskirts of the crowd, might be found two combatants who had gotten a little separated from the thickest of the fray and were having it out by themselves.

But, after a bit, the advantage which the settlers had became apparent. The soldiers were not used to this kind of warfare, and had no particular relish for it. They fought simply because they had orders to fight, and not because they loved the pastime.

The colonists enjoyed it. It was their opportunity to even things up a little, and they improved it to the utmost for five or ten minutes. By this time the soldiers outside were drawing off for repairs, and those just inside were reached for, drawn out and forcibly started off in the direction of their camp.

Then a separation of the mass of arms and legs and heads on the floor of the shanty began, and was continued until all had risen, or had been picked up and carried out.

Next to the last man in the pile to be found and lifted up was Mr. McKinley.

He was pretty badly battered up, but not in a worse condition than the soldier underneath him, with whom he had been contending since the fight began. Both had been bitten and clawed about the face, and both were covered with printer's ink until neither was recognizable by his comrades. It was not until Mr. McKinley had been dragged off the soldier under him and set upon his feet in the open air that he was identified, and they did not know him then until he spoke.

Wiping the ink from his face with his hand and then glaring at the retreating regulars, he drew himself up and remarked:

"I think that particular portion of the regular army will hesitate before again offering me an insult."

* * *

The reader may think it strange that a fight with fists such as is above described—should actually occur between citizens and soldiers, and no arms be used. Yet, such a fight did occur; and there is nothing very strange about it when all the attending conditions are kept in the mind's eye.

The soldiers wished to remove the citizens without taking life. Failing to overawe them, they attempted to arrest the leaders in a manner such as would not provoke the use of bullets.

On the other hand, the settlers respected the fact

that those who sought to arrest them wore the uniform of the United States, and so wished, if possible, to avoid taking their lives, yet were determined not to be driven off their claims.

Here, then, was the strongest possible incentive on both sides not to take life, but on the one hand to arrest and on the other hand to resist arrest without bloodshed ; and when the soldiers found they could not effect the arrest without precipitating a fight with arms, they got out of it as easily as they could, which was not so easily as they could have wished, as many of them carried black eyes and swollen heads and a banged-up front generally for days.

But many of the home defenders were in the same fix, so the fight may properly go down into history as a drawn battle.

Both armies slept that night upon the same ground which they had occupied in the morning, and both slept upon their arms.

———:o:———

DRESSING MR. MCKINLEY'S AND PHIL'S WOUNDS.

CHAPTER XXI.

MR. M'KINLEY GOES TO JAIL, AND FINALLY RETURNS TO THE BANKS OF THE WABASH.

On the morning following the day on which the rough-and-tumble fight had occurred the soldiers were withdrawn, and the settlers were at liberty to return to their families.

At first very few of them were inclined to regard the result of the fight as a real victory.

True, they had given rather more black eyes and broken heads than they had received in return, and the enemy had now withdrawn from the field of battle; but still they had a feeling that the end was not yet, and what added to this feeling was that the soldiers had not withdrawn toward Fort Reno, whence they came, but had moved away in the direction of Fort Russell, where it was known that a considerable body of United States troops were stationed.

Among the few who took a more cheerful view of the matter, and who believed that they had really conquered a peace, was Mr. McKinley. Perhaps he was the only one who looked at it in that way at the very first, but if so he soon inspired others with his own views of the case, and pretty soon one and another began to look at it as he did and to regard the matter in the light of a great victory.

He would say:

"I tell you, gentlemen, they are licked—licked, Sir —and they will not come back. And if they do, we'll lick 'em again. We can do it—do it easy. Why, if you men outside the shanty had fought the way me and the Captain and Phil Johnson did, there would n't be any of 'em left now. They were three to one agin us when the fight commenced—yes, Sir, three to one and more, too —but you ought to see the way we piled 'em up—yes, Sir, piled 'em up. Why, me and the Captain and Phil Johnson and old man Jones piled 'em up in a pile, and then fell on to 'em and pounded 'em till we was tired— yes, Sir, till we was tired. You just ought to have seen the way we did it.

"And as for their retreatin' in the direction of Fort Russell, that 's nothing strange. They 're 'fraid and 'shamed to go back to Fort Reno, and own that they got licked. Like as not some of 'em died last night of their wounds—some of 'em was hurt mighty bad—and they 're just goin' off that way to bury 'em on the sly, so 's not to have it known. Don't you be afraid; they aint coming back. Reckon they 've got sense enough to know when they 're licked, if that 's all they have got."

It is never very hard to make men believe that which they wish to believe, and the faith which Mr. McKinley possessed that the regulars had abandoned the contest and left not to return imparted itself to others, and soon a voice somewhere in the crowd made an attempt at a cheer.

Like other cheers which are without support, this particular "hip-hip" sounded weak to start on, and it grew weaker as it progressed, but it was not long before the spirits of the crowd had raised sufficiently to induce some one else to start a cheer, which this time was joined in by half the company, and grew in volume as it went until the last "hurrah" gave indication of having a good deal of confidence in itself.

Now, while the majority of them were feeling their spirits rise with the departure of the troops and with the hopeful view of the situation which Mr. McKinley insisted upon everybody's taking, there were those among them who felt that, now the need for suffering in silence was over, they would like very much to have their hurts and bruises attended to.

Among them there were several who had received wounds of a painful character.

Phil Johnson had received quite a long and deep gash across the scalp, apparently made by a column rule, wielded by some one who in the general melee had happened to get his hand on it. Old man Jones, the president and a dozen others had bruises and cuts that were painful, though not of a dangerous character, none of which had as yet received any attention, except that Phil had bound up his head with a handkerchief.

The handkerchief had answered very well, so long as there was a necessity of remaining on guard against another possible assault ; but, now that the soldiers had gone, Phil felt that he needed something further in the way of attention to his injuries. He repaired to the McKinley home, that being the place where he felt certain of receiving the consolation which his wounds now required.

Of course, he received it.

Nettie furnished the consolation, and her mother the iniment and bandages, and between them they fixed him up as good as new ; in fact, they made him feel that he should be tempted to have his head laid open every once in a while, just for the pleasure of having it repaired again.

Mr. McKinley also required and received careful attention at the hands of his wife and daughters.

He was not very seriously hurt—not quite so badly as he wished he was when he saw that Phil's having his head tied up was accepted as proof that he had been where the fight raged hottest.

He had, however, some black-and-blue spots on his person and about his face, from one of which a few drops of blood had issued and dried, and a sight of the red stain made upon the cloth with which his wife was striving to remove the ink from his face satisfied him. He had fought and bled for his country, and he was now content.

Two or three hours were required to get the printer's ink out of his hair and off his person. His wife and daughters soaped and scrubbed away diligently, without causing him to utter a complaint of any kind. He felt that he was having his wounds dressed, and that the time spent over him was evidence of the undaunted bravery with which he had led the contest.

Mr. McKinley was now positive that he should never again run a ferry boat. If he was not called on to organize a regiment for the protection of the frontier of the Territory when it should be organized, he would accept a seat in the Legislature, and serve his country there with a dignity equal to the desperate courage which he had displayed in fighting for its independence upon this memorable occasion.

Thus was Mr. McKinley mentally occupied while his devoted wife was conducting the work necessary to his physical repair and rejuvenation. Sorry was he when, this task finished, he realized that matters of grave concern demanded his immediate attention. His was the usual regret attendant upon the sudden termination of a day-dream.

* * *

The unsettled feeling among the colonists that came as a consequence of the events just recorded caused another postponement by Phil and Nettie of their intended wedding.

There was no one living in the settlement who was legally authorized to officiate at weddings; and in the uncertainty of what might be, they delayed their proposed trip to a place at which they could be united and begin their honeymoon.

They felt the better contented to do this now that Phil was spending most of his time at Mr. McKinley's house, being for several days quite unfit to do any thing, and for a still longer period suffering severely from a rush of blood to the head whenever he bent over; so that he made little attempt to work on his claim, but kept himself closely in the house and suffered himself to be made much of and coddled without a murmur.

Neither did any of the colonists feel greatly inclined to go on with their intended improvement.

They tried to hope that the troops had gone not to return, but they doubted if they had. Even Mr. McKinley could not keep alive their belief that the soldiers had been too badly frightened to think of returning, and that the Lieutenant was sure to make such a report to his superiors as would discourage them from renewing the attack.

Hence they did little except to secure a small portion of their crops, and wait and watch for what the future had in store for them.

Now, if preference could be followed in this narrative, Mr. McKinley would be sustained in his belief that the government was too badly scared to take any further steps in the matter of removing squatters from Oklahoma ; but a stern resolve to adhere to the facts compels a different course.

The soldiers did return, and they came back six hundred strong, being reinforced by a detachment from Fort Russell ; and, still under the command of Lieutenant Knight, they surrounded the little band of colonists, who had learned of their approach and boldly set out to fight them.

Having surrounded them, the army sat down to starve

them into submission, a feat which it accomplished in a week by cutting off all supplies which their families attempted to carry to them and by preventing them from obtaining food for themselves.

And then they compelled them to pack up for the third time their household goods, put their wives and children into the wagons, and after setting fire to the printing office without having first permitted the removal of the press, type and other appurtenances, conveyed them out of the Territory in the same manner that they had done twice before.

At the State line all except the leader, Phil Johnson and Mr. McKinley were released and told to go where they would, so they did not return to the disputed territory. These three men were taken to one of the larger towns of the State, turned over to the civil authorities and put in jail.

After some delay the leader obtained bail for himself in the sum of $3,000, and as soon as he had secured his own release he set about obtaining the release of his two companions.

Mrs. McKinley had followed on with the family when she learned where her husband was, and thus Nettie saw her father and lover in jail.

Bail was at last secured for both, and they were then released. Again arose the question as to what should be done.

Should they again rally their **friends** and **enter Oklahoma at once?**

Where were the colonists who **had just been driven out?**

A portion of them, they learned, **were** still in camp, **or had scattered along the** borders of Kansas, awaiting another opportunity to enter Oklahoma and take possession of their claims. Others had become discouraged **or had exhausted their means, and could not return immediately.**

Leaving Mrs. McKinley and **the** family **at the town** where **the men** had been incarcerated, Phil and **the others went** to the vicinity where the larger portion **of the** colonists were, **and after** getting some of **them together asked** them what **their wishes were** regarding **an immediate** return to Oklahoma.

For themselves, they told **them** that they **were ready to** return **at once, but would have to be back at** the time **set for their trial.**

Many were in favor of going back at once, but others declared **such action** unwise. They thought some time **could** be spent advantageously in efforts to enlighten the country regarding **the** struggle between themselves, **as** representatives of **the people,** and the cattle syndicates, through the press and **by other** means.

It had been learned **that already a** partial knowledge **of** the outrages committed upon them **had** reached the public ear, and that there were several members in Congress who would respond to any request to bring the matter before that body.

It was finally resolved to refrain for the time being from again entering the disputed territory, and to devote the interval to agitating before the country the question: "Who Owns Oklahoma?"

Accordingly, arrangements were made for the establishment of permanent headquarters at Caldwell, Kansas, which is close to the territorial line. Fresh printing materials were purchased, and their newspaper, bearing now the name The Oklahoma War Chief, was started again and placed under the editorial management of a competent person, with orders to give it the widest possible circulation.

Petitions were also printed, asking Congress to take cognizance of the matter of protecting citizens in their right to settle in Oklahoma.

These petitions, published in such journals as were in possession of the facts of the case and friendly to the purpose of the petitioners, were passed from hand to hand among the friends of the colonists, and, signed by thousands, were sent rolling in upon the members of the House and Senate of the United States and upon the President.

This procedure frightened the cattle kings, and they hastened to send a representative to Washington to bring such influence to bear as would prevent any action that might be unfavorable to their interests or expose the means by which they had secured the aid of the military arm of the government and of the civil courts to enable them to hold possession of such great bodies of land, and to drive from their homes, arrest and imprison men who were acting in good faith, in accord with the homestead and pre-emption laws of the country and in full harmony with the practices in similar cases since those laws were enacted.

Nevertheless, the cattle kings were only partially successful.

Public sentiment was too far aroused and too much in sympathy with the colonists to allow the matter to be left untouched by Congress and the President.

Petitions continued to roll in, and more than one Congressman received hints from his constituents that it would be better for his future prospects if he would heed the demands of the people in this matter.

The politicians at length began to feel that it would be a good stroke of policy for the new Administration to make some show of being interested in the people, even if it went no farther.

Then came the President's order for everybody, cattle king and squatter, to get out of Oklahoma.

It was a field day for the colonists when they heard read the President's sweeping order in the matter.

Although they were now scattered widely, and only such as were connected directly with the work of putting a knowledge of these things before Congress and the country were at Caldwell, yet this news was to them, at whatever point located, a note of victory.

The colonists knew that if the cattle were removed there would be no objectors sufficiently strong to prevent the acknowledgment by the Interior Department of their right, and the right of all citizens who wished, to make homes upon the prairies and along the beautiful streams of Oklahoma and the Cherokee Strip.

The trial of the Captain, Mr. McKinley and Phil Johnson for violation of the laws in entering Oklahoma never came off. When the date set for the trial arrived they were present in court, but were discharged without a hearing, although they strongly protested against the nolle prosequi.

The colonists were anxious to be able to prove again, as once before they had proved in the District Court at Topeka, that there was no law under which any citizen could be punished for entering upon and improving the lands in question, and they denounced as unjust and an outrage their arrest, removal, imprisonment and arraignment, only to be discharged without opportunity to show proof of their innocence or expose the flagrant violation of civil law by the military in persecuting them at the bidding of the cattle kings.

But in nothing were they allowed opportunity to make themselves heard by the court. They were simply told that, since their followers had vacated the disputed territory, they would not be prosecuted. And in spite of their protest against this attempt to convict them without trial, they were compelled to bear it.

After the farcical ending of this pretended trial, and after it had been decided that the colonists would not return to their claims at once, but would await the action of Congress, if action could be obtained within such time as should be considered at all reasonable, Mr. McKinley's family thought it best for them to return to their old home on the Wabash, and await the further movements of the colony. They had not sold the old place when they left it—principally because no one wanted to buy it at much of a figure.

The little old town of yore was still a little old town, and the few acres which Mr. McKinley owned possessed no value other than as agricultural land. Not knowing how the West might please them, they had decided not to accept the only offer they had had for it, which was from a farmer who owned land adjoining, and would in all probability be as ready to purchase it a year or two later as then.

To the old home, then, Mr. McKinley's family had returned, with the exception of one of the boys, who obtained work with the team in Kansas, and decided to remain there until such time as the family would return to enter once more upon their Oklahoma claim.

Phil and Nettie had again postponed their wedding, but only for a little while.

When Phil decided that he must remain in Kansas for a time, and help to start the movement which was to bring a pressure to bear upon Congress to compel action in relation to Oklahoma, Nettie and he talked the matter over and came to the conclusion that, inasmuch as Phil must be constantly moving about for some months, it would be best not to marry until this part of the work was performed. Nettie decided, therefore, to return with her parents to the old home, and there wait for Phil's coming.

Equally with Phil, Nettie felt interested in the settlement of the question of right involved in the contest in which they were engaged with the cattle syndicates.

The wrongs done to the colonists, of whom she had been one, the insults and injuries heaped upon her father and lover, the memory of their having been tied with ropes like criminals—all these things had aroused the spirit of resistance within her, and she was as ready to make sacrifices for the good of the cause as was Phil himself.

And, besides, Nettie was in love with her Oklahoma home—or Phil's home, which she was to share with him—and she wished to be able to return there with him.

and with her father's family and the other colonists, among all of whom had grown up bonds of friendship which made them seem nearer than any could seem who had never rejoiced together in prospective peace and prosperity, as they had done, or sympathized with one another over the disappointments and losses that for the time had broken up all their plans and hopes.

She was, therefore, anxious that Phil and others should do all that could be done to bring about a peaceful removal of the difficulties standing in the way of the colonists' return and their permanent settlement of the country.

Nettie and Phil had spent one last evening together, taken one last kiss, exchanged vows of eternal constancy and adoration, and she, with her father and family, had returned to the old home, while Phil started out on his mission.

But he went with a light heart.

Just so soon as he could do the work he had undertaken in behalf of the colony, he also was to return to the old home—to his father's home—and to Nettie, who would then become his wife.

He went forth, too, with Mr. McKinley's blessing, for the dignified old gentleman's heart was warm toward his prospective son-in-law.

Phil was brave and ready, and the old man, in spite of some little weaknesses, was fully capable of appreciating courage and honesty of **purpose**; and, besides this, nobody treated him with more deference than did Phil.

Perhaps the reverence which, in his boyish days, he had felt for the **great man** who held commission from two States to run a **ferry** boat on the Wabash had never quite deserted Phil.

Still, beneath his appearance of ingenuousness were inaudible whisperings of policy, telling him it was wisest to keep on the good side of the father of the girl whom he loved.

Naturally, he had a high sense of the respect due to men older than himself. **In the** case of Mr. McKinley **he** probably saw more clearly than did others of his intimates a **true** inward dignity **in** the **man, to** which the outward dignity of his manner **was but an** ill-fitting garment.

When the old gentleman came **to bid** Phil good-by **his lips trembled a** little **and** his voice had the suspicion of a tremor in it.

The two men, the old man and the young one, had been in prison together; they had ridden together many a weary mile between lines of soldiers—their guards; they had slept side by side upon the green sward of the prairies, and—yes, they had fought and bled together in a cause sacred to both. In addition to these strong ties, Phil was soon to be **the** husband **of** the old man's **beautiful** daughter. And now that **they were to be parted for** a time, he would give the boy his blessing. Straightway he proceeded to do so.

His lips trembled a little at first, but he fought hard against a display of emotion, and before he had finished speaking all his dignity of manner and fluency of language had returned to him. He said:

"Go, Philip, and do the work which is for you to do. You have my blessing—the blessing of a man who has been honored by having shed his blood for his country and in defense of the sacred rights of the people to settle in Oklahoma."

CHAPTER XXII.

A FARMER-LOOKING INDIVIDUAL, WHO ALSO ENDURES A THREE-PRONGED FRONT NAME.

Phil was one day sitting in the office of a little hotel in one of the frontier towns of Kansas, whither he had gone on colony business, when a stranger dressed in the garb of a farmer entered.

This farmer-looking individual was a man apparently 55 or 60 years of age, well formed and preserved, and wore an unusually jovial countenance.

He paused for a second upon entering the door, and glanced around the room, as if hoping to find there some one to whom he could impart the impression—which he held—that this is as good a world as any one need wish to live in; or, if not that, it was just as well for a body not to be aware of that fact.

Seeing no audience other than Phil, he nodded familiarly and said:

"Howdy, stranger. Glad to meet ye."

THE FRIENDLY STRANGER.

To which Phil returned an equally courteous salutation.

Though a stranger to Phil, this man evidently was no stranger to the house. He was, in fact, a resident of the vicinity and owned a farm a few miles out in the country. Being in town on business, he had dropped into the hotel for dinner, as is the custom of those farmers who feel that they can afford to spend a quarter for a meal now and then when away from home at meal time.

After nodding to Phil he walked up to the office of the clerk and was in the act of reaching for one of those rusty, ink-corroded pens which usually furnish forth the desks of such hotels, and with which guests are expected to perform the next to impossible feat of legibly recording their names in the hotel register, when from a door opening into the room back of the counter the landlord entered and greeted the new comer with:

"Hallo, Johnson! That you? Glad to see you—was just wishing you would happen to drop in. Look here."

The last two words were spoken in a low tone, and with a kind of confidential air, and as he spoke the landlord turned the register around and shoved it in front of his farmer-looking guest, pointing to some entry on one of its pages.

Now, this register—supposed to be kept for the sole purpose of registering the names of guests and the time of their arrival and departure—had become something unique among hotel registers. Besides being a record, more or less accurate, of the arrival and departure of an occasional traveler from foreign parts—that is, from parts as far away as the next county seat town, or possibly a drummer or two from Kansas City—it contained the names of all the farmers who occasionally dropped in to dinner, of all the regular boarders written as often as it occurred to them to do so, and of all the loungers about town who made the hotel office their headquarters, and who, since they never patronized the house to the extent of so much as a meal of victuals, felt it to be a duty which they owed to the landlord to help him to maintain an appearance of brisk business by writing their names among those of the guests and the regular boarders at least once a week, and as much oftener as circumstances seemed to require it of them.

Some of them did still more to make their presence agreeable to the landlord and apparent to the traveler who might chance to register there.

Besides their own names, these occasionally wrote the name of a chum or of some business man or other citizen of the place, with a prefix denoting the enjoyment of civic or military honors. Others, apparently less ambitious, contented themselves with simply adding huge flourishes to their own names or in drawing aimless lines in ink or pencil across the pages. Still others there were who, with an eye to the beautiful in art, added ink sketches of the landlord or of any person or any thing that appeared to them as a good subject from which to draw inspiration.

Now, when Phil had this caricature of a register laid before him by the good-natured but unmethodical landlord, with a request to "give us your 'John Hancock,' stranger, please," the peculiar appearance of the page upon which he was thus asked to write his name struck him as requiring something more than ordinary in the way of a signature. Appreciating this requirement, he had written, with all the flourishes he could command and with a superabundance of ink:

"Philip P. P. Johnson."

This was the first time he had ever written his alliterative signature to any document as any thing but plain Philip Johnson. For this reason the peculiarity of the signature struck him as somewhat odd, and he stood with the pen still in his hand and looked at it for an instant, as if to photograph upon his memory some thing which he regarded as a kind of curiosity, the like of which he never expected to see again. Then he turned away and other matters engrossed him.

But now the landlord and his jolly guest were evidently looking at that signature and discussing the coincidence.

Their heads were close together as they leaned over

the counter from opposite sides, the landlord keeping his finger upon the open page of the register, at which his guest was looking intently.

During the inspection of the register Phil heard the landlord say, in a low tone: "That's him over there."

Then the deeply interested farmer also put a finger upon the pie-bald register, and appeared to be making a thorough study of it.

Phil could see the man's finger move along by steps or jumps, much as an inch worm "measures" his way across one's path or along a blade of grass. He was evidently studying Phil's chirography, and was moving his finger from one letter to another in an effort to make certain that there was no mistake about it.

When he had apparently satisfied himself that it was what it appeared to be, he turned to Phil, who was sitting on the opposite side of the room, and called out:

"I say, stranger, if it aint bein' too impertinent, would you mind tellin' me if this is your John Hancock that's wrote here?"

"I reckon it is," replied Phil, good-naturedly.

"An' your name's Johnson, an' you actily claim them there three P's that you've got attached to your name as your 'n, do you?"

"Yes, I reckon they honestly belong to me, though I don't often put 'em to use," Phil answered.

"Because," continued the other, as if he had not

heard Phil's reply, "you see, that's my name, too, and I thought I had all the P's in the Johnson dish on my own plate."

He raised his hand and brought it down on his thigh with a slap, and gave expression to his appreciation of his own joke in a loud guffaw, while his eyes twinkled and danced like those of the Santa Claus of our childhood days, and his whole body shook with merriment.

"Well, maybe you did," returned Phil, willing to aid the old gentleman enjoy himself. "Maybe you did have 'em, and they just warmed 'em over for me."

The effect of this sally was to break the old fellow up entirely.

He placed both hands upon his knees, shut his eyes and mouth and bent himself nearly double, while his whole person shook like a man with the ague. Then suddenly his mouth flew open, and a peal of laughter that could easily have been heard a block away rolled forth and shook the building. He straightened up with a jerk which gave a twist to his voice and compelled his laughter to end with a kind of "whoop-e-e-e, *ah!*"—a sort of a cross between the snort of a mad bull and the scream of a factory engine. And then his body came together again like a jack-knife, and the operation was repeated.

"W-h-a-t—what do your P's stand for, young man?" he asked as soon as breath would permit.

"Well, you see," returned Phil, who was becoming interested in the entertainment and anxious to have it continued, "the fact is I sort of inherited two of them. They were, so to speak, warmed over for me, in the first place."

Here the jolly man gave a snort, but held on to himself out of a desire to hear what Phil might have to say further.

"I was a triplet," continued Phil (another snort from the old gentleman), "and when the other two died I was allowed to keep the names which had been given to all three—because, you see, they did n't exactly know which of us had died and which was still living."

"And the names?" snorted the other, making effort to hold himself down.

"The bunch of young Johnsons were named Philip, Phineas and Philander," replied Phil.

"Then they're mostly fresh Peas," yelled the old gentleman. "Mine are Philip Peter Pendegast."

Away he went again, doubling up like a jack-knife, shaking all over for an instant and then opening out with a jerk and a "whoop-e-e-e, *ah!*"

His hilarity attracted the attention of every man in that end of the town, and brought a dozen of the least busy among them around to the hotel on purpose "to hear old man Johnson laugh."

This was not an entirely new experience with them,

for the old fellow was in the habit of coming to town about once a week, and whenever he was known to be in town everybody who felt a necessity for having a good laugh was sure to gather about him.

The old gentleman often declared, with a snort: "The blues and me have never camped under the same blanket."

When this last ebullition of laughter had subsided, the old fellow came over to where Phil sat and shook his hand.

"I 'm mighty glad to have seed you, young man," he said. "You are an honor to the name you bear, and I don't (with a snort) begrudge you the single warmed-up P of mine which your parients gin you; and, moreover, I reckon I have got something of more value—considering Peas is so plenty (another snort) in our family—that belongs to you. Now, if you will go out home with me, or, if you can't do that, if you will wait until I gallop out and back, I 'll turn it over to you 'thout sayin' any thing about what you 've got of mine. Maybe it aint your 'n, but I reckon it is. It 's a letter which I got outen the post office at Caldwell, two or three years ago —or, rather, one of the boys, a young fellow what lives with us, did—and I forgot all about it till just the other day.

"You see, we camped down near there once—when we first came to the State—and we had our mail come there. This letter I 'm telling you about came there and was taken out by one of my folks, as I was saying, who put it in his coat pocket, where it slipped down through the linin', where my wife found it only t'other day, when she was a-rippin' the thing up for to make carpet rags outen.

"She s'posed, in course, it was mine, and having a natural curiosity to know what was inside, she tore the thing open. But it was n't for me nor for any of my family, and I reckon it must be for you.

"I hope the loss on 't haint caused you any special oneasiness."

"Whether it has or not, you certainly are not to blame in the matter," replied Phil.

"I have not received many letters—at least, was not receiving many at the time you got this out of the post office at Caldwell—and it is difficult to tell what effect it might have had upon me. But it does not matter now. I imagine it is a letter from my mother, failing to get which I wandered off still farther, and have never since returned to the old home or seen any of my own people —not one."

"Are that a fact," the old man commented, rather than asked. "Wall, now, let me give you a little advice. We are sort of relations, you know—both Johnsons, and also we both got part of our P's from the same patch."

THE OLD LETTER. 343

Here the old man's eyes twinkled, and his body gave indications of the doubling up process.

"What I 'm wantin' to say to you is this: If that letter is your 'n, an' was writ by your mother, she 's a mighty good woman; an' if you are a good son you 'll not waste any time in goin' back an' givin' her another look at you.

"You see, wife and I read the letter, 'cause we could not exactly understand how there could be two Johnsons with so many P's to their names, and we kept wonderin' what it could all mean—the finding of it there, and all that—till finally the boy, who is older now and not afraid of owning up to any mistakes which he makes, told us how he remembered getting a letter out of the post office at Caldwell and losin' it, and then we guessed that this was that letter, and that it was writ to somebody else. So we read it all over again, tryin' to find out who writ it so as we could send it back, but it did n't have no name signed to it 'ceptin' just 'Mother,' and no place of startin' 'ceptin' just 'Home,' but it was full of lovin' messages, and if it had really been writ to me, and she that writ it was my mother, I 'd feel like skipping back pretty lively for fear she got tired of waitin' for me here, and crossed over the river to do the rest o' the waitin' where maybe it will be easier doin' of it."

"You see," he added, in an apologetical kind of a way, "you see, wife and I have got a boy out in the world somewhere—we don't know where—and that sort of enables me to understand how your parients must feel about you."

There was moisture in Phil's eyes when he put out his hand again and heartily shook that of the farmer-looking individual.

When they had shaken hands, Phil spoke with more than usual deliberation:

"I am going to start for the old home inside of a week. It shall not be longer. I ought to have gone a year ago. In truth, I should never have left my home on the Wabash."

If there had been no moisture in his own eyes, Phil might have seen something suspiciously like it in those of the reminiscent old farmer, as he took his proffered hand.

"That's right, young man—that's right. Go back to the old folks and let 'em set eyes on ye once more. They won't be ashamed of your looks—could n't be, if you looked a heap wuss than you do."

Here the moisture left the old man's eyes, and they began to twinkle again.

"Young man, take your parients my best compliments, and tell 'em if they want to use any more of my P's they 're welcome. Bein' they 've got Philip, they can have both Peter and Pendegast if they can find ekally good use for 'em."

And again he started off with a snort and ended up with a whistle.

* * *

After eating dinner together, Phil rode out home with his new acquaintance.

There he was handed the letter written to him by his mother four years before, and for the first time read the loving message which it contained.

CHAPTER XXIII.

BACK TO THE LITTLE OLD TOWN ON THE WABASH—THE
WEDDING BELLS RESOUND.

A week later Phil made his report at headquarters, and then took the next train for his old home in the State of Indiana.

It all seemed to him as if he were in a dream, as he went bowling along across the prairies and by the banks of the rivers and through the woodlands—seemed as if his whole life had been a dream, and as if he were not yet fully awakened.

Possibly it was a dream, and he had not awakened, but was still dreaming. Perchance that is true which is taught by the occultists, and which they claim to have proven, that the real is the spiritual and that which we regard as the real is but a dream—an illusion of the senses from which we shall awaken some time, to know the truth and to live it.

THE OLD FERRY ON THE WABASH.

Now, if it was a dream—this reverie of Phil's—it was twice dreamed. For as he rode along he went back in his thoughts over his whole life. He saw again each incident which had occurred since his earliest memory— his boyhood days, the happy days spent with Nettie on the ferry, the weeding of the truck patch, the hunting for hogs in the river bottom, the little incidents or accidents that brought him joy or sorrow, the running away and the life upon the plains, the herding and the stampede, the circle of cow boys about a hundred camp fires, the range and the stockade and the herd at the foot of the Guadalupe Mountains, the attack of the Apaches and—Brown.

His dream changed a little at the thought of Brown, and he changed the position of his body to correspond with it.

"I wonder how Brown is and how he is getting on? Too bad I did not answer his last letter," he told himself. "Reckon he 's all right, though ; said he 'd got a boy, and his name was Phil. Kind of Brown to remember his old pard in that way. But, then, Sam never was a man to forget his friends. He shall not get far ahead of me in that way, though. I 'll ask Nettie to name our first ———"

Again the current of his dream changed, and away he went on a new trail.

Arrived at his destination, he got off the cars at a

station five miles from the little town on the Wabash, and walked out.

He had not written to let the folks know at just what time to expect him, and consequently no one was there to meet him. He preferred walking to being taken out by a stranger.

Phil wanted to see the old town for the first time with no one by to break in upon his thoughts with idle talk, and he wanted to come upon the folks unawares, so that he might enjoy their surprise, as well as see if his parents and others who had not seen him since he was a boy would recognize him.

The country about the railroad station where he left the train was changed, of course. He expected to find changes there.

Railroads bring business; they push and hurry people; they whistle and roar and scream at folks; they compel them to be up and doing. One can not sleep in front of a railroad train nor fish from the rear platform.

If a railroad had been built through the little old town on the Wabash to which he was going, even it would have been compelled to wake up, and its inhabitants to cease to sit in the sun and fish.

Phil realized this, and he was not surprised to find the country about the railroad station so changed that he scarcely knew where he was.

As he drew away from it things began to look more

familiar—enough so that he could at least tell exactly what and where the changes were.

That is the same log house that was there when he went away, but the barn has been built since, and the orchard has grown—that is, the trees have.

They were only just coming into bearing when he left. He remembered that because he had once been tempted to hook a few apples from one of the trees at the lower end of the orchard, and had been deterred by the fear that he might be seen from the house, the trees being so small as not to screen one from observation, while now the house could not be seen at all from where he stood.

Over there, a little farther on, somebody had cut a field out of the river bottom. That must have been recently, last year or the year before; the stumps yet had the bark on them, and the ground had never been broken with a mould board, but just harrowed over probably, and seeded down for pasture. Some of the logs lay yet where they fell, or where ineffectual efforts had been made to consume them in heaps by fire.

It was almost sundown when he came in sight of the old home and the little town itself. He did not have to cross the river to reach it. He almost wished he did, and by the ferry, and he wondered whether, if he had had to do so, Nettie would have been there to ferry him across. She was here now, and living with her father's family in the little old cabin, just as they used to when me and she were children. There was a frame addition to it now.

As he approached the old home, his father's house, he began to wonder whether his mother would not be standing in the doorway, looking out for him, just as he had found her doing many a time when he had been late in getting in from the river bottom, or from an errand to a farmer's somewhere; and as he came nearer still, he looked again, half expecting she would be there in the door.

And was it really true—this seeming? Was that she, his mother? Was she really looking out, and had she been watching for him thus all these years?

Yes, it was she, his mother—older and grayer, but looking a good deal as she had done when he saw her last. She has shaded her eyes with her hand now, just as he had seen her do many times before at his approach, striving thus to see a little more clearly, that she might know whether he who approached was her long-absent Philip.

"Is it Philip? Is it my boy?"

The tones were trembling, eager, expectant. So Phil made haste to relieve her suspense.

"Yes, mother, it is your boy—come back to ask forgiveness for having gone away."

And in another instant she had her arms about her

son's neck, and each was weeping upon the other's shoulder tears of joy.

* * *

"Nettie is well, and so are all the rest of Mr. McKinley's folks," said Phil's mother.

The first greetings between Phil and the other members of his father's family were over, and Phil was seated in front of the old familiar brick fire-place, for which he used to cut wood when he was a boy. A little fire was smoldering in the great wide space between the two jams; for, although it was Spring again, and the grass was green and the flowers were in bloom outside, it was cool indoors, especially as evening approached. So just a little fire was allowed to smolder away among the ashes all the day through.

Phil looked down at the chair on which he sat to see if it was one of the same old splint-bottom affairs, with straight back, which he remembered as a part of the old household riches. But it was not. There might possibly be one or two yet about the kitchen, or in the bed chamber above, with the ladder leading to it; but there was not one in sight—a fact which Phil regretted.

Every thing else was just the same as he remembered

it before he went away. The same bed, with its woolen counterpane, in which there were woven in varied colors all sorts of improbable birds and beasts and vegetable growths, stood in the corner just as it did, and it had about it, and concealing the floor beneath it, the same, or what looked like the same, calico short curtains or "valances."

The same old clock stood upon the mantel, and swung its pendulum back and forth and ticked away in exactly the same tone of voice that it had when he first remembered it. Nothing was changed in the least that he could see—nothing but the chairs.

"Nettie will be over pretty soon, I reckon. She comes over pretty nearly every evening to know if we have heard from you," continued Phil's mother, not forgetting in her own joy at the return of the prodigal that he must be eager to see his sweetheart.

Oh, these mothers! Always looking and longing for the presence of your children; bound up in them; ever anxious for them; willing even to surrender your own happiness, that theirs may be increased!

Who, among us all, has ever appreciated the beauty and goodness of a mother's love?

Nettie came a few minutes later by the back way, and into the kitchen.

They heard a little "tat-tat," at the kitchen door, and then the latch was lifted and Nettie entered without waiting to be bidden. She came so often, and was so soon to be a daughter to Mrs. Johnson, that she was looked upon as one of the family.

Mrs. Johnson had always liked Nettie, and after Phil went away, and during the years in which they heard nothing of him, she and Nettie had consoled each other oftentimes.

Without asking or being told in words, Phil's mother knew that this girl loved her boy, and for that alone she was ready to love her in return, though in truth she did love her for herself, and grew to love her more with the passing years.

"Come in here, Nettie," called Mrs. Johnson from the room where they all were, at the same time starting toward the kitchen and dragging Phil's father along with her.

Meeting her at the door, she pushed Nettie in and her husband out, following him herself after waiting only long enough to hear the girl's little scream of surprise and joy as she saw who was there and to see Phil rise from his chair and stretch out his arms to enfold her.

Then she went to' work getting supper. And such a supper as she got!

From somewhere about the kitchen, or from the cupboard in the sitting room, or from the out-door cellar, there came forth stores of preserves and canned fruits and jams and other good things in such profusion as only housewives like Mrs. Johnson know how to make, and as only such set forth with equal lavishness when they would get a meal for those whom they love or desire to honor.

He who has never sat as the honored guest at such a table has missed one of the best things of life, and can know but little about genuine hospitality.

Nettie came from the sitting room after a time, and helped about the supper.

Her face was a little more rosy and her eyes brighter than usual, no doubt, but Phil's mother did not seem to notice it. Her own step was lighter, and there was a glow in her own eyes that had not been there before for years; and if there was in Nettie's also, it was nothing she need to appear to know of or to question.

After supper Mr. Johnson went over to Mr. McKinley's house and brought the whole family back with him, for he knew they would be uneasy about Nettie if she did not return soon, and anxious to see Phil if they knew he had arrived, and for that first evening they could not let Phil go from beneath their own roof—at least, his fond mother could not. And so the McKinleys all came over to the Johnsons.

The McKinleys were not all actually brought over by Mr. Johnson—not the younger ones. They broke across lots on the run as soon as they learned of Phil's arrival, and Mrs. McKinley only waited to throw a shawl over her head before she followed after, leaving her husband to return with Phil's father in a more dignified, though somewhat hurried, manner.

The greeting between Phil and the younger members of the McKinley family was a bit boisterous.

They regarded him as a brother, an older brother—but as one with whom there was no necessity for any reserve—and they exhibited none in their expressions of joy at meeting again. Even Mrs. McKinley kissed him, and turned away to wipe a few tears from her eyes with the corner of her gingham apron.

Phil was a son to her already, and one in whom she had learned to repose the greatest confidence and for whom she had the deepest affection.

Then came Mr. McKinley.

He entered the house with Phil's father, and as those already there and gathered about Phil gave way for him the two men clasped hands, and shook long and with honest warmth.

Then Mr. McKinley spoke:

"I welcome you back to your native town, Philip, and I have already told your parents and all who have inquired about you that you are an honor to the place of your birth; yes, Sir, an honor to the place of your birth."

And then, as a memory of the scenes and incidents through which they had both passed and the kindness and respect with which Phil had invariably treated him flashed upon his mind, he hastily passed the back of his hand across his eyes, and exclaimed :

"We 'll beat 'em yet, Philip. We 'll beat 'em yet, and we 'll all go back to the Canadian River together. A bill to make Oklahoma a Territory was introduced in Congress today."

* * *

Two weeks later the residents of the little town on the Wabash were all gathered together at the McKinley residence, on the bank of the river near the ferry, to see Phil and Nettie married.

By all the "residents" is meant only the citizens who are classed as belonging to the genus homo.

The other citizens, free and independent though they were, had not been included in the invitation, and for this reason they continued their usual vocations, as on other days.

The hogs rooted at will in the streets or else went on

excursions to the river bottoms in search for the roots of the wild pea, the same as they had done all these years since the little town first squatted there; and the dogs lay in the shade and contended with their enemies, the fleas—just as they will do to the end of this chapter, which is the end of the story.

The old ferry boat lay fastened to its moorings, with the same long line of canoes stretched out behind it that were there when Nettie and Phil used to run it years ago, for it was still a convenience to a few people. Though now no one tended it regularly, yet any one who chose to used it, and to those living close by it was worth the little repairs which it occasionally needed, as the mending of a broken plank or the replacing of a rope.

But now it was arched over with branches of trees and decked out with flowers and a flag—the flag of our country, the Stars and Stripes—which floated from a pole erected at what was the bow, as the old craft lay at its moorings.

After the ceremony and **after** everybody had kissed the bride, wished joy to the groom and eaten of the wedding feast until filled, Phil and Nettie—that is to say, Mr. and Mrs. **Philip Phineas** Philander Johnson—were escorted down to the landing and aboard the boat. As many of the company as could crowd on board with the bridal couple did so. The chain was then loosened, and they swung away across the stream.

Not once only, but a score of times, did they make the passage. Now Nettie held the tiller and now Phil, and now some one else among the gay crowd. When the dark of evening came they were yet at it, and for an hour later still the sound of laughter and singing came floating up from the landing.

At last, grown weary of the swinging back and forth across the river, the crowd was mustered into line to escort the bride and groom in becoming style to the residence of Johnson pere. This riding back and forth on the ferry boat was all there was to be of their wedding journey.

Neither of the high contracting parties desired more

"When Oklahoma is declared open by act of Congress," they said, "then we will make a longer wedding journey, across hill and vale and river and mountain, to our claim and our home in that fair country; and such of our friends as will may go with us."

THE PLAINS.

CHAPTER I.

FROM THE MISSOURI RIVER TO THE ROCKY MOUNTAINS—THE TREES—THE HERBAGE—THE BUFFALO—INDIAN WARRIOR AND HIS PONY—THE INSECTS—THE MIRAGE—WATER—THE WICHITA MOUNTAINS—THE INDIANS.

It is but a few years ago that every school boy, who was supposed to possess the rudiments of a knowledge of the geography of the United States, could give the boundaries and a general description of the "Great American Desert."

As to the boundaries, the knowledge seemed to be quite explicit: On the north, bounded by the Upper Missouri, on the east by the Lower Missouri and Mississippi, on the south by Texas, and on the west by the Rocky Mountains.

The boundaries on the northwest and south remained

undisturbed, while on the east civilization, propelled and directed by Yankee enterprise, adopted the motto:

"Westward the Star of Empire Takes Its Way."

Countless throngs of emigrants crossed the Mississippi and Missouri rivers, selecting homes in the rich and fertile territories lying beyond. Each year this tide of emigration, strengthened and increased by the constant flow from foreign shores, advanced toward the setting sun, slowly but surely narrowing the preconceived limits of the "Great American Desert," and correspondingly enlarging the limits of civilization.

At last the geographical myth was dispelled. It was gradually discerned that the "Great American Desert" did not exist; that it had no abiding place, but that within its supposed limits, and instead of what had been regarded as a sterile and unfruitful tract of land, incapable of sustaining either man or beast, there existed the fairest and richest portion of the National domain—blessed with a climate pure, bracing and healthful, while its undeveloped soil rivaled, if it did not surpass, the most productive portions of the Eastern, Middle and Southern States.

Discarding the name "Great American Desert," this immense tract of country, with its eastern boundary moved back by civilization to a distance of nearly three hundred miles west of the Missouri River, is now known as "The Plains." The Indian tribes which have caused the government most anxiety and whose depredations have been most serious against our frontier settlements and prominent lines of travel across The Plains infest that portion of The Plains bounded on the north by the Valley of the Platte River and its tributaries, on the east by a line running north and south between the 97th and 98th meridians, on the south by the Valley of the Arkansas River and west by the Rocky Mountains.

Of the many persons whom I have met on The Plains, as transient visitors from the States or from different parts of Europe, there were but few who have not expressed surprise that their original ideas concerning the appearance and characteristics of the country were so far from correct, or that The Plains in imagination, as described in books, tourists' letters and reports from various scientific parties, differed so widely from The Plains as they actually exist and appear to the eye.

Travelers, writers of fiction and journalists have spoken and written a great deal concerning this immense territory, so unlike in all its qualities and characteristics to the settled and cultivated portions of the United States; but to a person familiar with the country the conclusion is forced, upon reading these published descriptions, either that the writers never visited more than a limited portion of the country which they aim to picture or—as is most commonly the case at the present day —that the journey was made in a stage coach or railway car, half of the distance traveled in the night time and but occasional glimpses taken during the day. A journey by rail across The Plains is at best but ill-adapted to a thorough and satisfactory examination of the general character of the country, for the reason that in selecting the routes for railroads the valley of some stream is, if practicable, usually chosen to contain the road bed. The valley being considerably lower than the adjacent country, the view of the tourist is correspondingly limited.

Moreover, the vastness and varied character of this immense tract could not fairly be determined or judged by a flying trip across one portion of it. One would scarcely expect an accurate opinion to be formed of the swamps of Florida from a railroad journey from New York to Niagara.

After indulging in criticisms on the written descriptions of The Plains, I might reasonably be expected to enter into what I conceive a correct description, but I forbear. Beyond a general outline embracing some of the peculiarities of this slightly known portion of our country, the limit and character of these sketches of Western life will not permit me to go.

The idea entertained by the greater number of people regarding the appearance of The Plains, while incorrect so far as the latter are concerned, is quite accurate and truthful if applied to the prairies of the Western States. It is probable, too, that romance writers, and even tourists at an earlier day, mistook the prairies for plains, and in describing the one imagined they were describing the other. But the two have little in common to the eye of the beholder, save the general absence of trees.

From the Missouri River to the Rockies.

In proceeding from the Missouri River to the base of the Rocky Mountains the ascent, although gradual, is quite rapid. For example, at Fort Riley, Kansas, the bed of Kansas River is upward of 1,000 feet above the level of the sea, while Fort Hays, at a distance of nearly 150 miles farther west, is about 1,500 feet above the sea level.

Starting from almost any point near the central portion of The Plains, and moving in any direction, one seems to encounter a series of undulations at a more or less remote distance from each other, but constantly in view.

Comparing the surface of the country to that of the ocean, a comparison often indulged in by those who have seen both, it does not require a very great stretch of the imagination, when viewing this expansive ocean of beautiful living verdure, to picture these successive undulations as gigantic waves, not wildly chasing each other to or from the shore, but standing silent and immovable, and by their silent immobility adding to the impressive grandeur of the scene.

These undulations, varying in height from 50 to 500 feet, are sometimes formed of a light sandy soil, but are often composed of different varieties of rock, producing at a distance the most picturesque effect.

The constant recurrence of these waves, if they may be so termed, is most puzzling to the inexperienced plainsman. He imagines—and very naturally, too, he judging from appearances—that when he ascends to the crest he can overlook all the surrounding country. After a weary walk or ride of perhaps several miles, which appeared at starting not more than one or two, he finds himself at the desired point, but discovers that directly beyond, in the direction he desires to go, rises a second wave, but slightly higher than the first, and from the crest of which he must certainly be able to scan the country as far as the eye can reach.

Thither he pursues his course, and after a ride of five to ten miles, although the distance did not seem half so great before starting, he finds himself on the crest—or, as it is invariably termed, the "divide"—but again only to discover that another and apparently a higher divide rises in his front, and at about the same distance as the preceding one.

Hundreds of miles—yes, even thousands of them—may be journeyed over, and this same effect will be witnessed every few hours. The traveler who would avoid this optical illusion must post himself before starting.

The Trees and Grasses —"Long Forage."

As you proceed toward the West from the Missouri the size of the trees diminishes, as well as the number of kinds.

As you penetrate the borders of the Indian country, leaving civilization behind you, the sight of forests is no longer enjoyed. The only trees to be seen are scattered along the banks of the streams, these becoming smaller and sparser, finally disappearing altogether and giving place to a few scattering willows and osiers.

The greater portion of The Plains may be said to be without timber of any kind.

As to the cause of this absence scientific men disagree, some claiming that the high winds which prevail in unobstructed force prevent the growth and existence of trees and also the taller grasses. This theory is well supported by facts, as, unlike the Western prairies, where the grass often attains a height sufficient to conceal a man on horseback, The Plains are covered by a grass which rarely, and only under favorable circumstances, exceeds three inches in height.

Another theory, also somewhat plausible, is that the entire region called The Plains were at one time covered with timber more or less dense, but this timber, owing to various causes, was destroyed, and has since been prevented from growing and spreading over that area by the annual fires which the Indians regularly create, and which sweep over the entire region. These fires are built by the Indians during the Autumn to burn the dried grass and hasten the growth of the pasturage in the early Spring.

Favoring the theory that The Plains were at one time covered with forests is the fact that entire trunks of large trees have been found in a state of petrifaction on elevated portions of the country, and far removed from all streams of water.

While dwarfed specimens of almost all varieties of trees are found fringing the banks of some of the streams, the prevailing species are cottonwood and poplar trees (populus monilifera and populus angulosa). Intermingled with these are found clumps of osiers (salix longifolia).

In almost any other portion of the country the cottonwood would be the least desirable of trees. But to the Indians and also to United States troops, in many instances which have fallen under my observation, the cottonwood has performed a service for which no other tree has been found its equal. That is as forage for the horses and mules during the Winter season, when the snow prevents even dried grass from being obtainable. During the Winter campaign of 1868-9 against the hostile tribes south of the Arkansas, it not unfrequently happened that my command, while in pursuit of Indians, exhausted its supply of forage, and the horses and mules were subsisted upon the young bark of the cottonwood tree. In routing the Indians from their Winter villages, we invariably discovered them located upon that point of the stream promising the greatest supply of cottonwood bark, while the stream in the vicinity of the village was completely shorn of its supply of timber, and the village itself was strewn with the white branches of the cottonwood, entirely stripped of their bark.

It was somewhat amusing to observe an Indian pony feeding on cottonwood bark. The limb being usually cut into pieces about four feet in length and thrown upon the ground, the pony, accustomed to this kind of "long forage," would place one fore foot on the limb in the same manner as a dog secures a bone, and gnaw the bark from it.

Although not affording anything like the amount of nutriment which either hay or grain does, yet our horses invariably preferred the bark to either—probably because of its freshness.

The Herbage.

The herbage to be found on the principal portion of The Plains is usually sparse and stunted in its growth. Along the banks of the streams and in the bottom lands grows, generally in rich abundance, a species of grass often found in the States east of the Mississippi, but on the uplands is produced what is there known as "buffalo grass." This is indigenous and peculiar in its character, differing in form and substance from all other grasses. The blade, under favorable circumstances, reaches a growth usually of three to five inches, but instead of being straight, or approximately so, it assumes a curled or waving shape, the grass itself becoming densely matted and giving to the foot, when walking upon it, a sensation similar to that produced by stepping upon moss or the most costly of velvet carpets.

Nearly all graminivorous animals inhabiting The Plains, except the elk and some species of the deer, prefer the buffalo grass to that of the lowland, and it is probable that even these exceptions would not prove good if it were not for the timber on the bottom land, which affords good cover to both the elk and the deer. Both are often found in large herds grazing upon the uplands, although the grass is far more luxuriant and plentiful on the lowlands. This fact would seem to be sufficient to show a distinct liking for this grass, if not their preference as a food.

Our domestic animals invariably chose the buffalo grass, and experience demonstrates beyond question that it is the most nutritious of all the varieties of the many wild grasses of this extensive region.

The Buffalo.

The favorite range of the buffalo is contained in a belt of country running north and south, about 200 miles wide and extending from the Platte River on the north to the valley of the Upper Canadian on the south. In migrating, if not grazing or alarmed, the buffalo invariably moves in single file, the column generally being headed by a patriarch of the herd, who is not only familiar with the topography of the country, but whose prowess " in the field " entitles him to become the leader of his herd. He maintains this leadership only so long as his strength and courage enable him to remain the successful champion in the innumerable contests which he is called upon to undertake.

The buffalo trails are always objects of interest and inquiry to the sight-seer on The Plains. These trails, made by the herds in their migrating movements, are so regular in their construction and course as to well excite curiosity. They vary but little from eight to ten inches in width, and are usually from two to four inches in depth. Their course is almost as unvarying as that of the needle, running north and south. Of the thousands of buffalo trails which I have seen, I recollect none of which the general direction was not north and south.

This may seem somewhat surprising at first thought, but it admits of a simple and satisfactory explanation.

The general direction of all streams, large and small, on The Plains is from west to east, apparently seeking debouchement in the Mississippi.

The habits of the buffalo incline him to graze and migrate from one stream to another, moving northward and crossing each in succession as he follows the young grass in the Spring, and in the Autumn and Winter moving southward, seeking the milder climate and open grazing. Throughout the buffalo country are to be seen what are termed "buffalo wallows." The number of these is so great as to excite surprise. A modest estimate would give three to each acre of ground throughout this vast tract of country. These wallows are about eight feet in diameter and from six to eighteen inches in depth, and are made by the buffalo bulls in the Spring, when challenging a rival to combat for the favor of the opposite sex. The ground is broken by pawing—if an animal with a cloven hoof can be said to paw—and if the challenge is accepted, as it usually is, the combat takes place. After the fight the victor remains in possession of the battle field, and, occupying the "wallow" of freshly upturned earth, finds it produces a cooling sensation to his hot and gory sides. Sometimes the victory which gives possession of the battle field and drives a hated antagonist away is purchased at a dear price.

The carcass of the victor is often found in the wallow, where his brief triumph has soon terminated from his wounds.

In the early Spring, during the shedding season, the buffalo resorts to his "wallow" to aid in removing his old coat. These "wallows" have proven of no little benefit to man, as well as to animals other than the buffalo. After a heavy rain they become filled with water, the soil being of such a compact character as to retain it. It has not unfrequently been the case when making long marches that the streams would be found dry, while water in abundance could be obtained from the "wallows." True, it was not of the best quality, particularly if it had been standing long and the buffalo had patronized the "wallows" as summer resorts. But on The Plains a thirsty man or beast, far from any stream of water, does not parley long with these considerations.

The Indian Warrior and His Pony.

Surely no race of men, not even the famous Cossacks, could display more wonderful skill in feats of horsemanship than the Indian warrior on his native plains, mounted on his well-trained war pony, voluntarily running the gauntlet of his foes, drawing and receiving the fire of hundreds of rifles, and in return sending back a perfect shower of arrows or well-directed shots from some souvenir of a peace commission in the shape of an improved breech-leader. The Indian warrior is capable of assuming positions on his pony, the latter at full speed, which no one but an Indian could maintain a single instant without being thrown to the ground. The pony, of course, is perfectly trained, and he seems to be possessed of the spirit of his rider.

An Indian's wealth is most generally expressed by the number of his ponies. No warrior or chief is of any importance or distinction who is not the owner of a herd of ponies numbering from twenty to many hundreds. He has for each special purpose a certain number of ponies, those that are kept as pack animals being the most inferior in quality and value. Then come the ordinary riding ponies used on the march, about camp and when visiting neighboring villages. Next in consideration is the "buffalo pony," trained to the hunt, and only employed when dashing into the midst of the huge buffalo herds, when the object is either food from the flesh or clothing and shelter for the lodges, to be made from the buffalo hide. In the first grade, considering its value and importance, is the "war pony," the favorite of the herd—fleet of foot, quick in intelligence and full of courage. It may be safely asserted that the first place in the heart of the warrior is held by his faithful and obedient war pony.

Indians are extremely fond of bartering, and they are not behindhand in catching the good points of a bargain. They will sign treaties relinquishing their lands and agree to forsake the burial grounds of their forefathers. They will part, for due consideration, with their bows and arrows and their accompanying quivers, handsomely wrought in dressed furs. Even their lodges may be purchased at not an unfair valuation, and it is not an unusual thing for a chief or warrior to offer to exchange his wife or daughter for some article which may have taken his fancy. This is no exaggeration. But no Indian of The Plains has ever been known to trade, sell or barter away his favorite "war pony." To the warrior his battle horse is as the apple of his eye. Neither love nor money can induce him to part with it. To see them in battle, and to witness how the one almost becomes a part of the other, one might well apply to the warrior the lines:

> But this gallant
> Had witchcraft in 't. He grew into his seat,
> And to such wondrous doing brought his horse,
> As he had been encorpsed and demi-natured
> With the brave beast, so far he passed my thought,
> That I, in forgery of shapes and tricks,
> Come short of what he did.

The Insects.

Wherever water is found on The Plains, particularly if it is standing, innumerable gadflies and mosquitoes generally abound. To such an extent do these pests to the animal kingdom exist that to our thinly coated animals, such as the horse and mule, grazing is almost an impossibility. But the buffalo, with his thick and shaggy coat, can browse undisturbed. The most sanguinary and determined of these troublesome pests are the "buffalo flies." They move in myriads, and so violent and painful are their assaults upon horses that a herd of the latter has been known to stampede as the result of an attack from a swarm of these flies.

But here, again, is furnished what some reasoners would affirm is evidence of "the eternal fitness of things." In most localities where these flies are found in troublesome numbers there are also found flocks of starlings, a species of blackbird. These, probably more to obtain a livelihood than to become defenders of the helpless, perch themselves upon the backs of the animals, and woe betide the helpless gadfly who ventures near, only to become a choice morsel for the starling.

In this way I have seen herds of horses grazing undisturbed, each horse of the many hundreds having perched upon his back from one to dozens of starlings, standing guard over him while he grazed.

The Mirage.

About the first subject which addresses itself to the mind of the stranger on The Plains, particularly if he be of a philosophical or scientific turn of mind, is the mirage, which is here observed in all its perfection.

Many a weary mile of the traveler has been whiled away in endeavors to account for the fitful and beautifully changing visions presented by the mirage. Sometimes the distortions are wonderful, and so natural as to deceive the most experienced eye.

Upon one occasion I met a young officer who had spent several years upon The Plains and in the Indian country. He was, on the occasion alluded to, in command of a detachment of cavalry in pursuit of a party of Indians who had been committing depredations on the frontier.

While riding at the head of his command he suddenly discovered, as he thought, a party of Indians not more than a mile distant. The latter seemed to be galloping toward him. The attention of his men was called to them, and they pronounced them Indians on horseback.

The "trot" was sounded, and the column moved forward to the attack. The distance between the attacking party and the supposed foe was rapidly diminishing, the Indians appearing plainer to view each moment.

The charge was about to be sounded, when the discovery was made that the supposed party of Indians consisted of the decayed carcasses of half a dozen slain buffaloes, which number had been magnified by the mirage, while the peculiar motion imparted by the latter had given the appearance of Indians on horseback.

I have seen a train of government **wagons** with white canvas covers moving through a mirage, which, by **elevating** the wagons to treble their height and magnifying **the** size of the covers, presented the appearance of a line of large sailing vessels **under** full sail, while the usual appearance of the **mirage** gave a correct likeness of an immense lake or sea. Sometimes **the** mirage has been the cause of frightful suffering and death because of its deceptive appearance.

Trains of emigrants making their way to California and Oregon have, while seeking water to quench their thirst and that of their animals, been induced to depart from their course in the endeavor to reach the inviting lake of water which the mirage displayed before **their** longing eyes.

It is usually represented at a distance of five to ten miles. Sometimes, if **the nature** of the ground is favorable, it is dispelled by advancing toward it; at others it is like an ignis fatuus—hovering in sight, but keeping beyond reach. Here and there throughout this region are pointed out the graves of those who **are** said to have been led astray by the mirage until **their** bodies were famished and they succumbed to thirst.

Water.

The routes usually chosen for travel acro⸺ .he Plains may be said to furnish, upon an averag.. w⸺⸺r ⸺**very** fifteen miles. In some instances, however, and during the hot season of the year, it is necessary in places to go into what is termed "a dry camp"—that is, to encamp where there is no water. In such emergencies, with a previous knowledge of the route, it is practicable to transport from the last camp a sufficient quantity to satisfy the demands of the people composing the train, but the dumb brutes must trust to the little moisture obtained from the night grazing to quench their thirst.

The animals inhabiting The Plains resemble in some respects the fashionable society of some of our larger cities. During the extreme heat of the summer they forsake their accustomed haunts and seek a more delightful retreat. For, although The Plains are drained by streams of all sizes, from the navigable river to the humblest brook, yet at certain seasons the supply of water in many of them is of the most uncertain character. The pasturage, from the excessive heat, the lack of sufficient moisture and the withering hot winds which sweep across from the south, becomes dried, withered and burnt, and is rendered incapable of sustaining life. Then it is that the animals usually found on The Plains disappear for a short time, and await the return of a milder season.

The Wichita Mountains.

Having briefly grouped the prominent features of the central Plains, a reference to the country north of Texas and in which the Wichita Mountains are located, a favorite resort of some of the tribes, is here made.

To describe as one would view it in journeying upon horseback over this beautiful and romantic country and picture with the pen those vast solitudes—so silent that their silence alone increases their grandeur—to gather inspiration from Nature and to attempt to paint the scene as my eyes beheld it, would comprise a task from which a much abler pen than mine might shrink.

The scene was a beautiful and ever-changing panorama which at one moment excited the beholder's highest admiration and at the next impressed him with speechless veneration.

Approaching the Wichita Mountains from the north, and after the eye has perhaps been wearied by the tameness and monotony of the unbroken Plains, the tourist is gladdened by the relief which the sight of these picturesque and peculiarly beautiful mountains affords.

Here are to be seen all the varied colors which Bierstadt and Church endeavor to represent in their mountain scenery. A journey across and around them on foot and upon horseback will well repay either the tourist or the artist.

The air is pure and fragrant, and as exhilarating as the purest of wine.

The climate is entrancingly mild, the sky clear and blue as the most beautiful sapphire, with here and there clouds of rarest loveliness, presenting to the eye the richest commingling of bright and varied colors.

Delightful odors are constantly being wafted upon the breeze. The forests, filled with the mocking bird, the colibri, the humming bird and the thrush, constantly put forth a joyful chorus.

The sights and sounds all combine to fill the soul with visions of delight and enhance the perfection and glory of the creation.

Strong, indeed, must be that unbelief which can here contemplate Nature in all her purity and glory and, unawed by the sublimity of this closely connected testimony, question either the Divine origin or purpose of the beautiful firmament.

Unlike most mountains, the Wichita can not properly be termed a range or chain. They can be correctly designated a collection or group, as many of the highest and most beautiful are detached and stand on a level plain "solitary and alone."

They are mainly composed of granite, the huge blocks of which exhibit numerous shades of beautiful colors—crimson, purple, yellow and green predominating. They are conical in shape, and seem to have but little resemblance to the soil upon which they are founded. They rise abruptly from a level surface—so level and unobstructed that it would be an easy matter for one to drive a carriage to any point of the circumference at the base

—and yet so steep and broken are the sides that it is only here and there that it is possible to ascend them.

From the foot of almost every mountain pours a stream of limpid water of almost icy coldness.

The Indian.

If the character given to the Indian by James Fenimore Cooper and other novelists, as well as by the well meaning but mistaken philanthropists of a later day, were the true one ; if the Indian were the innocent and simple-minded being which he is represented to be—more the creature of romance than reality, imbued only with a deep veneration for the works of Nature, freed from the passions and vices which must accompany a savage nature ; if, in other words, he possessed all the virtues which his admirers and writers of fiction ascribe to him and were free from all the vices which those best qualified to judge assign to him, he would be just the character to complete the picture which is presented by that section of the country which embraces the Wichita Mountains.

Cooper, to whose writings more than to those of any other author are the people speaking the English language indebted for a false and ill-judged estimate of the

Indian character, might well have laid the scenes of his fictitious stories in this beautiful and romantic country.

It is to be regretted that the character of the Indian as described in Cooper's interesting novels is not the true one. It is not a pleasant task to dispel the glamor that he threw about the noble red man.

But as, in emerging from childhood into the years of a maturer age, we are often compelled to cast aside our earlier illusions and replace them by beliefs less inviting but more real, so we, as a people, with opportunities enlarged and facilities for obtaining knowledge increased, have been forced by a multiplicity of causes to study and endeavor to comprehend thoroughly the character of the red man.

So intimately has he become associated with the government as a ward of the Nation, and so prominent a place among the questions of national policy does the much-mooted "Indian question" occupy, that it behooves us no longer to study this problem in works of fiction, but to deal with it as it exists in reality.

Stripped of the beautiful romances with which we have been so long willing to envelop him, transferred from the inviting pages of the novelist to the localities where we are compelled to meet with him—in his native village, on the war path and when raiding upon our frontier settlements and lines of travel—the Indian forfeits all claim to the appellation "noble red man."

We see him as he is, and, so far as all knowledge goes, as he ever has been—a savage in every sense of the word. He is not worse, perhaps, than would be his white brother similarly born and bred, but is one whose cruel and ferocious nature far exceeds that of any wild beast of the desert.

That this is true no one who has been brought into intimate contact with the wild tribes will deny. Perhaps there are some who, as members of peace commissions or as wandering agents of some benevolent society, may have visited these tribes or attended with them at councils held for some pacific purpose, and who, by passing through the villages of the Indians while at peace, may imagine their opportunities for judging of the Indian nature all that could be desired.

But the Indian, while he can seldom be accused of indulging in a great variety of wardrobe, can be said to have a character capable of adapting itself to almost every occasion.

He has one character—perhaps his most serviceable one—which he preserves carefully, and only airs it when making his appeal to the government or its agents for arms, ammunition and license to employ them.

This character is invariably paraded, and often with telling effect, when the motive is a peaceful one.

Prominent chiefs, invited to visit Washington, invariably don this character, and in their "talks" with the

A SUBJECT FOR STUDY. 383

"Great Father" and other less prominent personages they successfully contrive to exhibit but this one phase.

Seeing them under these or similar circumstances only, it is not surprising that by many the Indian is looked upon as a simple-minded "son of Nature," desiring nothing but the privilege of roaming and hunting over the vast and unsettled wilds of the West, inheriting and asserting but few native rights, and never trespassing upon the rights of others.

This view is equally erroneous with that other which regards the Indian as a creature possessing the human form but divested of all other attributes of humanity, and whose traits of character, habits, modes of life, disposition and savage customs disqualify him from the exercise of all rights and privileges, even those pertaining to life itself.

Taking him as we find him—at peace or at war, at home or abroad, waiving all prejudices and laying aside all partiality—we will discover in the Indian a subject for thoughtful study and painstaking investigation back through some centuries.

In him we will find the representative of a race the origin of which is, and promises to be, a subject for ever wrapped in mystery; a race incapable of being judged by the rules or laws applicable to any other known race of men ; one between which and civilization there seems to have existed from time immemorial a determined and unceasing warfare—a hostility so deep seated and inbred with the Indian character that in the exceptional instances where the modes and habits of civilization have been reluctantly adopted such adoption has been at the sacrifice of power and influence as a tribe, and the more serious loss of health, vigor and courage as individuals

CATTLE AND RANCHING.

CHAPTER II.

GAINS IN CATTLE RANCHING—HOW TO START IN THE BUSINESS—THE **STOCK COUNTRY**—THE RANGES—THE RIGHTS OF SETTLERS—**THE** DASHING COWBOY.

Away from the haunts of men one seldom meets any of the upper and educated classes, and the pleasures of social and literary intercourse are for the time superseded. The life is sometimes pleasant and sometimes dreary; there is plenty of exposure and not a little discomfort; there is generally good health, and consequent good temper; there are all sorts and conditions of men, who meet you on perfect equality, whether better or worse than yourself; your wants are few, as generally you have to satisfy them yourself.

It is wonderful how you lop off necessities when they burden your time and occupations.

You have entered on a new life in a new world. It

is not all admirable, for good and **evil are everywhere** balanced. With freedom in forming **new opinions, you are apt** to grow disdainful **of the small niceties of civilization.** The trammels of society are cast off, leading to a dangerous drop into rude habits and ill-restrained language. The impossibility of fulfilling all the refir.ements of the toilet engenders a disregard of personal neatness. Much can not be helped; some things might be avoided.

Young men **are** naturally the more **easily** influenced by their surroundings, and fall too readily into the habits and tricks of **speech** most honored on **the** prairies. This is the main educational disadvantage to young men starting alone in the West, for good breeding has to be nurtured by descent and association. **Coarseness** may be learned in a day.

The Gain in Cattle Ranching.

We have all **heard** of the gains in cattle ranching. ιs not 30 per cent a common return?

The fact is pointed out that Maverick, one of the cattle kings, began with a single steer and a branding iron. Now his herds browse on a hundred hills.

There is money in that.

How can we do likewise? The times for these marvels of money getting are gone by.

After the war a vast number of unclaimed cattle were running loose. They were the spoil of whoever could rope them. Those who bought even ten years later got their herds at the very low average of $7 or $8 a head.

If you have plenty of room and good feed, you may expect 80 or 90 per cent of calves to cows. If, at the same time, the all-round price advances to $22 or $24, the chances have been much in your favor.

Now the expenses in a crowded country of searching out your cattle at the different round-ups and in parts of the country lying sixty miles from your range foot up such a total that with less than 5,000 head the stock owner's profit is far below the normal.

Men still do start with small numbers, but they have first to seek a very secluded spot, and then must be constantly riding around and driving the cattle back on the home range. This injures the cattle, there is great loss of labor in doing continually over again the same work, and the rancher is forced to lay in a stock of hay to feed his cattle in the Winter time, as he can not allow them to roam at liberty and shift for themselves.

How to Start in the Cattle Business.

There is still room, and whether you wish to amuse yourself, find occupation or try a new life there are openings. The main point is to be careful and in no hurry; settle and wait. To be on the safe side, if you have capital leave it at home. Learn the business you wish to follow by working at it with your own hands. Pay no premiums, but hire yourself out. If active and willing, you are worth your keep. At the end of two months, if he is a sensible man and meaning to get on, your employer will be glad to give you wages, for steady men are scarce. Many know their work, but few will do it, and still fewer are to be trusted out of sight.

You will soon be able to save money—a very little, no doubt, but enough to make you think of investing.

This will set you to inquiring into prices and into the chances of a return. You will probably by one or two bad deals pick up experience, and will learn that saddest lesson—a distrust of men.

After a couple of years you may venture an independent start. You can take up 160 and 320 acres at a very little expense, under the government land laws; or, you may buy out some one who has pre-empted a claim suitable to your purposes. Your money will help you to stock it and buy farm implements.

The tenderfoot who takes his dollars in his trouser pockets is a lost man.

Every old settler with a poor farm, a worn-out wagon and horses, a valueless mine or property, will make a dead-set at the coin, and they are not easily shaken off. Their tricks are dark but not vain, and their victims are legion among those not wise in their generation.

The Stock Country.

In Denver you are in the middle of the stock country. North, south, east and west cattle have been raised and are still running on the prairies where the grass has not been fed off.

The prairies include all the unsettled parts. They are sometimes grass land, sometimes covered with sage and other brush, among which grass is found. The term takes in flat table lands, the slopes of mountains, and what are called bad lands, which are the wildest jumble of hills, ravines, small flats of excellent grass, and stretches of almost bare lava rocks. The name is derived from the French, who wrote on their maps: "Terres mauvaises à traverser."

In the hurry of business the first two words only were translated, and consequently left a wrong impression, for these lands often afford excellent cattle ranges. The grass is rich, water is to be found in many deep ravines, and the broken ground gives good shelter against storms.

The Cattle Ranches.

At the cattle ranches, where a half-dozen cowboys may have to spend the winter, fair-sized rooms are put up, the accommodations being increased and improved year by year. Bunks occupy one end of the room, a huge fire-place the other, from which the mound of hot ashes, topped by two enormous logs, fills the room with light and warmth. A large area of ground is fenced near the ranch, in which horses likely to be required are turned loose. The range lies outside this, its extent depending on the cattle man's ideas, tempered by the opinions of his near neighbors.

Settlers' Rights.

There are, of course, no absolute rights. The land is all government—often even that which is fenced—and there is little attempt to segregate the herds. Some of the Territories have passed laws acknowledging settlers' rights on streams, or to pieces of land they have inclosed ; but this is contrary to State law, and latterly a circular was issued in California pointing this out, and distinctly laying down the law that others could enter on such land without trespass.

Among stock raisers, however, there is much give and take. The first settlers naturally try to keep out new comers. They must end in accepting the inevitable— that is, so long as there is grass cattle will crowd in.

But the great enemy to stock is the plow. The farmers are coming slowly but surely from the eastward, and parts of Kansas and Nebraska have gone over to tillage.

Stock must give way and disappear into the mountains and rugged country.

The Dashing Cowboy.

Formerly the man who shouted the loudest, galloped hardest and was quickest in drawing his "gun" was considered the most dashing cowboy.

In the days gone by if a cowboy, coming up on the Texas Trail, had failed to kill his man, he was held to have wasted his opportunities.

But times are changing for the better.

Now only in the South—for instance, Arizona—is the term cowboy equivalent to desperado.

CHAPTER III.

CATTLE ON THE RANGES—CATTLE IN WINTER—ADVAN-
TANGES OF CATTLE RAISING OVER HORSE RAISING—
THE ROUND-UP—"CUTTING OUT"—THE COW PONIES
—BRANDING CALVES—BRANDING CATTLE—INCREASED
VALUE OF CATTLE HAS INTRODUCED MORE CARE AND
GENTLER HANDLING IN THEIR MANAGEMENT.

While roaming on the range the less the cattle are interfered with the better, particularly in the Winter. In this half wild state they can take much better care of themselves and find shelter and food; whereas, if they were herded—that is, controlled in any way by men—they would probably starve.

The cows, which in cowboy language includes all sexes and sizes, split up into bunches and take possession of some small valley or slope where water is procurable at no great distance. The shallowest spring bubbling up through mud will satisfy a small lot, if they get it all to themselves—a spring so small that, knowing it must exist

from the presence of the cattle, you would scarcely find it unless for their tracks, and when you reach it there is nothing fit for you to drink, and most likely your horse will refuse the mixture of mud in alkaline water which pleases the cow.

If water is scarce the cattle must make long tramps, and the country is then crossed by deeply trodden paths, which are an unerring guide to the thirsty horseman. The cattle come down these paths just before the sun gets hot, have a drink and then lie down till the evening, when they go off again to the pasture at some distance, and feed most part of the night.

Cattle in Winter.

In the beginning of Winter the cattle leave the high ground, and the appearance of a few hundred head in the valley which the day before was empty tells the tale of severe cold or snow storms in the mountains.

They like the shelter of heavy timber, which they find along the banks of streams, and here at some rapid or at the tail of a beaver dam is their latest chance for getting water. They can not, like the horse, eat snow, nor does their instinct suggest to them to paw away that covering to reach the grass beneath. In fact, the cattle will sometimes attach themselves to a herd of horses, sustaining life by following in their footsteps.

When times are hard the cattle will subsist on grease wood and eat almost any thing, but until the young sprouts begin to shoot there is on the prairie little to find after the snow covers the ground. Bare cottonwood trees line the streams. On the bark of these trees horses will manage to keep alive, but the cattle are far less hardy than the horses. These will come through the exceptional Winters when 20 per cent of the cattle have been lost.

The Advantages of Cattle Raising Over Horse Raising.

In the matter of breeding cattle and horses, the former have some advantages. There is, and must always be, an increasing demand for beef, and in the disposal of your live stock there is a great convenience in being able to ship any number by a train load to Chicago. There they can be disposed of in a day. Horses must, generally, be sold in small lots. Besides, the losses by horse thieves, both red and white, are greater than from cattle thieves.

The Indians often shoot a calf for food in Winter, being altogether easier to find and better to eat than are deer and buffalo. Some stockmen believe they lose a large number from the redskins, but these are decreasing in numbers every year, and are being restricted continually to smaller reservations, in which they are more successfully watched.

The Round-Up.

A round-up is the general arrangement among cattlemen in a given district to work the cattle by a common establishment. Each owner sends one or more cowboys to represent his brand and to take charge of all animals belonging to his herd.

The management is placed in the hands of an experienced foreman, and the ground to be covered is of a great extent, occupying the men from a couple of months to an entire season.

The main plan is, each day, to drive the cattle out of all outlying valleys into some central level spot. From the mixed mass the different brands are separated, commencing with the largest herd. This mode is a distinct advantage to the large owners, as the principal object of the general round-up is to get at the young calves.

While these are being "cut out," as it is called, the cattle in the main bunch are churned up, so that calves get separated from their mothers; and, as the only title to a calf is that it is following a cow with your brand, those who cut out last will naturally lose some which belong to them.

"Mavericks."

Any unbranded calf which is found not following a cow is called a "maverick." All such belong either to the man on whose range they have been found or are shared according to local custom.

"Cutting Out."

The process of cutting out a cow and calf is very pretty, if neatly done. One man can do it, but two men are seldom too many on the task.

The cowboy rides through the gathering of cattle till he sees a cow and calf which belong to him. He follows these quietly, trying to shove them to the edge of the herd. As he gets them moving he quickens his pace, and when on the outside he will endeavor to push them straight out of the mass. But the cow is disinclined to leave her companions, and generally tries by running around to break back into the main bunch. This move the cowboy has to prevent by riding between the cow and her object.

Cow, calf and horse are soon going their best, and the cowboy must be ready to turn as quickly as does his game. He must, however, be careful not to separate the young one, for should this happen his labor is lost.

"CUTTING OUT."

In that event he must let the cow rejoin the herd and recover her calf.

Each batch of cows thus separated is kept a certain distance off—say, 200 yards—and is watched by a man to prevent them rejoining the main herd, or from mixing together.

If the cowboy has been successful, the cow is soon blown, and, finding herself checked in doing what she wishes, will yield. Then, seeing another lot of cattle which she is not interrupted from joining, she will trot contentedly toward them, and, having her calf alongside, will settle down quietly.

This cutting out goes on all day long, until the whole herd is divided. It is hard work on the men, and particularly hard on the horses, which have to be changed two or three times during the day. The quick turning and stopping must shake their legs, and certainly bring on sore backs. Their mouths do not suffer. Riding with very severe bits, the cowboy has necessarily a light hand, and hardly uses the reins for turning. The horses know the work, and a touch on the neck brings them around at a pace which sends the beginner out of his saddle. Cowboy and pony should be trained together.

The Cow Ponies.

The cow ponies are rather small animals, and half disappear under the big saddles of the cowboys, which often weigh forty pounds.

The progenitor of the cow pony is the bronco, which came into this region with the cattle driven up from Texas. They have, however, been much improved in latter years. The biggest are by no means the best. A short and compact pony of about fourteen hands works more quickly than a larger animal.

Some of them, with small and well shaped heads and bright eyes, are really comely animals. Their manes and coats are shaggy, showing coarse breeding, and their tempers are not to be trusted. Each boy, when out cow punching, rides from six to ten horses, using them in turns, and without the slightest compunction riding one horse fifty or sixty miles, of which a good deal may be fast work.

After the day's duty he takes off the saddle and the bridle, and without further ado lets the horse loose. The pony, after a good roll, takes up the scent and rejoins the herd of horses. His turn for work will not come around again for several days.

Of course, they get nothing to eat but the grass they pick up, and they are seldom shod. Their half-wild origin is attested by the majority of duns and sorrels. The heavy saddles are believed to be a benefit to the horse, as on account of their size and solidity they distribute the weight of the rider and his kit over a larger portion of the animal's back. There is truth in this, and for long journeys probably the ease of the big saddle more than compensates for the extra weight. But in roping cattle the heavy saddle is an absolute necessity. There are often two girths. These must be well tightened, and even then the jerks try the horses severely. The end of the rope is held fast by a turn around the horn, which stands six inches above the pommel. Often the rider has to hang heavily over the farther side to prevent the chance of the whole saddle being turned round.

The big spurs do not hurt the horses. To make them effective at all the cowboy reaches his heels forward and spurs his horse in the shoulder.

Branding Calves.

If there is still time, it is best to brand all the calves the same day, as, after that operation, the cattle may often be turned loose to run on the same range in which they were caught. But if the outfit to which they belong has its principal range at some distance, the batch must be taken off and driven and watched until they arrive on their own range. It is not absolutely necessary to have a **corral to** brand in, but if you can run your bunch into one it saves trouble. **The** corral is roughly and strongly **made of posts and rails,** about five feet high. **It should be large enough to hold** your bunch **of cattle and leave** room for **working. Just** outside a fire is **lit,** and one man keeps the **brands hot, which** he passes through the rails as they **are** called **for. In a** small corral one man on horseback is enough **inside,** and he can be dispensed with unless there are large calves to handle. A man, armed with a rope lasso, catches a calf by throwing it over his head. **If a** little fellow, the **calf is** dragged to one side, caught **and thrown down, cut** and branded in a very short time. But **a calf of two or** three months even is not always easily managed. **The noose** having been **tightened on his neck,** the end **of the** rope is then passed around **one of the rails.** The **calf** gallops up and down the arena at **the** fullest length of his tether, jumping and bellowing as **if he** knew his end **was coming.** By slow **degrees the rope is** overhauled, and the length which **gives the calf play is** shortened. One of the men will then go up to **it,** catching it by the rope around the neck in one hand, and, passing his hand over its back, by the loose skin on its flank near the stifle, with the other.

The more the calf jumps the better, and if he is slow **and** stupid he will get a shake to arouse him. There**fore,** taking the time by the calf, the man seizes the opportunity of one of **his prances,** puts **a knee** under him to turn his body over, and then lets him drop to the ground on his side. Another man catches hold of a hind leg, which is stretched out to its full length. The first man sits near the calf's head, with one knee on the neck, and doubles up one fore foot.

The calves generally lie quietly, and do not bellow, even when they feel the hot iron. But a few make up for the silent ones by roaring their best.

A good-sized calf gives a lot of trouble. After the rope around the neck has been drawn up, another noose is thrown to catch one of the hind legs, which should be the one not on the side to be branded. This rope is also passed around a rail, and is hauled tight till the animal is well extended. Somebody takes hold of his tail, and with a strong jerk throws him onto his side. A hitch is taken with the same rope around his other hind foot and the noose is loosened around his throat, but the man leans his best on the calf's neck and holds his fore leg tightly. He must look out for the brute's head, as the calf throws it about, and if it should strike the man's thigh instead of the ground, as it is very liable to do, he will receive a bruise from the young horns which he will not have the chance of forgetting for a good many days.

The brand should not be red hot, and when applied to the hide should be pressed only just sufficiently to keep it in one place. The brand, if properly done, shows by a pink color that it has bitten into the skin, through the hair. Some of the stock, in the early Spring, have very shaggy coats, and a brand applied only so long to their hide as would answer in most cases would leave a bad mark which would hardly show next Winter.

The calf, when finished with, generally gets up quietly, so soon as it feels the rope loosen, and rejoins the others. The cows seldom interfere to protect their progeny, but when you do find one on the war path she makes the ring lively, and all hands are prepared, at short notice, to nimbly climb the fence or jump over.

To keep steadily at catching, throwing and branding is hard work. The sun is hot, the corral is full of dust from the cattle running round and round, and your clean suit is spoiled with the blood and dirt of the operations. You may have, besides, a tumble yourself when throwing a calf. The process is still worse if rain has fallen, and the cattle have probably, for want of time the day they were corralled, been shut up through the night. As they run round and round to avoid the man they see swinging his lasso, the whole area is churned into mud. The animals dragged up get covered with filth, which is passed on to the men at work.

There is a certain excitement about the business. The cowboys will work at it very hard and through long hours. The boss is a great sight, and never tires, running backward and forward between the fire and the struggling calves. Each time he slaps on the brand he seals a bit of property worth $10 to $15. He would like to work at this all day long. If the corral is very large the ropes are thrown by a man on horseback. So soon as a calf is caught he takes a turn with the end of the rope around the horn of his saddle, and the horse drags the animal to the right spot.

A cow accustomed to men on horseback will sometimes run after her calf with her nose stretched down toward it—no doubt inquiring the nature of its trouble, with probably a "What can I do for you?" But when she nears the men on foot the cow stops, and leaves the calf to its fate.

If branding is done in the open, one man holds the bunch together, and the lassoist picks out the unbranded calves and drags them off to the fire.

Branding Cattle.

If large cattle have to be branded you can not expect to do any thing without horses. The lasso should be thrown over the horns only. Three or four men are required to hold the animal after it is down. When it comes to an old bull, and he declines to be maltreated, he has his own way. A couple of ropes thrown over his horns and tied to a post he snaps like a pack thread. A brand can be put on him by a man on horseback with a not iron in his hand, following the bull into the thick of the herd. Jammed in the corner of the corral, the bull can move but slowly, and there is time to press the brand, and to leave a mark. Throwing the big cattle does them no good. For all purposes it would be a better plan to arrange the corrals with pens and shoots for both separating the different brands and for doing the necessary cutting, branding, etc.

One man should be able to catch, throw and brand a cow on the plain, but even with two or three men the object is not always accomplished very speedily. Should one man dismount, the enraged cow makes for him. If the rope is held tight there is no danger outside the ring, but sometimes the rope breaks, or in the charging and shifting the man on foot may get between the animal and the horse. The cow will make a rush, and the man is lucky if he can escape a tumble and a kick.

When the cattle in one place have been settled with, the round-up moves on. The camp is broken up, the wagons packed, and a string of four-horse teams makes a start.

The cowboys, with their schaps—that is, leather leggings and flopping, wide-brimmed hats—are trooping off in different directions, puffing their cigarets and discussing the merits of their mounts.

On both sides moving clouds of dust half conceal a mob of trotting horses, which are the spare animals that are being taken along to the next halting station, where similar scenes are again enacted.

Soon the place which was lively with bustle is left deserted, marked only by the grass trampled down and the heaps of dirt around the old camp.

The coyote will sneak in and have his pickings on the offal, scraps of leather and ends of lariat. Then all will be quiet until the Autumn round-up, or even until the next Spring.

———:o:———

CHAPTER IV.

ON THE TRAIL—NIGHT WATCHING—SHIPPING BY RAIL—
JOURNEY TO CHICAGO.

After the calves, the fat cattle have to be separated from the herd and driven off in the direction of the railway. This drive may occupy one or two months, and it must be done with deliberation and quietness.

The seed-bearing grasses are very fattening, and the tendency of all the cattle is to grow rounder and sleeker till late in the Autumn. This condition is natural and very necessary to enable them to live through the Winter. The steers, mostly three and four years old, having been collected into a band, are moved slowly from day to day, care being taken that they cross plenty of grass and water.

At first they are wild, and even the men on horseback have to hold back a little distance, showing themselves

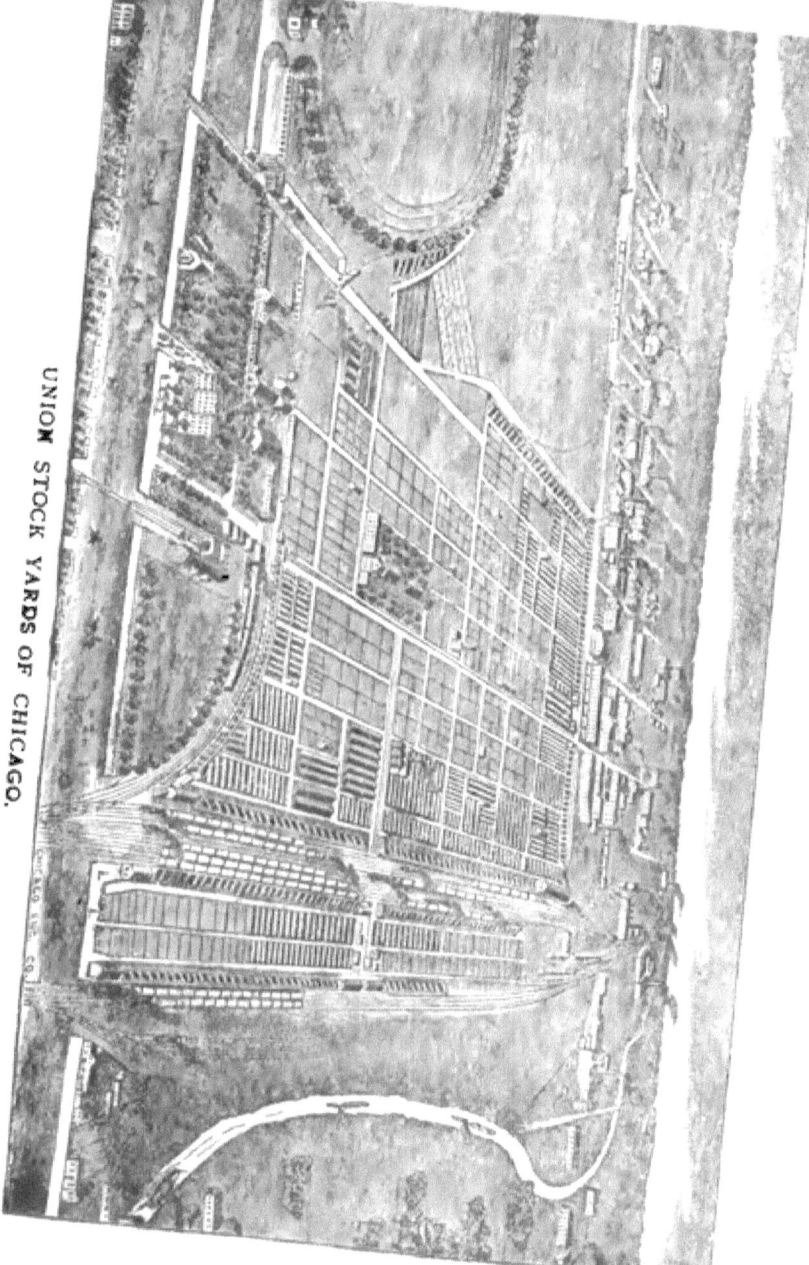

UNION STOCK YARDS OF CHICAGO.

just enough to keep the herd headed in the right direction. All galloping and shouting are discouraged, for nothing must be allowed to startle the steers. A man on foot would possibly drive the whole herd off into a mad stampede.

A few old bulls that are past work are often included in the bunch of fat cattle. A low price per pound is paid for them in Chicago, but they weigh heavily. On the trail they are useful as setting an example of steadiness. If the steers are kindly handled and never overdriven—being young, fat and frisky—they are ready to romp. Should they stampede, the bulls—heavy and old and not easily scared—hang back and look about for the cause of the run. They will stop, and the steers near them will follow suit.

The cattle of the northern territories have the character of being easily stampeded, but they seldom run far. On the other hand, the Texan cattle go for miles.

One or two men must be continually in advance to drive off the range cattle, which might otherwise mix themselves with the steers, and give much trouble in cutting them out.

On the actual journey the herd is encouraged to string out. The leaders find their place every day, and it is only necessary to keep them along the right trail. A boy on either side and two at the end to work up the stragglers are sufficient, though the line may be over a half-mile long. When halted to feed, the herd should be surrounded, half the men doing this work in turns, the other half getting dinner—if in luck's way. But as it is necessary, both for food and to avoid disturbance, to take the cattle by the most unfrequented routes, the wagon may have ten miles to go around in addition to the march of the herd. In these cases breakfast must last until supper time, except the snack which the boys carry with them.

Night Watching.

It is important that the herd should never be left unwatched. When at night it is thought time, they are driven onto a bedding ground and bunched up. So soon as they have steadied down, one or two men are left on watch, whose duty it is to ride round and round the herd and prevent any straying. If the weather is not too cold, the night watch not too long and the cattle behave well, this is not disagreeable work.

The cool air is refreshing after the long day's heat and glare. You walk your horse at a little distance from the cows, with an occasional short scamper after some rebels. You must, however, keep moving, and show yourself constantly on all sides.

To hear the human voice seems to quiet the cattle, and the man on watch will often sing or call quietly.

One by one the animals lie down. You hear a great puff, as if all the wind was let out of a big air cushion. It is a steer settling down onto his side. More puffs— the shadows sink low—and at last there is none to be seen standing.

The quiet of all these huge animals is impressive, and seems in keeping with the sleeping earth and calm sky. The voices of the men in camp hardly reach you. A flicker from the fire catches the higher part of the wagon, and just marks its position.

Provided nothing extraneous disturbs the peace, the cattle will lie still up to 11 or 12 o'clock at night, while you circle in the darkness around the black patch on the ground, keeping a sharp lookout for any shadowy object sneaking off in the gloom, and often riding to investigate a suspicious object, which turns out to be only a bush.

Before midnight, under some special ordinance of Nature, the cows are restless and get on their feet. A few will try to feed out. These you must drive back again. But before that time, if holding the first watch, you have probably been relieved, and are back in your bed. Each man has a horse saddled and picketed near the camp all night, for if any thing frightens the herd or a storm comes on, all hands must turn out and mount. If the cattle are really away, you must be after them without delay, and so soon as you can stop them bring them back to camp—provided, always, you know where it is. Any one left behind will make a good bonfire to direct the boys, but a dark night with rain prevents your seeing far, and the camp has often been chosen in a sheltered spot, which makes it more difficult to discern the blaze. The main thing is to keep the herd together, whether still running or halted.

If matters have been well managed, and no serious disturbances have occurred, the herd makes up and sets out at daylight. You string them out along the trail, and take a count, or see that all the bulls and other animals with distinguishing marks show up present at the roll-call, and move off on another day's expedition.

Shipping by Rail.

When approaching the railway station at which the steers are to be shipped, three or four days' notice will secure you a train. At the appointed time the herd is driven into the railway stock yard.

This is a large inclosure, with passages communicating with pens which hold just the number you can cram into a car. The pens are placed at exactly the distance apart of the length of a car.

When the business of loading is commenced the pens are filled. The steers are driven up a chute and enter the cars. The last one or two have to be prodded and forced to find themselves room. They should then all be fairly distributed throughout, their heads up and legs clear of each other. A cow hanging its head will get its horns entangled in some other's hind leg, and when the head is lifted the leg must come too. A steer may often be seen caught by a hind foot over a rail five feet above the floor. This has happened in trying to kick itself free from the horns of a brother in difficulty, and until the foot was pushed out there it must have remained.

When all are properly disposed the bar is dropped, the door shut, and the next pen is emptied into its car. The top of the palisade of the stock yard is planked, so that you can walk all around and look down onto the cattle. When the last ones have been cooped in, the bell rings and the train starts.

On well arranged lines the cattle trains are run as fast as any, and allowed to take precedence of most other traffic, but every day the train must halt, and the cattle be taken out for several hours to feed and drink.

At most large stations there are cattle pens with water running through them, and deep mangers all filled with hay. At these cattle get a chance to eat and slake their thirst.

On first getting out of their cars they are more disposed to lie down than to do any thing else, for while traveling they are so crowded that they get little rest. As for lying down in the car, that would never do, and during any halt of the train the boys accompanying the herd must take a look around, and, with their poles, prod any cow that is resting, and force it to get up. This is done in their best interests, for any animal once down can not rise, and is almost sure to be trampled to death, missing the ultimate glory of becoming beef. The carcasses of those that die in transit are thrown out at sidings and are eaten by hogs.

The work of loading and unloading along the journey is very expeditious. The new experience of being cooped up and shaken, or some instinct of their impending fate, has sobered the steers. They are no longer the sleek, shining, frisky inhabitants of the prairie. Bones begin to show; their hides are dirty from close quarters and lying down in pens. They can not eat food enough in the short time at their disposal, so their sides flatten and they walk in and out of their cars with the utmost docility and dejection.

Twenty minutes' time is sufficient to load up a train of 200 or 300 beasts. Each day of a journey the right number files into the car with less squeezing.

Delays are annoying to the owner, who hates to see his cattle shrinking. Every pound of flesh lost is money out of pocket, but so long as Chicago is the main market for cattle they must travel six or seven days by rail from the railway point nearest to their range.

The Journey to Chicago.

The railway journey is as uncomfortable as it can be to the men accompanying the herd. The only accommodation is the caboose, which is often quite crowded by railway working people and travelers by favor of the conductor. The employes of the railway are often disobliging, and the mere fact of the cowboys being of secondary consideration to their charges makes the trip a disagreeable one.

The night is no time for sleep. At each halt you must jump out—one man with a lantern, both with goads—walk along the rough ballast, and peer into each car to discover a cow which requires stirring up. Having found an offender you poke her, prod her, twist her tail, and do your utmost to make her rise. In the midst of your efforts the bell rings, and the train starts. You climb up the side of the car onto the roof, and make the best of your way back along the top of the train to the rear car. This little trip in the dark is not one to enjoy. There may be twenty cars, each forty feet long. Before you have crossed two or three the train is going at full speed. Only one man has a lantern. You are incommoded by a heavy overcoat, as the air at night is keen. The step from car to car requires no more than a slight spring, but it is dark, or, probably worse, the one lantern is bothering your eyes. The rush through the air makes you unsteady; no doubt your nerves are making your knees feel weak. It is a hard alternative to get back to the guard's caboose or to sit down in the cold on the top of the train until you reach a halting place. Having tried both, it seems that neither can be cheerfully recommended. If you do not climb onto the roof you must take your chance of jumping onto the step of the last car as it goes by. This would be the reasonable way if you were allowed to do it, but as the driver does not care to look back you must consider whether you are sufficiently an acrobat to rejoin.

Having reached Chicago, there is an end of the business. The cattle are turned into the big stock yards and sold on commission.

To visit these stock yards and witness slaughtering there are an important part of the sight-seer's orthodox duties in Chicago, and need not be mentioned here.

CHAPTER V.

QUEENS OF THE RANCH—BRIGHT WOMEN WHO MAKE STOCK RAISING PAY.

Of the women who have had the courage to make a bold departure for themselves some few have been successful. Conspicuous among the rich women of the country is Mrs. Bishop Hiff Warren, who is credited with being the wealthiest woman in Colorado. She is worth $10,000,000, and has made it on cattle, with no other adviser than her own wit.

Another cattle queen, who is said to have amassed about $1,000,000, is Mrs. Rogers, the wife of a minister in Corpus Christi, Texas. Her husband ministers to the spiritual wants of a widely scattered congregation, but Mrs. Rogers, whose talents are of the business order, went into stock raising on a small scale, experimentally, some years back. She gave her personal attention to the business from the start, leaving very little for the overseer. She bought for herself, sold for herself, knew how her cattle were fed, learned to be a fearless rider, and was over the range about as frequently as the cowboys she employed, and more carefully. She enlarged her enterprises every season, and her business is still growing today.

Two rich widows, who have inherited ranches from their husbands, are Mrs. Massey of Colorado and Mrs. Mary Easterly of Nevada. Mrs. Massey went to Colorado as agent for a life insurance company, married a man with 150,000 head of cattle, and it is said she now manages them quite as well as he did. Mrs. Easterly has not a large herd, but her stock is of a fine grade, and she gets good prices for it. She is worth, probably, $300,000.

Mrs. Iliff, widow of John Iliff, a cattle king, and Mrs. Meredith, widow of Gen. Meredith of Illinois, are excellent business women, and making money on stock.

Of unmarried women, there are Clara Dempsey of Nevada and Ellen Callahan of newspaper fame—the one worth $20,000 and the other less—which they have earned from the initial dollar, and are young women to have made so fair a start in the world.

The Marquise de Mores enjoys life on the ranch with her husband. She is a good shot and fine huntswoman.

The number of women who have gone West and made money is large, and it grows every year.

CHAPTER VI.

CALIFORNIA AS A CATTLE RAISING STATE—LAWS—CONCERNING WATER RIGHTS.

California, after having been one of the best ranges for stock, is by degrees turning everywhere, except in the mountains, into an agricultural State.

This of necessity follows from the greater profits of husbandry and the diminishing profits of cattle farming to men of small capital. So soon as the soil becomes valuable and the choicer portions are taken up by individuals, the cattle are no longer free to roam over the country, costing nothing for food. They must be looked after and herded, hay must be put up for their sustenance in Winter, and a few days in the Spring and Autumn must be given up by the farmer. His boys are no longer sufficient for guarding his interests, nor for keeping track of his property, which are driven by the inclosing of the former pasture grounds to wander farther afield.

In the golden days of old, which in California are days of memory and not of tradition, the quantity of land actually purchased or taken up, whether under the laws or merely held by a sort of squatter right, would be limited to an occasional ranch along the fertile valleys of the big rivers and to inclosures of meadows where the natural dampness of the soil or primitive irrigation gave large quantities of hay.

The owners would let their horses and cattle run at perfect liberty to feed themselves, and would only round them up when it was desirable to brand the young calves and colts or to pick out horses or fat steers for the purpose of sending them to market.

There are still a few wide ranges, the property of companies or of individual millionaires. The land is owned, however, and if not fenced is constantly ridden over by the boys, who drive off outside cattle and carry on a perpetual warfare with the Basque and Portuguese owners of bands of sheep which have to traverse the ranges on their way to the mountains or to the railroad.

Those halcyon days of the California stock raiser can never return.

Land has grown exceedingly in value. Water taken out of the rivers is led by large canals over a wide tract of country. Emigrants have crowded in, some purchasing small lots of twenty-five to forty acres at high prices from the pioneer farmers and far-seeing land speculators, who by ingenious manipulation of the land laws, backed by the power of ready money, succeeded in acquiring considerable tracts at an early date.

California Laws.

So long as a State is but sparsely settled, the stock interest is sufficiently strong to make laws favoring that industry ; but when the numbers of farmers have increased the law making, following the balance of votes, is taken into the new hands, and one of their first acts is naturally in the direction of safeguarding their pockets. Whereas, before the land owner had to protect his crop from the roaming herds, subsequently the stock raiser is held responsible for any damage caused by his cattle, and therefore has to look to this. Practically, it is found convenient by the farmers to protect themselves, and, either in combination or singly, they soon begin to inclose the land where the more valuable crops are to be grown, and in the older settled districts fencing is the order of the day. The cattle are thus shut out of the water, and they lose the protection of the copses and fringes of trees which border the valley streams. They leave the bottoms and range far back in the mountains, where they find small springs, and put up with the shelter of broken ground.

Formerly timber was cheap, and it was mostly used

for fencing, but now barbed wire of different patterns is more common.

The laws which concern stock, though they differ in the various States and Territories, have been in each case made by people who know exactly what they want. From the local standpoint they are excellent—that is, they suit the majority and benefit the framers. This, no doubt, appears the best ends of justice to men struggling for wealth in a primitive society. The basis of equity may be neglected. Each must look after his own interests, and if a man does not like the laws he can move.

If the stock owners are in power, they say to the small rancher: "Fence your fields." If the farmers preponderate, they turn on the stockman and say: "Herd your cattle." Meanwhile all combine against the stranger within their bounds.

Laws are useful to those who command the market, and who can thereby profit themselves or frustrate the commercial competition of outsiders. At least, such is the hearsay evidence of the inhabitants and one of the leading topics of their newspapers. It is a common saying that the rich man may secure a verdict.

With all this fencing and irrigation the lawyers in California have their hands full of work, with a harvest which lasts all the year round.

Water Rights.

The ranchers living farther down a river find the volume of water on which their crops and stock depend gradually diminishing as the upper reaches are settled and new canals are laid out. Suddenly, in some particularly dry year, there is no water at all in the lower channel of the river, and the crops suffer and the cattle must be driven to the hills.

In the old days the injured party was apt to set out with his shotgun and argue the matter in person. Now the majesty of the law favors the long purse, and the man who wins his case recovers just enough to pay his lawyer.

There is no more fruitful source of litigation than water rights, and in purchasing land the buyer must be extremely careful to know that his title to water, and to a fixed quantity thereof, is undoubted; otherwise, he may be called upon by his neighbors to join in a lawsuit to protect their common rights, or perhaps find that he has bought the privilege to fight single-handed a large owner who has strong influence in the courts and is prepared to appeal as a pure matter of business.

CHAPTER VII.

SHOWING PROFITS ON CATTLE RAISING IN TEXAS, AS THE BUSINESS WAS FORMERLY CONDUCTED.

As the cattle business was conducted many years ago the cost of raising cattle was but a trifle.

To start in business, it was only necessary to have a good pony and a couple of men experienced with the lasso to catch mavericks and brand them, the cost being about 50 cents per head.

These cattle would run at large, feeding on government pastures, and would be rounded but once a year. The owner then branded all calves following the cows. This brand was registered at the county seat, and all the cattle bearing it were recognized property of the owner of the brand.

The natural increase of stock is so great that in a few years a daring and adventurous man would have a large herd arising from the capital shown in the cost of the brand and the wages of a few men.

In after years the Eastern capitalists began to embark in the cattle business. They bought these registered brands, figuring five head of cattle to every calf branded at the last round-up. The price usually paid for this stock averaged $10 per head, so $9.50 per head profit was realized. Some of these herds had increased to 50,000 head.

Many of the cattle kings of Texas started in this way, and still hold their stock, and are now the millionaires of Texas.

But the days for starting in the cattle business in this simple fashion are now past.

The Eastern capitalist, though termed "tenderfoot" in this section, is very wary of how he invests, and prefers to see the cattle rounded up and counted before he parts with his money.

———:o:———

CHAPTER VIII.

THE PROFITS ON CATTLE RAISING AS THE BUSINESS IS AT PRESENT CONDUCTED.

The cost of raising cattle at the present time is more than in olden times. More attention is given to providing them with shelter in the Winter months and furnishing them with hay.

Yet the stock matures better and is of more value because of this care and attention, so the stockman is fully compensated in the additional price that his stock will bring in the markets. The average cost of raising three-year-old cattle in large numbers is about $4.50 per head. This stock may be marketed in Chicago at an additional cost of $6 per head, making the cost, laid down in Chicago, $10.50 per head.

The average weight of Texas cattle sold on the Chicago market is about 900 pounds, and the average price is about $3 per hundred, leaving a net profit to ranchmen of $16.50 per head.

Another way of making money in the cattle business by those who are familiar with the "ropes" and market in Chicago is to purchase droves of fat cattle from the ranchmen and ship to Chicago. One who understands his business and is a judge of stock may make on a fair market in Chicago $6 per head in this way.

The popular and surest way of succeeding in the cattle business is to locate a ranch near a good water right and start in the business yourself. For instance, one may purchase 100 cows, and the increase from this stock in ten years would amount to 2,500 head. This stock could all be marketed in Chicago in thirteen years. It will cost the ranchman $4 per head there on the ranch, or $10,000. It will cost him $6 per head to ship to the Chicago market, allowing 3 per cent for loss, which will make the gross cost to him, laid down in Chicago, $10 per head, or $25,000 for the bunch of 2,500.

These cattle would bring, at the present low rates in Chicago, $3 per hundred, or $27 per head, making, after deducting cost and expense, a grand total of $67,500. The ranchman's net profit would be $42,500.

These figures show what can be done in ten years, with a start of only 100 head of cattle. The ranchman will have, in addition to this—as it will require thirteen years to market the same—the increase of the last three years.

These figures are based on the present depressed condition of the cattle markets of the world, which is not likely to continue always.

A war of magnitude in Europe would increase prices of stock, and would have its effect on stock and beef sooner than on any other commodity, with the possible exception of pork.

In that case the value of these cattle would be not less than 50 per cent greater than estimated.

It is proper in any business to consider the average prospects for and against the chances of success.

Besides, the ratio of increase of the world's population is greater than the increase of cattle, as pasturage is growing less by reason of the plow. All these causes will tend ultimately to advance the price of beef and improve the chances of success.

CHAPTER IX.

ADVICE TO COWBOYS—WAGES PAID TO THEM AND THEIR NECESSARY EXPENSES OF OUTFIT.

Wages received on The Plains in the capacity of a cowboy vary from $15 to $60 per month, according to experience and the section of country in which employment is sought.

The farther North you go the better the wages, but the expense of living is greater, as the clothing must be heavier, and other expenses are greater than they are in the Southern country.

Formerly it was the habit of the cowboy to spend from $300 to $500 in an outfit for himself. For example, a $100 saddle, a $75 revolver, a $25 silver-mounted hat, expensive belts and sometimes as much as $25 for a horse.

But the cowboy has learned that it is better for him to save his money, and start with an outfit costing not to exceed $100, never forgetting that part of this money should be expended for a good revolver, as this weapon certainly commands respect on The Plains.

If you are industrious and watchful of the interests of the man for whom you are working, you will soon be getting better wages and be given an opportunity of investing your savings in cattle.

The owner of the drove will allow your cattle to run with his. Possibly he may charge you $1 per head per annum for this privilege.

At the low prices for which cattle can be purchased, if you save your wages and do not spend your money for whisky, gambling or sprees of any kind, you will soon have quite a herd of cattle of your own.

In a few years, if you maintain your habits of sobriety, economy and thrift, you will have a competence.

SHEEP.

CHAPTER X.

SHEEP DRIVING—SPANISH MERINOS—PROCURE CERTIFICATE FOR TAXES—THE OUTFIT—TAKING THE HORSES THROUGH MOUNTAINS—HIRING DRIVERS.

Texas has lately been a good outlet for some of the surplus stock of California. Young sheep have been bought and sent by rail half way, and afterward driven into that State.

For many years previously large bands have left both the northern and southern parts of California for the newly settled States of Colorado, Wyoming and Montana. The numbers run up to many hundreds of thousands each year.

The bands start from every county, but generally cross the Sierra Nevada over three main passes. The pass north of the Central Pacific Railway is the outlet for sheep from the Sacramento Valley. Southeast of San Francisco the sheep cross a little to the north of the Yosemite. Those from the direction of Los Angeles turn the lower end of the range, and, taking a northward direction, subsequently join the second route. The second trail joins the first near the head waters of the Humboldt River. From here the trail crosses a corner of Idaho and Utah, and then splits. One road leads north into the western portion of Montana and the other goes east into Wyoming and Colorado.

If rain does not fall, the sparse grazing to be picked up in ordinary years along the road, on which animals must depend while traveling, has totally disappeared after the passage of a few herds. There is naught but dust, under which sheep for a time will continue to find scraps and pickings, though not a blade is observable to the human eye. This, of course, does not last long. To buy sheep in such a season is a mere lottery. Rain may fall, and then your transaction turns up trumps. Rain may hold off, and then your sheep, unless singularly well managed, will weaken. Once they begin dying, they depart by hundreds.

Spanish Merinos.

The better bred sheep have been mostly improved with Spanish merinos. They are small sized sheep, but carry a heavy fleece. They are thought more hardy than French merinos and are close feeders, finding something to eat on the most barren looking plains.

Cértificate for Taxes.

Before starting, have the man of whom you purchase procure two certificates that the taxes for the year have been paid on them. These certificates should come from the county office. They are the most informal documents, merely stating that Mr. John Doe or Richard Roe has paid his taxes for the current year.

Nothing is added to say that the sheep taxed are the same which are now your property, or that they bore a particular mark. Often they are not dated.

I will, however, speak well of them, for I was once called on to show my tax receipts, and after some very proper objections to the informality of the documents they were allowed to pass.

People moving from one neighborhood to another should carry their tax receipts along with them, as they are liable to be stopped, wherever there is a collector, and asked to show cause why they should not pay the county taxes on the value of their horses, wagon, and outfit, and also something in the shape of poll tax upon each individual for the construction and improvement of roads throughout that particular county.

The Outfit.

Besides the sheep, it is necessary to get an outfit. This ordinarily consists of a wagon and pair of horses, two riding ponies, cooking and eating utensils, saddles, harness, a few tools and a stock of food to start with.

When the boys shall have thrown their bedding and bags in the wagon, the whole will make a solid load for the team.

The wagons all over the West are imported. They are very much alike, regardless of the makers, and vary mainly in diameter of wheels and size of axles. The driver's seat has a pair of springs and hooks onto the sides of the wagon box. The body is painted green and the wheels and working parts red.

You will see them in dozens at most railway stations, lying in parts. They are quickly put together.

There is a large demand for these wagons. They are much lighter than the ordinary English farm wagon, but they are weak and do not last. Their early break-down is due to the hastily dried wood of which they are made. The usage they receive is rough. They are frequently loaded far beyond the maximum which even the makers will guarantee, and are rattled along with four horses by a reckless young fellow, who cares not for his employer's property nor his own neck, over a nominal road full of ruts, washouts and boulders.

But our lad has driven from the time he could hold the reins, and he is at home on the box. Perched up there, with one foot dangling over the side and resting on the handle of the brake, he sends the team along.

The wagon leaps and swings and sidles, steered as well as may be past the big boulders and then checked through the washouts by a heavy pressure on the brake.

The journey is lively, and the driver has quite a time in recovering his seat when thrown out by a jolt or slid to the farther end by the sway in turning a corner or in changing his ruts.

This is something like driving, and as a science is far ahead of any skill called into play in the jog-trot travel along our hum-drum and excellent roads.

Taking Horses Through the Mountains.

There is a heavy expense in taking horses through the mountains, for not only is barley expensive, but, as there is little grazing, hay has to be freighted out to the different points, and varies from $1\frac{1}{2}$ to $3\frac{1}{2}$ cents a pound. When it comes to feeding big horses, thirty or forty pounds do not go far.

I receive a letter from my temporary foreman, sent by the hand of a traveler who has just crossed, saying that he has hired a range, besides entering upon other transactions, and asks for a big sum of money. This is a serious matter. If I will only give him time he will, I feel sure, like an electioneering agent, study my interests by getting rid of any amount of money with the greatest industry. I therefore determine to leave the wagon at the foot of the pass, and to ride over the team horses.

A large sheet of canvas, which serves as a tilt to the wagon in rainy weather, is eminently serviceable. On The Plains, where nothing stands higher than a bush which hardly gives shade from the hot sun to a dog, this canvas is stretched from the wagon bows to pegs in the ground, and gives a little shelter.

A mess box is fitted into the hind end of the wagon. It is made with shelves, and holds a supply of daily wants. The door is hinged at the bottom, and when lowered it is propped by a stick. This makes a fairly good table, on which food can be prepared for cooking, out of the dust. But you eat your meals on the ground, as there is more room for everybody. Besides, at noon you want the shade of the tilt; morning and night, the light and solace of the camp fire.

Hiring Drivers.

The important affair is to hire men. Settlers in California have come to employ Chinese labor almost wholly for indoor work, and to a great extent for any outdoor work which is continuous—not, as one might suppose, that there is any economy therein. The Chinaman is a thoroughly self-satisfied being; he considers his work "allee same like Melican man," and lets you know that he is not to be hired for less than white man's wages. I would assert that Chinese labor is neither in quantity nor quality equal to that of the average European. All over the world the Chinaman is a copyist. He invents nothing and improves nothing. His aim is to produce a facsimile; he can never excel.

Notwithstanding this inferiority, he is preferred for the reason that he is more to be depended on—mainly in the matter of sobriety. As a household servant he looks clean and is fairly willing, but he is far behind the class of domestics in European houses on the other side of the Pacific.

Nevertheless, he has a solid footing in California, and you find a smutty, yellow-faced cook in small farm houses, where elsewhere in the States the wife and daughters do the household work.

In choosing sheep herders, the best will be found among the Mexicans, Basques or Portuguese. These latter two do not, as a rule, take service except with their own people. Their aim is ultimately to possess a share in the herds, and to rise to the position of owners.

The Mexicans enter into service willingly enough, but

they dislike to leave the temperate parts of California. It is a great advantage when employing them to be able to talk Spanish. They can seldom be persuaded to join a drive which takes them off into unknown regions, for they are profoundly ignorant of the geography of the world beyond their districts.

There is, besides, little inducement to travel with stock for good men, who are sure of employment locally. They have to undergo hard work, exposure and some privation.

And for what result?

None!

Every cent a man can earn above ordinary California wages will go to pay his railway fare, even by emigrant train, on his return to California.

A herd of 5,000 sheep requires about six men, besides the cook,—an important member of the outfit.

CHAPTER XI.

SHEEP SHEARING—ON THE ROAD THROUGH SAN JOAQUIN VALLEY—SCAB—DIPPING.

In California the sheep are shorn twice a year. It is necessary to take their wool off before starting. The band is driven out onto a barren plain, where a few tumble-down open sheds guide you to the shearing corral. The first thing to do is to go around and rearrange panels and make fast ties and block holes, so as to keep the sheep in the pens.

A mixed band of Mexicans and Chinese do the shearing. Each man is careful not to catch any sheep which, on account of size or wool, is likely to prove slightly more troublesome.

A badly boarded floor is all the men work upon. The fleeces, having been rolled up and tied, are thrown into a long bag hung on a stand, and are filled in by stamping on them. The bags are then carried to the railway.

where they are either sold to brokers or shipped to an agent in San Francisco.

On the Road.

Preliminaries are completed and the herd is started on the road, which lies at first along the railway running through the San Joaquin Valley. As the land is all owned, the drover has no right beyond the width of sixty feet. Where there are no fences it is futile to try to keep a large flock within such narrow limits. The sheep will spread across some 200 yards, and so long as they are kept going it is hoped that the land owners, most of whom are owners of sheep which have to be traveled twice a year, will not object. As a rule, large owners do not trouble traveling bands much. But a man with a small holding, whose land borders the road, will mount his horse on the first sight of the column of dust which announces the approach of a band of sheep, and ride to meet it. He is all on the fight. First he wants you to go back, then to go around, and last to manage the herd as you might a battalion of soldiers, and march them past his grazing ground in a solid pack, on a narrow strip of road. It is a lucky day's travel in which you have not to go through some annoyance and jaw.

Each year driving becomes more difficult, grazing increases in value, the fields are fenced, and more land is broken up. It would be difficult to take sheep on the drive, close along green crops, without their breaking into them. Here troubles begin with the farmer's opportunity of claiming compensation. As a matter in which he may have to go to law, he must exaggerate the damage. He can always find neighborly friends who will swear to his complaint and assess the loss arising from a few hundred sheep crossing a corner of his field at the price of a crop from twenty acres of wheat.

Scab in Sheep.

Before taking the sheep out of the country it is necessary to dip them to check scab. The Californians are not careful in eradicating this disease. I do not know of any practical system, as in Australia, for dealing with the malady or for detecting its presence in certain flocks and compelling the owners to effect a cure. Most owners dip their sheep at least once a year, after shearing. Yet hardly in any band you pass can you omit noticing marks of the disease on some of the sheep. In some of the Territories laws have been passed and scab inspectors appointed. The attention of the latter is directed mainly to overhauling bands passing through. Provision is generally made by the county or State to pay these inspectors of sheep for detection of scab in sheep.

Dipping—How It Is Done.

The use of a dipping station must be procured. This consists principally of a trough lined with wood, twenty-five to thirty feet long, five feet deep and about two or three feet wide at the top. This is sunk in the ground. At one end is a shed roofed over to shelter the men at work. The floor is boarded and has a slight slope to the trough. At the other end the sheep walk out of the trough by an inclined plank onto the dripping platform, which is divided into pens. This is also boarded, so that the water which runs out of the fleece may fall back into the trough, and save material. At either end is an inclosure to hold the sheep that are being worked. Iron tanks for heating water stand conveniently near, for hot water must be used with some of the scab-curing ingredients. The number of sheep which can be handled in a morning are folded in a large inclosure. Then smaller bunches are cut off and penned near the shed, which will hold thirty or forty sheep. So many are driven in as to crowd the place tightly. The gate is shut, and two men step in, standing near the outlet which overhangs the trough. The sheep naturally turn their heads away and press more closely to the upper side. This is just what is wanted. The men catch them one by one by the hind leg, with a good pull and final jerk drag each one toward the trough, turn him around and tumble him, head first, into the fluid. It is rough work, but they get through the business at a fair pace.

When properly done, the sheep souses, head first, in the trough, and comes up turned in the proper direction. Seeing the others swimming in front, he follows, and walks up the sloping plank onto the dripping platform. Sometimes it happens that a sheep will fall in backward, and floats with feet up in the air, no doubt feeling particularly uncomfortable with the composition of the dip— half chemical and turbid with grease and mud from the fleeces—filling his mouth and nostrils. A man stands alongside the trough, armed with a long pole which has a crutch at one end. It is his duty to restore these acrobats right side up, to push the heads of those not wetted properly under water and to keep the line of bathers moving on. When one compartment of the dripping platform is full, a gate is shut, and while the alternate pen is filling the former lot of sheep stand and shake themselves, sneeze, cough and generally strive to recover their mental equilibrium. Soon their turn arrives to be let out into the larger inclosure. Here they ought to remain till nearly dry, as the dipping mixtures are more or less poisonous, and should not be scattered on the feeding ground, as would happen from wet fleeces.

The dip mostly used is lime and sulphur, which is effective in killing scab, but makes the wool brittle. It has the merit of cheapness. A decoction of tobacco and sulphur is also common. Both of these have to be used with hot water, which is a great additional trouble, as the appliances at most dipping stations are of the rudest. A weak solution of carbolic acid and a patent Australian chemical are also used for dipping. These can be mixed in cold water. Some men put their sheep through the natural hot mineral waters which abound in the West. Each farmer will swear by his own spring. It cures scab in sheep, removes corns and rheumatism in men, and is of universal efficacy. He nurses a pleasant dream that some day its virtues will be apparent to an Eastern capitalist, who will develop it and create an establishment like the White Sulphur Springs, with a vision of shares, purchase money and a snug monopoly for the rest of his days.

About noon the sheep penned in the morning are through, and the men knock off for dinner. Although there are three reliefs in plunging the sheep into the dip, the work has been hard. The sun is bright and hot, and the air is close inside the shed. The work of driving the sheep into compact bunches in the pens is tedious, and when you have jerked forty or fifty sheep by the hind leg you find yourself winded and your back aching.

CHAPTER XII.

SHEEP DRIVING FROM **CALIFORNIA TO** SONORA—TOLLS—**CROSSING** THE SIERRAS—THE BEDDING GROUND—THE SAN ANTONIO DESERT.

After having dipped the **band they are all marked** with a brand, and next day **you start off.**

Driving sheep is simple enough—in **theory.** The herd is marched from day to day **a distance of eight or ten miles, feeding as they go, starting very early so as to travel in the cool,** and, if possible, reaching **the banks of a stream before the sun grows hot. Through the heat of the day the sheep do not care to feed or to travel.** If full, they will lie down, seeking **some shade,** or drooping their heads under the shadow of each **other's** bodies. This is called nooning. It may begin **as early as 8 A. M.** in the height of Summer, and last until **4 or 5 P. M.** It is a regular part of the day's business, and is often very troublesome, when you have **a little distance yet to go,** to find the sheep stopping in bunches, some lying down and the whole baaing their protest against further exertion. If you want to reach your point now is the critical time. When the sheep baa shout at them and hustle them a bit with the dogs. Beware of a check, for if the flock once gets bunched up your chances are over. You may then let the sheep lie, for they will not travel again until evening.

There is a disagreeable feeling of helplessness when handling sheep. They are the boss, and in your own interest you must study their whims.

Suppose, however, your arrangements have been good. You have brought the sheep to water, and they have been pleased to approve the quality and to drink at once, without wandering off in search of something clearer, fresher, warmer or different. It is not always we can understand their fancies. They will feed again for a little while, after which you may bunch them up where you can conveniently watch them. You will see some standing in a line, each head under the belly in front. Others gather around a bush, with their heads together in the shade and tails out. Some lie down to sleep, but many stand with vacant eyes, noses stretched to the ground, and ease their feelings by heavy panting.

In the afternoon, so soon as the sheep show a tendency to scatter out and feed, they are headed in the desired direction, and they travel slowly until nightfall,

SHEEP DRIVING. 445

when they are rounded up in a bunch and expected to sleep. A good driver will, as much as possible, fall in with the inclinations of the herd, and let them start, travel and feed as much as they are disposed—always, of course, with due regard to the prime necessity of getting over the ground. There are, besides, certain factors of which the sheep can scarcely be expected to be aware with regard to the situation of water and feed, and it will often be desirable to drive them even a couple of miles after they show a desire to noon, so as to reach water.

Sometimes, to get across a desert, you may drive the sheep as much as twenty miles a day, but this has to be done at night if the weather is warm, and can seldom be ventured for more than two or three days.

Crossing the mountains, the sheep are often as much as four or five days on the snow without losing many of the band. After reaching good grass on the farther side they soon recover themselves.

At night the sheep, if well fed, will lie still; but as a rule, when traveling, they should be watched.*

Leaving the main road is not, on the whole, a success. The feed is better, but on the country road you

---

*A cruel necessity is disposing of the newly born lambs. New arrivals are *de trop*, and more likely to injure the ewes than be of any benefit themselves. There is nothing to be done but to knock the flicker of life out of the little things, and drive the mothers on. The latter **never make any fuss.** At all times these merinos are careless parents **during the first few days after the** birth of **their young.**

are more on your rights and meet with fewer annoyances from small farmers, whose object often seems merely to exhibit "cussedness," though to the credit of the few it must be said that their intention is elevated into the region of common sense by the motive of extracting a few dollars.

At one place you may be amused by a woman running out of a farm house and calling to her husband:

"Give 'em h—ll, Jack."

These are little incidents, but will serve to illustrate the dislike which farmers have against sheep and the petty annoyances they are not above putting in practice on the drovers.

To see the worst side of the character of settlers in California, I could not suggest a better plan than moving a band of sheep through one or two counties. After that you may try any thing else and enjoy the change.

The objective point of the drive is Sonora, which stands at the west end of the only road over the Sierra Nevada Mountains which is passable by wagons in this part of California.

Tolls—Exorbitant Charges.

There are several rivers to cross, where the only convenient points of crossing are farmed to some man who works a ferry and taxes sheep exorbitantly. The rates permitted by the charter often reach as much as 10 cents a head for sheep and pigs. This the collectors reduce to about 3 cents in their printed rates, but are generally satisfied with about half. Even these amounts, when they recur three or four times, together with the road tolls, add a heavy percentage to the original cost of about $2 per head.

These annoying charges can only be avoided by crossing the mountains over out-of-the-way and very difficult passes, which are known to but few people. The farmers who have lived many years near the hills and have sent their flocks up regularly hazard these passes, notwithstanding the risk of spending several days in the snow, rather than pay the heavy tolls.

From Sonora onward, except for a few miles at the beginning, the road runs through the forest, and is quite unfenced.

This is about the most difficult part of the drive, on account of the loss from sheep straying into the bush.

Generally a few extra hands are hired, who are often Indians. The latter belong to the Digger tribe, and some of them are not averse to work, either on the farm or in town. They are not all equally civilized, and one of their little settlements of a few miserable hovels, with granaries of pine-nuts in the shape of bee hives four feet high, enclosed by a poor fence made of brambles, cut down and thrown into a line, gives a notion of their aboriginal and miserable style of living. The picture will be completed by supposing an ancient and wrinkled hag sitting on a flat rock in the grounds, pounding the pine-nuts into flour, the mortar being a hole in the rock.

For a few marches out there are corrals, in which the sheep can be placed at night, and out of which they can be counted in the morning. This, however, takes so long a time that, as a rule, it is done only every second or third day. Counting the black sheep and those with bells is thought a sufficient check for intermediate occasions.

It is quite possible for a bunch of 400 or 500 sheep to disappear out of a band of as many thousands, and the ordinary herder will not notice their absence, even in an open country, where he can see his flock together.

Crossing the Sierras.

Crossing the Sierras, a very small portion of the band travel on the road. Most of the sheep are scrambling along the hillside in a parallel direction, browsing on the young shoots or wildly climbing in search of the young grass.

With all this bush to contend with, it is hard work to keep the sheep together, and it is no unusual sight to see a band, as if gone mad, mounting higher and higher toward the hill-top, scattered everywhere in groups of ten to twenty, striving to out-run or out-climb some bunch with a slight advance, baaing and rushing as if quite distraught, and all because they have come on a patch of wild leek or green snow bush, butter weed or brier.

Now is the occasion for the shepherds to show their activity. They must outpace the sheep in climbing the hill, and strive to turn them in fifty places, or they will have a small chance of collecting the rabble without sustaining great loss.

In such moments a dog is of more use than three men —not only that he gets more quickly over the ground, but the sheep mind a dog, whereas they have no fear of the men.

When started on one of these escapades, they will stand and dodge a herder, or turn only so long as he is driving them. Others will sneak into the bushes, or hide in some little ravine, while nature aids the troublesome brutes in exhausting the men, who are often taken in by the appearance of rocks far above them, and thinking to catch a band of strays, do not find out their mistake till they have had a long climb.

Toward evening the sheep follow well. It would be as difficult to separate them now as in the day time it was hard to bring them together.

No longer in search of food, they come down to the path, succeeding each other in endless line.

For a quarter of a mile the road is a solid mass of

woolly heads and backs, with wisps joining in at intervals from out the dusk through some gap in the bushes, or down a broken ramp in the bank.

The Bedding Ground.

A bedding ground has been chosen already, and so soon as the leaders reach the farther limit they are all stopped. The rest crowd in, and are made to close up their ranks. The men and dogs walk around and check the usual discontented ones who now want to go foraging.

There is plenty of dead wood, and soon a half-dozen fires blaze at various points, lighting a small portion of the forest and picking out, with a ruddy glare, the outlines of the men and pine trees. By and by cook shouts "Supper!" One man is left on guard, and we gather around the piece of oil-cloth spread on the ground, on which are laid the exact number of tin plates. After the supper is served the watch is settled for the night. We all turn in, except the cook, who is left washing up and getting every thing ready for the most speedy preparation of breakfast next morning.

After ten days' travel through the mountains, the herders are pretty well tired out by the unwonted exercise of chasing vagrant and skittish yearlings along the steep and rocky slopes, or in slowly pushing their way in the rear of a straggling bunch through a labyrinth of tangled manzanita or bull brush. Here you have to contend each step with the tough branches, forcing the upper ones apart with your arms, while you feel with your feet for some firm footing in a mixture of low ground stems, roots and loosely holding stones.

It is bad enough to work your way down hill, but if you have to mount upward with a band of a hundred sheep to watch and bring them back to the road; to head off those which foolishly fancy an outlet by some small clearance to one side; to keep the leaders in view and in the right direction; to persuade those lagging behind to follow at all, you will enjoy no small trial of your calf muscles, and a moral victory if you repress the bitter anathemas on the whole race of sheep.

Sheep driving is no dashing occupation. It requires endless patience.

The San Antonio Desert.

The San Antonio Desert can be crossed in several places, but nowhere is it less than forty miles wide, unless you skirt its upper end, to do which you must go around the sink of the Carson River, which adds to the length of the whole route.

It is not a desert in the sense of a sandy waste, for much bunch grass grows in little tufts throughout, but water there is none, except in rare and tiny springs far up in the hills.

Along the road you intend to travel there are several of these small springs, which will suffice for the camp and the horses. The sheep must do without until you reach the farther side. For yourselves, too, you must often carry water.

In this matter of crossing the desert, an ounce of experience is worth a ton of theory.

Sheep should be moved quietly—early in the morning and late at night.

CHAPTER XIII.

DRIVING SHEEP IN NEVADA—FOOD IN CAMP—THE COOK'S DUTIES—SHEEP DRIVERS' CLOTHING—BATHING—THE SHEEP DRIVER'S BED—TEMPERATURE—SLEEPING IN CAMP—SHEPHERD DOGS—PRAIRIE DOGS.

It would not be in the least interesting to detail from day to day the recurring duties and inevitable annoyances.

Nevada is a thirsty land. The little water which is to be found along the road is being monopolized by individuals, so that stock of all sorts—but more particularly sheep, which are violently disliked by farmers—have a bad time when following the Emigrant Trail.

Where there are rivers the water is taken out for irrigation, and the approaches to the banks are fenced. On some of the down-stream farms the people, after the Spring freshets, must content themselves with very little water. The upper sluices may be closed once a week to allow a supply to run down to them, which supply has to be ponded, and it then becomes unfit in a few days for most uses.

Food in Camp.

The food out in camp is simple and coarse. Nothing but the wonderfully pure air and hard exercise would make it palatable to, or digestible by, the ordinary mortal. There is, however, no choice. Rich and poor, master and man, all sit down to the same provisions, fare alike, and—enjoy their food.

The stock for camp consists of flour, baking powder, necessary but more or less deleterious, coffee, tea, sugar and bacon.

With a wagon we can afford to carry tins of tomato, green corn and fruit, a bag each of rice and beans, some dried apples and peaches and a gallon of syrup. These are luxuries ; more would be superfluous.

The bacon serves the double purpose of supplying the grease in which to fry any meat or fish that we can get on the road and of taking the place of fresh meats when the latter are unobtainable.

The Cook's Duties.

The cook's chief qualities should be cleanliness and

THE COOK'S DUTIES. 455

dispatch. Skill comes third—it requires so little and the boys are so hungry. When the meat is fried and the coffee is boiled, a piece of oil-cloth is stretched on the ground, and the necessary number of plates, tin cups, knives, forks and spoons are set out. The word is given: "Grub pile." Every man washes his face and hands, and, seizing his *couvert*, he helps himself and eats. The cook hands around the coffee.

After the meat a clean place is scraped in one corner of the plate for syrup, fruit or pudding, so long as these luxuries hold out. The boys are moderate, except when any thing new tickles their palate. Then they like to finish it at once. If, then, the wagon comes within reach they ransack the mess box, and supplement three hearty meals by an extra lunch. The cook, however, should be a despot, and stand them off. This raid upsets his calculations, and may lead to a second baking It is the same with whisky. No self-control will prevent them finishing any given quantity at best speed, though it is all theirs, and might easily last longer.

Clothing.

While traveling through this parched and waterless country your condition, as may be guessed, is somewhat grimy. Your outer clothing is made of canvas, which can be bought in every store. The overalls of the herders are generally blue, worn either without undergarments or over a pair of cloth trousers or red flannel drawers, according to the state of the weather. One or two flannel shirts, usually dark blue, with a turn-down collar and some ornament, either lacing or buttons, in front, a brown canvas coat lined with flannel, a felt hat with a wide brim, strong highlows, and a stick. There is seldom any difference in the men's working dress from the above. These are the kind invariably provided for the Western market, and the woolen goods are worse than inferior. The overalls are soonest worn out and to be replaced.

On leaving every town some of the boys will appear in a new pair of blue trousers. A light-colored patch, sown into the waist band behind, represents a galloping horse as trade-mark, and informs all concerned that the wearer is clothed in "Wolf & Neuman's Boss of the Road, with riveted buttons and patent continuous fly." Then come two figures—say, 36 and 34—which refer to the size of waist and length of leg. If short and stout, you buy a large man's size and turn up the bottom of the leg. If, on the contrary, 32 would suit you for waist, in a country store you are often compelled to take 40, so as to secure the other dimension. An odd size, however, leads to a tailoring in camp, which is an unprofitable employment. For this reason most men start with at least one extra pair of overalls to fit. The patch is left —either from idleness or as a memorandum of one's measurements.

For the rough and rusty work of driving, whether on horseback or on foot, these canvas suits are the most efficient. They turn wind and dirt, and can be washed. Where you must follow stock in a cloud of dust and have the ground as your only seat, woolen outer garments would be objectionable. In cold weather, therefore, you put the canvas overalls and coat over the woolen ordinary clothes. They make a great difference, and help immensely in keeping you warm.

Bathing.

Whenever sufficient water can be found and a little leisure secured, it is a great achievement to have a bath. Dust is so penetrating that the least said about one's condition is best said. It is a great consolation that it is clean dirt, for after having washed thoroughly a quarter of an hour at the tail of the herd would blacken you as before. In truth, the occupation is so laborious, the hours so long and the attention must be so unremitting that a bath is often out of the question, even after the proper quantity of water is found, for those who have to do the work. The middle of the day is the only time available, as the drives are arranged for the stock to get water at that time. The wagon generally gets ahead in order to fill up kegs before the stock come in and trample the stream into mud, which takes but a few minutes after they arrive. Where no provision is made for the men beforehand, they must go a half-mile to get clean water. To bathe in the evening, long after sunset, or in the early morning, when you should have finished breakfast by sunrise, is out of the question. First, you are too tired; second, it is too cold among the hills, even in Summer.

You are very seldom camped on water. When by good luck you find yourself near a deep and slowly flowing stream, in which the water is warmed a little by the sun, it is a festive day.

There is generally feed on the banks. The sheep, which prefer slightly warm water to a cold rivulet, are content to stop around. You can then go in for real luxury—bathe, change and wash the clothes you remove. In the evening you are again as before—the bath but a memory.

The natural result of these circumstances is that the boys seldom look to ablution beyond washing their faces and hands. They are careful in this.

Barring dust, it is a clean country, and there is fresh air all around. Dirty men abound, and at least one is to be found in every outfit; but his habits are sharply criticised, and sharing of bedding or clothes is carefully avoided. It is fate that he should be there. You must put up with him—at least, for a time.

Beds—Rocky Improvisations.

The bedding consists of blankets or quilted counterpanes. Your pillow is a bag stuffed with your spare clothing. If possible, the whole should be contained in a sheet of extra stout canvas, sufficiently long that it can be spread underneath you, and when brought over to cover you fully. The width must allow a wide margin, being tucked under the sides. About fifteen feet by seven answers well. At night you spread your bed on the ground, and if the sides are properly tucked in, should it come on to rain you draw the upper fly over your head and lie snug; the canvas is fairly waterproof. In the morning you turn the edges inward on top, roll up the bed and strap or tie it tightly. The canvas keeps the bedding clean and dry, protecting it against dust and objectionable emigrants, who find themselves crowded in other blankets. Usually the boys sleep in pairs, which increases their resources and saves weight. The bedding is the most bulky part of the load in the wagon. Your night toilet consists in taking off your coat and boots. The coat you may imagine a pillow, and your boots must be tucked away safely to keep them dry and beyond the reach of coyotes, which will steal into camp at night and carry off anything made of leather. Without your boots you would be in a very poor fix on the prairies.

Temperature.

As in all elevated countries, the difference of temperature during the day in the sun from that at night is very great. Although you may work in a single flannel shirt, it is proper to have plenty of blankets for your bed.

Sleeping in Camp.

It is the cook's duty, after fetching camp in the evening, having unhitched the team, to tumble all the beds out of the wagon onto the ground. Each boy at night carries his bed to a spot he likes and there unrolls it. He is limited to some definite direction, from which he is supposed to assist in guarding the sheep. It is not always a search which ends successfully. When you start after supper in the dark, carrying a heavy load of bedding for the purpose of making your bed, the ground may slope and be thickly covered with sage brush. There are hollow and stony places, but no level spot, even six feet by three. You are a little out of breath with the weight on your shoulders. It leans against your head, which you hold sideways. You can not see clearly, and stumble against bushes or trip over stumps in the dark. You drop your bed carelessly with a flop, and—up jump the sheep. Having jumped up, they begin to stray from their bed ground in search of feed. Your first business must now be to drive them back and watch them till they lie down and are still again. You may then return to your bed, and after spreading it out as much as can be done in a narrow space between the bushes, you pull off your boots and creep inside the blankets.

But where is comfort? A root stump is under the very middle of your bed—invisible to your eyes in the dust, but prominent to your present feelings. It is, however, a very aggressive stump that makes you shift your quarters. You are far too tired to mind a little bullying. If by means of bending yourself into a C or an S curve you can avoid the knotty point it is good enough; at any rate, you will not move.

Granted that your expectations are accomplished; suppose the sheep have fed and drunk well during the day, and therefore are not inclined to move that night; say that there is no wind storm to disturb you and the plaintive coyote is dumb—then the hours pass away too quickly. You wake in the dull gray light of day-break. A little flame is seen flickering in camp, and the cook's call is heard: "Roll out!" You jump up, but before you have time to dress and pack your bed the second call is heard: "Breakfast!" You carry your bedding to the wagon and dump it down somewhere. Having washed your face and hands, you take a place near the fire. Some one throws on a bush to make a blaze, and you eat a hearty meal of fried meat, bread and coffee. Long before you are ready the sheep are on the move, and break up their camp. If they travel in the right direction you can let them go, but if they are wandering one man must start at once and take charge. The other boys finish breakfast, fill their canteens with water, grab their sticks and follow the herd. The cook is left in sole possession. He must wash up, reload the wagon, feed and water the team, and then follow the trail of the herd and be up with them in time to cook dinner.

Shepherd Dogs.

Well bred and well broken dogs fetch a good price, if you can hold them till you find a purchaser who is really in want of such an animal. The day-dream of a herder is to get a dog that will watch the sheep at night, for to wake and hallo even a few times makes a bad night, and no one need envy the man whose fate compels him to walk, half-chilled, round and round a lot of fractious and pig-headed sheep; to find the same brutes leading off again and again, bunches watching him, and standing still as statues in his presence, but stealing out from the corner on which he has just turned his back. If he sits down on a stone for ten minutes the whole work may have to be done over again. He comes on a band that he has already headed back several times. They wait till the last minute and trot into the herd just about a yard in front of him; so soon as he is past they walk out again.

You must take matters slowly. Impatience would do more harm than good. The sheep you drove in with a rush would startle ten times their number among those which, perhaps, had been lying down. They then pack and squeeze on the center—heads inward and tails outward. The chief culprits have knowingly secured places quite out of reach. The lot can not remain so, and to lie down must open out. You have to leave them.

Quietness, patience and persistency—these are the cardinal qualities. Keep on turning them back until they are all lying down. You may then go to bed.

In the first place, use judgment in choosing your bed ground. Have room enough for the herd to lie down without crowding. They will lie more quietly with elbow room. Any place does not suit a sheep's idea of comfort.

If a big wether sees a smaller sheep in a spot which he fancies, he will touch him with a fore foot as a signal to clear out. If the sheep will not take the hint the big one will butt him out.

On several occasions, when the sheep had been particularly well fed and were proportionately content, they spread out their ranks till in the morning they were seen lying all around the men's beds, and quite close thereto. But at these times they did not care to feed at night.

Properly handled, sheep like nothing better than to carry out their role, which is to grow wool and grow fat. It is for the men to help them to do so.

Good dogs are of great assistance on a drive. They are scarce in California in the early Summer, when every band going to the hills needs two or three dogs. Some owners pretend they would rather be without dogs.

It is possible that in driving fat sheep on The Plains the man would work the herd more quietly than would the average dog, but the dog is a necessity where the ground is rough and covered with bush, and if the sheep, attracted by some new food they are fond of, are liable to scatter, dogs get them in more quickly than any man can do, and by turning those heading in a wrong direction at once save time and save the sheep an unnecessary journey.

Sheep, too, will mind a single dog when they would not be controlled by several men. They watch the latter, and dodge them so soon as their attention is engaged elsewhere. A dog which has nipped them once or twice instills a wholesome fear, and for him they will turn at once.

In bad hands a dog is liable to be rough. A lazy man will spoil his dog by over-working him. The dog soon learns bad tricks, when he feels that he is misused, and saves himself by cutting across little bunches, instead of going outside of all.

The Prairie Dog.

Prairie dogs are not common in Nevada. There are plenty on the prairies in Wyoming and Montana.

Their bark is more like a chirrup.

They are fat and pretty little beasts, as seen sitting upon the mounds which surround the mouths of their burrows. They eat the grass very close around their village, but they are otherwise harmless.

On the other hand, as they are of no use to you as food, you naturally slight them.

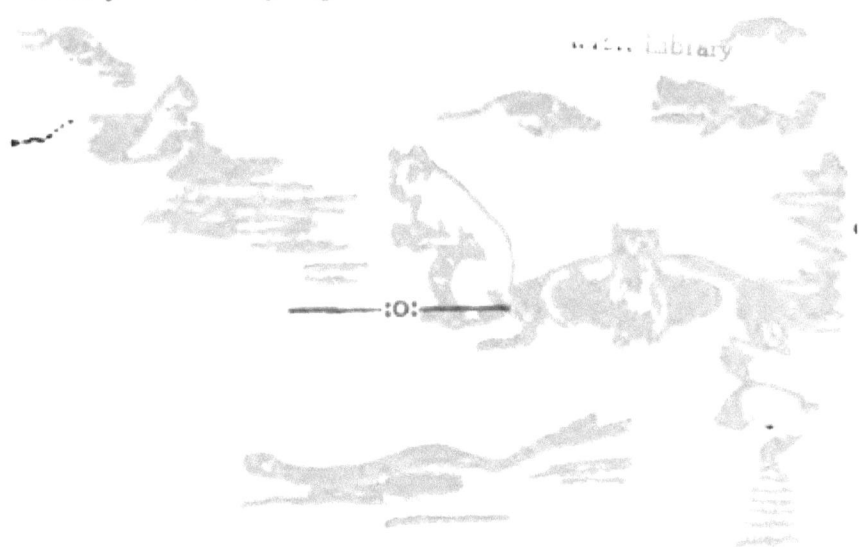

CHAPTER XIV.

DRIVING SHEEP IN IDAHO—THE LARAMIE PLAINS—NEAR THE GREAT SALT LAKE—HOW TO MAKE MONEY ON SHEEP IN UTAH.

As you get into Idaho there is a marked improvement in the country. Grass and water are more plentiful.

There are cottonwood and birch trees all along the streams and in fringes on the hillsides. Wherever a hollow has retained snow after its general disappearance from the ridges of the hills and from open spots the late moisture has encouraged the growth of every thing that is green.

But the Autumn is decidedly fading into early Winter. The higher ranges have been once or twice capped with snow; the leaves are changing from green into colors more lively; the sun, even in the middle of the day, is occasionally feeble, having probably over-worked itself in scorching us through the Summer. It is high time to consider where the sheep shall be wintered. Your choice lies between taking them south to the country which borders the Salt Lake and pushing on either to Green River or to the Laramie Plains. The Green River country is said to have been overstocked for many years, and though ranges may still be found, good ones are scarce.

Without plenty of feed a band of sheep, more particularly one which has traveled up north from a warmer climate, would have a poor chance in the extreme cold of these parts.

The Laramie Plains.

These comprise a portion of the highest table land between the oceans. Although subject to as bitter cold as any other place in the Northwest, its exposed position, liable to be swept by strong winds, enables stock to live, for the reason that, the snow being blown off, the herbage is laid bare. This is the case in ordinary winters.

Animals which start healthy and in good condition pull through on these plains fairly well. But in every season there are severe snow storms and piercing winds, during which it is impossible to take out sheep and when cattle and horses can not do better for themselves than to turn tail to the blast and drift slowly before the storm.

The chinook, which is a warm wind, blows at times and melts the snow, but the greatest danger to all stock is when such a partial thaw is followed by sharp frost The surface of the snow is then ice-bound, and it is impossible for any animal to care for itself. To meet these cases a sufficient quantity of hay must be provided for the sheep. If this is not done, the chances are that the whole herd will be starved and frozen to death. Even with hay in hand, it is not always a good plan to feed it to the herd, for they will not in future take the trouble to hunt for themselves, but idle all the day and wait for the hay in the evening—a proceeding that is exasperating to the most even-tempered herder, but all in a piece with the general behavior of sheep.

Near Salt Lake.

The climate of the country lying to the south of and surrounding Salt Lake is much milder than that of the nearest portions of Idaho and Wyoming. The snow does not lie deeply, and the plains, besides grass, bear the white sage, which is very nutritious. The latter, after it has been nipped by frost, is apparently much relished by all stock.

A light fall of snow here is an advantage, as it permits the herds to push out into the plains, which are waterless. The sheep can eat snow, and the herders melt it.

On these trips the herders live in a small canvas house, which is built onto the wagon. In this there is a stove. The bed is on a low shelf across the hind end. The entrance is on one side. With the traps and supplies of a couple of men, two horses only are required. The wagon does not move every day, and often the journeys are short.

How to Make Money in Utah.

To men who are not averse to a solitary life and do not fear rough times and exposure this wintering with sheep may be tolerable.

A man who understands the work, and can be trusted to do it, should always be able to secure something better than good wages. There are plenty of men in Utah who, having saved money, would like to invest it in a band of sheep. The sheep, to live, must travel Summer and Winter. It is impossible for a man resident in town and with a business to see after his sheep in person. He must look around either for a herder to manage for him or a joint owner to share in the speculation.

The current expenses are not heavy. Two men can through the year easily drive 2,000 or 3,000 sheep, with a little help at lambing time. The returns from wool and increase are not exaggerated at 25 per cent. As the profit with sheep, much more than with other stock, is dependent on the care and success of the men in charge, the man who knows has a power which in some cases transfers the flock from the owner's hands into his own in three or four years.

The alternative to the proprietor who can not accompany his own herd often lies between seeing his property destroyed through ignorance or transferred through unscrupulous acumen.

There is a good opening for any man thoroughly up in sheep to make his way in Utah.

A short stay in Salt Lake City satisfies most persons. It certainly may be called a pretty town, the trees and gardens having a good effect. But how long would the latter be retained should the land become valuable? At present worse places can easily be found, and when the burning question is settled the town may start afresh.

* * *

I think I have given a truthful picture of the manner of life which must be followed on the trail.

It is not everywhere so dry and dusty as in Nevada. But, with due allowances for the more pleasant aspects of affairs in journeying through a better grassed and better watered country, any one can fancy for himself how far he is likely to appreciate the life. There may be difficulties special to that portion of the territories lying farther north, owing to heavier timber and bush, into which sheep might stray, and to the greater cold and deeper snow which prevail through a longer Winter.

But wherever it is followed the business of driving or looking after sheep is rude and tiresome. The outdoor life is healthy and exhilarating. The roughing does not show too disagreeably.

Young men who are fitted out with good spirits and manliness have nothing to dread.

The West is a Land of Hope.

It is well to go and try it for yourself.

Many persons who are now being educated by signs, have sufficient hearing to be taught with the Audiphone articulate speech instead. Truly yours

Paris France
Dec 1st 1880.

R. S. Rhodes.

TEACHING THE DEAF TO SPEAK.

THE TEETH THE BEST MEDIUM AND THE AUDIPHONE THE BEST INSTRUMENT FOR CONVEYING SOUNDS TO THE DEAF, AND IN TEACHING THE PARTLY DEAF AND DUMB TO SPEAK.

ADDRESS DELIVERED BY R. S. RHODES OF CHICAGO, BEFORE THE FOURTEENTH CONVENTION OF AMERICAN TEACHERS OF THE DEAF, AT FLINT, MICHIGAN.

MR. PRESIDENT AND LADIES AND GENTLEMEN:

I would like to recite some of the causes which led to my presence with you to-day.

About sixteen years ago I devised this instrument, the audiphone, which greatly assisted me in hearing, and discovered that many who had not learned to speak were not so deaf as myself. I reasoned that an instrument in the hands of one who had not learned to speak would act the same as when in the hands of one who had learned to speak, and that the mere fact of one not being able to speak would in no wise affect the action of the instrument. To ascertain if or not my simple reasoning was correct, I borrowed a deaf-mute, a boy about twelve years old, and took him to my farm. We arrived there in the evening, and during the evening I experimented to see if he could distinguish some of the vowel sounds. My experiments in this direction were quite satisfactory. Early in the morning I provided him with an audiphone and took him by the hand for a walk about the farm. We soon came across a flock of turkeys. We approached closely, the boy with his audiphone adjusted to his teeth, and when the gobbler spoke in his peculiar voice, the boy was convulsed with laughter, and jumping for joy continued to follow the fowl with his audiphone properly adjusted, and at every remark of the gobbler the boy was delighted. I was myself delighted, and began to think my reasoning was correct.

We next visited the barn. I led him into a stall beside a horse munching his oats, and to my delight he could hear the grinding of the horse's teeth when the audiphone was adjusted, and neither of us could without. In the stable yard was a cow lowing for its calf, which he plainly showed he could hear, and when I led him to the cow-barn where the calf was confined, he could hear it reply to the cow, and by signs showed that he understood their language, and that he knew the one was calling for the other. We then visited the pig-sty where the porkers poked their noses near to us. He could hear them with the audiphone adjusted, and enjoyed their talk, and understood that they wanted more to eat. I gave him some corn to throw over to them, and he signed that that was what they wanted, and that now they were satisfied. He soon, however, broke away from me and pursued the gobbler and manifested more satisfaction in listening to its voice than to mine, and the vowel sounds as compared to it were of slight importance to him, and for the three days he was at my farm that poor turkey gobbler had but little rest.

With these and other experiments I was satisfied that he could hear, and that there were many like him; so I took my grip and audiophones and visited most of the institutions for the deaf in this country. In all institutions I found many who could hear well, and presented the instrument with which this hearing could be improved and brought within the scope of the human voice. But at one institution I was astonished; I found a bright girl with perfect hearing being educated to the sign language. She could repeat words after me parrot-like, but had no knowledge of their value in sentences. I inquired why she was in the institution for the deaf, and by examining the records we learned she was the child of deaf-mute parents, and had been brought up by them in the country, and although her hearing was perfect, she had not heard spoken language enough to acquire it, and I was informed by the superintendent of the institution that she preferred signs to speech. I was astonished that a child with no knowledge of the value of speech should be permitted to elect to be educated by signs instead of speech, and to be so educated in a state institution. This circumstance convinced me more than ever that there was a great work to be done in redeeming the partly deaf children from the slavery of silence, and I was more firmly resolved than ever that I would devote the remainder of my life to this cause.

I have had learned scientists tell me that I could not hear through my teeth. It would take more scientists than ever were born to convince me that I did not hear my sainted mother's and beloved father's dying voice with this instrument, when I could not have heard it without.

THE AUDIPHONE.

It would take more scientists than ever were born to convince me that I did not hear the voice of the Rev James B. McClure, one who has been dear to me for the last twenty years, and accompanied me on most of my visits to institutions spoken of above, and who has encouraged me in my labors for the deaf all these years, say, as I held his hand on his dying bed only Monday last, and took my final leave from him (and let me say, I know of no cause but this that would have induced me to leave him then), "Go to Flint; do all the good you can. God bless your labors for the deaf! We shall never meet again on earth. Meet me above. Good-by!"

And, Mr. President, when I am laid at rest, it will be with gratitude to you and with greater resignation for the active part you have taken in the interest of these partly deaf children in having a section for aural work admitted to this national convention, for in this act you have contributed to placing this work on a firm foundation, which is sure to result in the greatest good to this class.

You have heard our friend, the inventor of the telephone, say that in his experiments for a device to improve the hearing of the deaf, (as he was not qualified by deafness,) he did not succeed, but invented the telephone instead, which has lined his pocket with gold. From what I know of the gentleman, I believe he would willingly part with all the gold he has received for the use of this wonderful invention, had he succeeded in his efforts in devising an instrument which would have emancipated even twenty per cent. of the deaf in the institutions from the slavery of silence. I have often wished that he might have invented the audiphone and received as much benefit by its use as I, for then he would have used the gold he derives from the telephone in carrying the boon to the deaf; but when I consider that in wishing this I must wish him deaf, and as it would not be right for me to wish him this great affliction, therefore since I am deaf, and I invented the audiphone, I would rather wish that I might have invented the telephone also; in which case I assure the deaf that I would have used my gold as freely in their behalf as would he. [The speaker then explained the use of the audiometer in measuring the degree of hearing one may possess. Then, at his request, a gentleman from the audience, a superintendent of one of our large institutions, took a position about five feet from the speaker, and was asked to speak loud enough for Mr. Rhodes to hear when he did not have the audiphone in use, and by shouting at the top of his voice, Mr. Rhodes was able to hear only two or three "o" sounds, but could not distinguish a word. With the audiphone adjusted to his teeth, still looking away from the speaker, he was able to understand ordinary tones; and repeated sentences after him; and, when looking at him and using his eyes and audiphone, the speaker lowering his voice nearly as much as possible and yet articulating, Mr. Rhodes distinctly heard every word and repeated sentences after him, thus showing the value of the audiphone and eye combined, although Mr. Rhodes had never received instructions in lip reading. The gentleman stated that he had tested Mr. Rhodes' hearing with the audiometer when he was at his institution in 1894, and found he possessed seven per cent. in his left ear and nothing in his right.

The "Hard-of-Hearing" Speechless Children in our Schools for the Deaf.

Paper Read by R. S. Rhodes, of Chicago, at the Fourteenth Convention of American Teachers of the Deaf, at Flint, Michigan.

"In what manner can we best serve the interests of those pupils in our institutions, who have a good degree of hearing?" I find this question asked in the reports of the superintendent of one of our large institutions, issued June 30, 1894. I also find in this report a statement that of "384 children whose hearing was accurately tested, 60 had a record of hearing varying in degrees up to ten per cent.; 35 a record varying between ten and twenty per cent.; 47 between twenty and thirty per cent.; 18 between thirty and forty per cent.; 7 between forty and fifty per cent.; and 16 of fifty per cent. and over"—in all, 183, or nearly fifty per cent. of all children tested, are not totally deaf, but are simply hard-of-hearing people.

In 1879, I visited many schools for the deaf in this country, and tested the hearing of many deaf children, and in 1880, I visited many institutions and schools in Europe, and have made accurate tests of the hearing of the deaf children wherever I have been; and I find that forty per cent. of the children in the institutions and schools throughout the world possess ten per cent. and over of hearing, and are capable of being educated to speak through the sense of hearing with mechanical aid. This being the case, and this question being asked by the superintendents of several of our institutions, showing a willingness on the part of the superintendents of these institutions to utilize this hearing and teach aurally to speak, well, then, may this convention pause to consider this question, affecting the interests of half of the children in the institutions represented by you gentlemen present. And let me say that it not only affects the interests of those children in these schools at the present day, but will affect the interests of those in all time to come, not only in this country, but other countries throughout the world. Most of you have up to the present time ignored the fact that these children could hear, and have treated them as totally deaf children, and they have been graduated as such, and in most institutions in the world to-day are being graduated as such. Well, I say, may we consider " in what manner we can best serve the interests of those children who have a good degree of hearing," and well may this convention give much of its time to this important question, and let us answer wisely. God has bestowed upon half the children whose welfare is in your charge ten per cent. and over of nature's own means of learning to speak. This being known, shall we longer ignore the fact? We see adults on every hand, more deaf than many of the children in your schools, using mechanical aids to hearing, and enjoying the use of their own voices, and understanding others well. What they can do with mechanical aids, you can teach these children, with an equal degree of hearing, to do. Forty per cent. of the children in your schools hear better than I can. My degree of hearing in the left ear is about seven per cent., and nothing in the right, and I can hear with the audiphone, at conversational distances, almost perfectly, and can hear my own voice, when speaking against it, quite perfectly. You will allow that if the deaf can hear others and can hear themselves, there is no reason why they cannot be educated aurally, if they have mental capacity. No, there is no reason why they *cannot*, but there is a reason, and a potent reason, why they *are* not, and that reason lies with you, the teachers of the deaf. But you cannot be wholly blamed for this, because I allow that even with this instrument which I carry, you, with perfect hearing, find no improvement. But those with imperfect hearing will find great improvement. You hand the instrument to one who has never enjoyed the benefit of hearing, in learning articulation, and you find he answers you that he can hear but little, and you use his judgment and say that he cannot hear sufficiently with it to learn to speak, when you should know that they who have never learned to speak know nothing of the value of sound, and are perfectly ignorant as to how well they should hear to enable them to learn. You know you are succeeding in some degree in teaching them to speak when they hear nothing; if, then, they may by any means acquire simply the vowel sounds of our language, by hearing them, what a great advantage would this be to them in learning to speak! And I assert that where a person enjoys one per cent. only of natural hearing, this instrument will improve his hearing to a degree that will enable him to acquire a knowledge aurally of the vowel sounds, and thus enable you to teach him to speak. Sixteen years ago when I visited the institutions in this country and Europe, for the purpose of urging that the hearing be appealed to, and carried with me this device, and selected classes that could hear, and freely presented this instrument for their use, every child was being instructed as though it were totally deaf, and in some instances I was told that a slight degree of hearing rendered a child more difficult to teach by "our" method. That may be very true, for some of these children possessed twenty or thirty or even fifty per cent. of hearing, and I should suppose that it would be natural for them in such cases to be at first inclined to listen, and it would be some trouble to overcome this inclination. As for me, I believe that ten per cent. of nature's means, ten per cent. of natural hearing power, is worth more in learning valuable speech than one hundred per cent. of substituted methods. I could teach to speak two languages to a bright student, with ten per cent. of hearing, before you could teach him to speak one with all methods ever used, without the hearing. Yes, ten per cent. of a sense that God has endowed us with is too valuable to throw away, and we have no right to ignore even one per cent., when we have a device which will improve it and make it valuable to us, as in this sense of hearing we certainly have. I am sure the audiphone will improve thirty per cent., and bring one per cent. within the scope of the human voice, and valuable speech may be taught. With the audiphone one may speak to a dozen or two dozen, or three dozen, at one time; and the sounds that reach the listener with the audiphone, according to my judgment, are far more natural than those reaching the listener by any other instrument. Music itself is perfectly enjoyed with the audiphone, whereas, there is no other instrument that will reveal the harmonies of music in their perfection, and therefore, I say, it is the preferable instrument for teaching, but it is not the only instrument.

Each child carries an instrument of value, which I believe has never before been spoken of or used, and which I would like to explain to this convention. You may simply allow a deaf child to close his teeth firmly; this brings the upper jaw in tension, and when his teeth are firmly closed, he may speak and hear his own voice more distinctly. You will not hear him so well, but he will hear himself better, and he may study in this manner, with his teeth firmly pressed together, until he can acquire the knowledge of every sound in the English language, and one must be exceedingly deaf—I would say totally deaf—if he cannot hear himself speak with his teeth firmly closed together. Now, you gentlemen of perfect hearing may try this; you will find it gives you no results, but do not decide at once that what I have said is not true. Let those who are deaf try it, and they will find that they can hear. Thus, the deaf have some advantages; it requires a deaf person to hear through his teeth. This may be one reason why some teachers decide that the audiphone is not of value to the deaf, simply because they of perfect hearing cannot hear with it. With the double audiphone you speak between the discs, and you get back to yourself the double power of your voice—that is, the deaf will get it back. One with perfect hearing will see no results, because the same result will be attained through the natural organ first, but one with defective hearing will receive the results. I would place the audiphone in the hands of each child with any degree of hearing remaining, and have him study his own voice at his seat, while speaking against it. He would have to study aloud, as it is *his* voice we wish to cultivate. It is more important that the child should hear himself speak than that it should hear others, and when the child comes to recite, its articulation of mispronounced words may be corrected. Very slow progress would be made if it was required to speak aloud only at recitations, and very hard work on the part of the teacher could be avoided by having the child study the sounds it produced at its seat, and while studying its lesson. I would advise that where many are being taught, the class should pass into a quiet recitation-room. It has been my experience in institutions I have visited that I have been able to teach classes of a dozen children to speak plainly thirty to one hundred words in two or three days, whether they have received previous instruction in articulation or not, and at this rate it would require but a very short time to give them a vocabulary that would be of practical value to them. I have, however, selected those possessing the most hearing, and that would be faster than the average could be taught; but all intelligent children, with five per cent. of hearing can be taught as valuable speech as I possess. My articulation may be defective, but I think you have been able to understand what I have said, and, poor as it is, I would not part with it for all the possessions any one of you may have. And here, gentlemen, you are depriving half of the children in the institutions that you teach of an articulation that might be as valuable to them as mine is to me, or as yours is to you.

I have known institutions where the teachers themselves have used this audiphone, and have taught children who could hear naturally better than themselves, and did not allow them to use it. By what line of reasoning they can justify this I do not know; or why they should deprive the innocent child of the blessings they appropriate to themselves. And these poor children, ignorant of the value of the slight degree of hearing God has conferred upon them, are sent to the schools for the deaf for instruction, and thousands are being sent forth from these institutions ignorant still of the great value the hearing they have would have been to them had it been utilized in teaching them to speak. Teachers, will you continue to do this? Will you continue to graduate this large class of hard-of-hearing children as children perfectly deaf? If you do, you commit a grievous offense and an offense which will not be forgotten or forgiven. You will deprive fifty per cent. of the afflicted children given to your care of valuable speech and an education to articulate sounds. You deprive them of the enjoyment of God's most valuable gifts, speech and hearing. You in a great measure deprive them of the means of making a livelihood. The hard-of-hearing, speaking person will succeed well in most callings. The responsibility for the present rests with you; in the future this will all be done. Are you prepared to say, "We will not do it; we will leave it to the future; we will continue in our old methods," or will you rise equal to the occasion and deserve the blessings of future generations? As for me, I would rather be the inventor of this little device I hold in my hands, and the author of these few words I have addressed to you, knowing them to be true, and feel the satisfaction I feel in having devoted the past sixteen years of my life to this cause, than to be the inventor of any device that merely serves commercial purposes. Commerce may be benefited in a thousand ways, whereas an affliction may be alleviated in but few.

A Vote of Thanks.

On motion it was

Resolved. That the thanks of this convention are due to Mr. F. S. Rhodes for his valuable paper.

Rhodes' Audiphone

Enabling the Deaf to hear through the medium of the Teeth.

FOR THE DEAF
THE AUDIPHONE

An Instrument that Enables Deaf Persons to Hear Ordinary Conversation Readily through the Medium of the Teeth, and Many of those Born Deaf and Dumb to Hear and Learn to Speak.

INVENTED BY RICHARD S. RHODES CHICAGO. MEDAL AWARDED AT THE WORLD'S COLUMBIA EXPOSITION, CHICAGO.

The Audiphone is a new instrument made of a peculiar composition possessing the property of gathering the faintest sounds (somewhat similar to a telephone diaphragm), and conveying them to the auditory nerve through the medium of the teeth. *The external ear has nothing whatever to do in hearing with this wonderful instrument.*

Thousands are in use by those who would not do without them for any consideration. It has enabled doctors and lawyers to resume practice, teachers to resume teaching, mothers to hear the voices of their children, thousands to hear their minister, attend concerts and theatres and engage in general conversation. Music is heard perfectly with it where without it not a note could be distinguished. It is convenient to carry and to use. Ordinary conversation can be heard with ease. In most cases deafness is not detected.

Full instructions will be sent with each instrument. The Audiphone is patented throughout the civilized world.

PRICE

Conversational, small size,	$3.00
Conversational, medium size,	3.00
Concert size,	5.00
Trial instruments, good and serviceable,	1.50

The Audiphone will be sent to any address, on receipt of price, by

RHODES & M'CLURE PUB. CO
AGENTS FOR THE WORLD,
CHICAGO, ILL

PUBLISHED BY
RHODES & McCLURE PUBLISHING CO.
CHICAGO

All handsomely bound in the best English and American cloths, with full Silver embossed side and back stamp, uniform in style of binding. Together making a handsome library, or, separately, making handsome center-table volumes.

Price $1.00 each.   Sent post paid.

ABRAHAM LINCOLN'S STORIES AND SPEECHES; in one volume complete. New (1897) edition handsomely illustrated; containing the many witty, pointed and unequaled stories as told by Mr. Lincoln, including Early life stories, Professional life stories, White House and War stories; also presenting the full text of the popular Speeches of Mr. Lincoln on the great questions of the age, including his First Political Speech," Rail Splitting Speech," "Great Debate with Douglas " and his Wonderful Speech at Gettysburg, etc., etc.; and including his two great Inaugurals, with many grand illustrations. An instructive and valuable book; 477 pages.

MOODY'S ANECDOTES; 210 pages, exclusive of engravings. Containing several hundred interesting stories, told by the great evangelist, D. L. Moody, in his wonderful work in Europe and America. Hundreds of thousands of copies have been sold. Illustrated with excellent engravings of Messrs. Moody, Sankey, Whittle and Bliss, and thirty-two full-page engravings from Gustave Dore, making an artistic and handsome volume. "A book of anecdotes which have thrilled hundreds of thousands."
—*Pittsburg Banner.*

MOODY'S GOSPEL SERMONS. As delivered by the great Evangelist, Dwight Lyman Moody, in his revival work in Great Britain and America. Together with a biography of Mr. Moody and his co-laborer, Ira David Sankey. Including, also, a short history of the Great Revival. Each sermon is illustrated with a handsome, full-page engraving from Gustave Dore. The book also contains an engraving of D. L. Moody, Ira D. Sankey, Mr. Moody Preaching in the Royal Opera House, London, Chicago Tabernacle (erected for Mr. Moody's services) and "I Am the Way." A handsome and attractive volume of 443 pages.

MOODY'S LATEST SERMONS. As delivered by the great Evangelist, Dwight Lyman Moody. Handsomely illustrated with 24 full-page engravings from Gustave Dore. 835 pages.

MOODY'S CHILD STORIES. As related by Dwight Lyman Moody in his revival work. Handsomely illustrated with 16 full-page engravings from Gustave Dore, and 106 illustrations from J. Stuart Littlejohn. A book adapted to children, but interesting to adults. A handsome volume. Should be in every family. 387 pp.

STANDARD PUBLICATIONS, $1 EACH, BOUND IN CLOTH

SAM JONES' GOSPEL SERMONS 346 pages exclusive of engravings. Sam Jones is pronounced one of the most sensational preachers in the world and yet among the most effective." His sermons are characterized by clearness, point and great common sense including "hits" that ring like guns. Printed in large type, and illustrated with engravings of Sam Jones and Small, and with nineteen full-page engravings from Gustave Dore.

SAM JONES LATEST SERMONS. The favor with which Sam Jones' Gospel Sermons has been received by the public has induced us to issue this book of his Latest Sermons. Each sermon is illustrated with a full-page illustration from Gustave Dore's Bible Gallery. The book is bound uniformly with his Gospel Sermons and contains, besides illustrations, reading matter of 350 pages.

SAM JONES' ANECDOTES; 300 pages. An exceedingly interesting and entertaining volume, containing the many telling and effective stories told by Mr. Jones in his sermons. They strike in all directions and always impart good moral lessons that can not be misunderstood. Adapted for the young and old. A book which everybody can enjoy.

MISTAKES OF INGERSOLL, and his Answers complete; newly revised popular (1897) edition; illustrated, 482 pages Containing the full replies of Prof. Swing, Judge Black, Munro Gibson, D. D, Chaplain McCall, Bishop Cheney, Dr. Thomas, Dr. Maclauglan, Dr. Goodwin and other eminent scholars to Ingersoll's Lectures on the "Mistakes of Moses," Skulls." "What Shall We Do to be Saved?" and "Thomas Paine," to which are appended in full these Ingersoll lectures and his replies. A fair presentation of the full discussion.

GREAT SPEECHES OF COL. R. G. INGERSOLL, complete, newly revised (1897) edition; 400 pages, Containing the many eloquent, timely, practical speeches of this most gifted orator and statesman, including his recent matchless "Eulogy on Abraham Lincoln,' 'Speech on the Declaration of Independence." To the Farmers on Farming," Funeral Oration at his Brother's Grave, etc., etc. Fully and handsomely illustrated

WIT, WISDOM AND ELOQUENCE OF COL. R. G. INGERSOLL, newly revised popular (1897) edition, illustrated; 336 pages. Containing the remarkable Witticisms, terse, pungent and sarcastic sayings, and eloquent extracts on popular themes from Ingersoll's Speeches; a very entertaining volume.

THE FIRST MORTGAGE; 310 pages. A truthful, instructive, pleasing and poetical presentation of Biblical stories history and gospel truth; fully and handsomely illustrated from the world-renowned artist Gustave Dore, by E. U. Cook, the whole forming an exceedingly interesting and entertaining poetical Bible. One of the handsomest volume ever issued in Chicago.

Standard Publications, $1 Each, Bound In Cloth

TEN YEARS A COW BOY. A full and vivid description of frontier life, including romance adventure and all the varied experiences incident to a life on the plains as cow boy, stock owner, rancher, etc., together with articles on cattle and sheep raising how to make money, description of the plains, etc , etc. Illustrated with 1oo full-page engravings, and contains reading matter 471 pages.

WILD LIFE INTHE FAR WEST By C. H. Simpson, a resident detective, living in this country. Giving a full and graphic account of his thrilling adventures among the Indians and outlaws of Monana—including hunting, hair-breadth escapes, captivity, punishment and difficulties of all kinds met with in this wild and lawless country. Illustrated by 3o full-page engravings by G. S. Littlejohn and contains reading matter 264 pages.

A YANKEE'S ADVENTURES IN SOUTH AFRICA (In the diamond country) By C. H. Simpson. Giving the varied experiences adventures. dangers and narrow escapes of a Yankee seeking his fortune in this wild country, which by undaunted courage, perseverance, suffering, fighting and adventures of various sorts is requited at last by the ownership of the largest diamond taken out of the Kimberly mines up to that time, and with the heart and hand of the fairest daughter of a diamond king. Containing 3o full-page illustrations by H. DeLay and reading matter 22o pages.

WIT Contains sketches from Mark Twain, witticisms from F. H. Carruth Douglas Jerrold, M. Quad, Opie Reid, Mrs. Partington, Eli Perkins, O'Malley, Bill Nye, Artemus Ward, Abe Lincoln Burdette Daniel Webster Victor Hugo Browner Gardner, Clinton Scollard, Tom Hood, L. R. Catlin, Josh Billings Chauncey Depew and all humorous writers of modern times. Illustrated with 75 full-page engravings by H. DeLay, and contains reading matter 407 pages.

BENONI AND SERAPTA A Story of the Time of the Great Constantine, Founder of the Christian Faith. By Douglas Vernon. A religious novel showing a Parsee's constancy and faith through many persecutions, trials and difficulties, placed in his way by priests nobles and queens of his time and his final triumph over all obstacles. Being an interesting novel intended to show the state of the religious feelings and unscrupulous intrigues of those professing religion at the time of the foundation of the Christian faith. Illustrated with 88 full-page engravings by H. DeLay, and contains reading matter 280 pages.

A NEW BOOK.

1910 PUBLICATION.

CLOTH BOUND, - - - $1.00

Captain W. F. Drannan, Chief of Scouts, as Pilot to Emigrant and Government Trains Across the Plains of the Wild West of Fifty Years Ago.

This book, being a sequel to the famous "Thirty-one Years on the Plains and in the Mountains," of which over 100 editions have been printed in less than ten years, does not need any recommendation; the author being an abundant warrant as to its value.

So we launch this little volume into "The Public Sea" with perfect confidence that it will float with flying colors, and soon share the honor of wide-spread popularity with its elder brother.

The book contains over 400 pages of reading matter, and is illustrated with ten full page engravings from original drawings by E. Bert Smith.

Standard Publications, $1.00 each, Cloth-bound.

BIBLE CHARACTERS. A collection of Sermons by the most renowned divines of their times on these subjects. A beautiful and inspiring book, that ought to find its place into every home where good and elevating literature is sought after. Henry Ward Beecher, Dr. Talmage, Joseph Parker, Dr. Guthrie, etc. 32 full-page illustrations from the famous paintings by Gustave Dore. 894 pages.

GLIMPSES OF HOOSIERDOM. A selection of Humorous and Pathetic Poems, which, together, give a most vivid and delightful description of the life, the thinking and feelings of the farmer of Indiana. The Poems are truly original, and show that the author is a resident of the State he sings about, and has lived through most of the incidents he depicts in a truly fascinating way. Copiously illustrated Deamor R. Drake. 268 pages.

PLOTS AND PENALTIES. A selection of Political stories, taken from life, and told by W. H. Hinrichsen, "Buck," a man who held the position of Secretary of State of Illinois. These stories do not give a one-sided view of the Comedies and Tragedies that occur in Politics but will prove of value and highest interest to the Democrat and Republican alike. True Humor and deepest Pathos go here hand in hand, and the book, once opened, will be rarely laid aside without that feeling of true satisfaction that comes after the perusal of literature, based on real life, and built by genius. Copiously illustrated. 458 pages.

THE PIONEER'S HOARD. A Thrilling Romance of the Ozarks by Scott Van Gorden A vivid, graphic tale of the reign of the Outlaws in those Mountains of the West, and their downfall and final extermination by the Regulators. Combat and Bloodshed, Indian warwhoops, and wild, dark night scenes blend most luckily with courtship and love-making, and offer a story to lovers of sensational literature that will hold them spell bound from beginning to end. Illustrated with twenty-three full page engravings by H. S. De Lay. 500 pages.

STANDARD PUBLICATIONS, $1. EACH, CLOTH-BOUND

They are idols of home and of household;
They are Angels of God in disguise,
His sunlight sleeps in their tresses;
  His glory still gleams in their eyes.

STORIES FOR THE LITTLE ONES AT HOME. 320 pages. "This handsomely ilustrated book has been compiled and arranged by one who is best able to tell what is good for the instruction and amusement of the children."—A MOTHER. Many of the rhymes are original, but a large number are old favorites that will interest the old folk as reminiscences of their childhood days. The illustrations are numerous and designed to amuse and interest the little ones at home.

GEMS OF POETRY. 407 pages. Finely illustrated. Contains a very choice and varied selection of our most popular, beautiful and time-honored poems, written by the poets of all ages and climes. A magnificent gift book for a friend; a splendid book for the holidays; appropriate for a birthday or wedding present; a fine center table book, interesting to all.

KIDNAPPED: OR, SECRETS OF A GREAT MYSTERY. By A. Stewart Manly. Illustrated by H. S. De Lay. 428 pages.

SOCIAL KNOTS UNTIED. A Series of Practical and Popular Sermons delivered by T. De Witt Talmage, D. D. Handsomely illustrated. 475 pages

LUCKY TEN BAR OF PARADISE VALLEY. His humerous pathetic and tragic adventures. Copiously illustrated by H. S. De Lay. His travels by reproductions from photograpbs, constituting almost a Pictorial America. By C. M. Stevens. 600 pages.

PEARLS FROM MANY SEAS. A collection of the best thoughts of four hundred writers of wide repute. Selected and classified by Bev. J. B. McClure. Illustrated with 51 full page engravings selected especially for this work from the great art galleries of the world. A volume of rare value and interest to all lovers of good literature. Reading matter 588 pages

A TEN DOLLAR DICTIONARY FOR $2.45

The Original Webster's Unabridged Dictionary
Thoroughly Revised and Greatly Enlarged and Improved

By CHAUNCEY A. GOODRICH, D. D., and NOAH PORTER, D. D., L. D.

WITH an Appendix of useful tables and a supplement of more than 5,000 words, including the newest inventions, as: "wireless telegraphy," etc.

Classified selection of pictorial illustrations; population statistics; ancient alphabets.

Over 1,750 pages; weigh, nine pounds.

3,000 illustrations.

Handsomely bound in sheep; marble edge; thumb index; printed on good paper in clear type.

The Very Best and Up-to-Date on the Market for the Money

ALSO, ALL KINDS OF POCKET DICTIONARIES

Sold by RHODES & McCLURE PUBL. CO.

106 SO. JEFFERSON ST., CHICAGO, ILL.

www.ingramcontent.com/pod-product-compliance
Lightning Source LLC
Chambersburg PA
CBHW031944290426
44108CB00011B/674